THE
HUNDRED DAYS
TO
HITLER

THE
HUNDRED DAYS
TO
HITLER

by Roger Manvell and Heinrich Fraenkel

St. Martin's Press   New York

Contents

Introduction

Our purpose in writing this book has been to show, in greater detail than has hitherto been available in any single volume, the day-by-day events and political manœuvres which led up to Hitler's seizure of power. The final, intensely dramatic period—from the downfall of Gregor Strasser on 7th December 1932 through to the passage in the Reichstag on 23rd March 1933 of the Enabling Act which finally gave Hitler his dictatorial powers—we have called 'the hundred days to Hitler'. (In fact, the time-span was 107 days, but the title is used broadly to emphasize how fast and how successfully Hitler worked as a master-tactician once he felt the ball was at his feet, and his alone.)

We have given the reader the full text of the most significant documents (notably the vital Hitler-Meissner interchanges of November 1932), which are usually only alluded to or represented by brief quotations in the general histories of the Nazi Party and the Third Reich. These documents show, better than any comment, how Hitler's mind worked during this, in some ways the most crucial and testing period in his career. We have quoted from unpublished material (such as Hans Schaeffer's diary preserved at the Munich Institut für Zeitgeschichte and Hinrich Lohse's memoranda preserved at the Hamburt Forschungsstelle für die Geschichte des Nationalsozialismus) which offers an illuminating gloss on these intense and complex events, as well as quoting numerous testimonies (such as Papen's) which offer personal accounts of what happened. The devious nature of so much of this testimony is in its way more revealing than if it were all truthful and objective.

We have examined afresh the nature and degree of the threat to Hitler's position which Gregor Strasser's faction in the Nazi Party really represented in the last weeks of 1932. And we have re-examined the evidence concerning the Reichstag fire, which we remain firmly convinced was the work of the Nazis, using the partially crazed incendiarist, Marinus van der Lubbe, as their willing tool.

From this reappraisal of the events of 1932–3 in Germany, and the

7

aftermath of vengeance in 1934 in what the Nazis called the Night of the Long Knives, we show (beyond any doubt, in our view) that Hitler towered head and shoulders above all his opponents in Germany both as a political tactician of instinctual genius and as a personality of unique, if wholly negative, quality. Equally, he towered over his ablest supporters and advisers, and reduced opposition within his own ranks to mere pinpricks. In the end, he alone refused to compromise, in spite of continuing pressure to do so from opponents and supporters alike. He emerges, we think, as a genius in the tactics of the *coup d'état*, one of the truly unique men in Europe's history, albeit evil, amoral, and ultimately inhuman.

We must acknowledge the help we have received in writing this, as in all our other books on Nazi history and its personalities. Of particular interest was the personal evidence given to Heinrich Fraenkel by the late Franz von Papen, Hjalmar Schacht, Count Schwerin von Krosigk, all ministers in Hitler's early cabinets, and by others closely involved with Hitler at this period, such as the late Karl Kaufmann (Nazi Gauleiter of Hamburg, and one of the principal supporters of the Gregor Strasser faction in the party), Eugen Ott (one of Schleicher's principal advisers), and Otto Strasser. We are also deeply grateful to the following archives and their officials, to whose patience and skill we are so continually indebted:

the Institut für Zeitgeschichte at Munich, and especially to Dr H. Hoch;
the Bundesarchiv in Koblenz, and especially to Dr H. Boberach and Frl. Kinder;
the Military Section of the Federal Archives at Freiburg, and especially to Dr Stahl;
the Forschungsstelle für die Geschichte des Nationalsozialismus at Hamburg, and especially to Dr Jochmann;
and to the Librarian and her assistants at the Wiener Library in London, especially Mrs Christa Wichmann.

We would also like to thank Mrs Prudence Hutton for undertaking the typing of a difficult manuscript.

London,　　　　　　　　　　　　　　　　　　ROGER MANVELL
　　October 1973　　　　　　　　　　　　HEINRICH FRAENKEL

Principals in the Action

BRAUN, Otto (1872–1955). Prussian Premier when deposed by the 'Papen coup' of 20th July 1932.

BRÜNING, Heinrich (1885–1970). German Chancellor March 1930 to May 1932; member of the Centre Party. As Chancellor special interest in restoration of the German economy, and resolution of the war reparations problem. Emigrated 1934 to the U.S.A., becoming a professor at Harvard. After World War II, returned to Germany for a while to become Professor of Political Science at Cologne.

DIETRICH, Josef (Sepp) (1892–1966). Col. Gen. SS. Commander Hitler's SS bodyguard, 1928. Army Commander 1944–5. Sentenced to twenty-five years' imprisonment in 1946. Released 1955. Subsequently he was charged with the murder of Roehm.

DIETRICH, Otto (1892–1954). A journalist, joined Hitler's entourage 1931 with special responsibilities for the press. Head of the press section in the Ministry of Propaganda from 1937. Interned after the war; released 1949.

DÜSTERBERG, Theodor (1875–1956). Co-leader of the Stahlhelm (Steel Helmets).

FRANK, Hans (1900–46). Minister of Justice in Bavaria at time of the Night of the Long Knives. Later Reich Commissioner for German Law, and during the war period Governor-General of Poland. Executed following the International Military Tribunal at Nuremberg, 1946.

FRICK, Wilhelm (1877–1946). Nazi Party leader in the Reichstag. Reich Minister of the Interior, January 1933–August 1943. Executed following the International Military Tribunal at Nuremberg, 1946.

GEREKE, Günther (1893–1972). Reichstag deputy, jurist, landowner. Organizer of the 'Hindenburg Committee' during the 1932 Presidential election. Reich Commissioner for Re-employment in Schleicher's cabinet, and retained by Hitler, January 1933, but excluded the following April. Jailed later and involved in the July plot of 1944.

GISEVIUS, Hans Bernd (1903–   ). Official in the Gestapo, 1933. Later in Police Department, Ministry of the Interior, 1934. During the war member of the German resistance movement against Hitler, escaping to Switzerland in January 1945 following the abortive attempt on Hitler's life, July 1944. Gave important evidence at the International Military Tribunal.

GOEBBELS, Josef (1897–1945). Gauleiter for Berlin from 1926; Nazi Reichstag Deputy and head of Party Propaganda from 1928. Minister for Propaganda and Public Enlightenment in Nazi Germany 1933–45. Committed suicide along with his wife following Hitler's suicide, May 1945.

GÖRING, Hermann (1893–1946). Captain in the German Air Force, World War I; air ace, awarded Pour le Mérite decoration. Principal adviser to Hitler, and head of the SA prior to the Munich *Putsch*, 1923. In exile 1923–7; became morphine addict; partially cured 1927. Rejoined Hitler; Reichstag deputy for Nazi Party, 1923. Principal adviser to Hitler in industrial and military matters, and in dealings with President Hindenburg. President of the Reichstag from 1932; Minister without Portfolio in Hitler's Cabinet; Minister for the Interior for Prussia from 1933; Prime Minister for Prussia, April 1933. Held many offices for Hitler 1933–45, including control of the Air Ministry, the Luftwaffe, and the German war economy. Appointed Hitler's official successor 1939. Committed suicide following sentence of hanging at the International Military Tribunal, 1946.

GROENER, Wilhelm (1867–1939). Minister of Defence and of the Interior for Brüning, 1931–2. Retired as Minister of Defence May 1932 following 'treachery' by his protegé Schleicher, due to disagreement with him over banning of the SA.

GUERTNER, Franz (1881–1941). Reich Minister of Justice from 1932, continuing in office under Hitler until his death.

HESS, Rudolf (1894–   ). Hitler's aide and close associate from 1921. Hitler's Deputy as Head of Party from April 1933, and Minister without Portfolio. Dispossessed of all Party offices after flight to Scotland, May 1941. Sentenced to life imprisonment by the International Military Tribunal in 1946. Has been imprisoned in Spandau jail, West Berlin ever since.

HEYDRICH, Reinhard (1904–42). Chief of Himmler's SS Intelligence, the SD, 1931–4. Chief of Security Police and SD, 1934–9; and of all police, including Gestapo, 1939–42. Protector of Bohemia-Moravia September 1941 until his assassination the following year. Held rank of General in the SS.

HIMMLER, Heinrich (1900–45). Served in Munich *Putsch* in junior capacity. Reichsführer SS from 1929. Police President Bavaria 1933. Chief of Reich Political Police from 1935. Minister of the Interior from 1943. Committed suicide while in the hands of British forces May 1945.

HINDENBURG, Field Marshal Paul von (1847–1934). Monarchist and Right-wing nationalist. Field Marshal and Chief of the General Staff, and responsible for advising the Kaiser to abdicate after the First World War. Became last President of the Reich, April 1925 at the age of 78; re-elected 1932. Confirmed Hitler's succession to his office.

HINDENBURG, Oskar (1883–1961). Principal adviser to his father.

HITLER, Adolf (1889–1945). After nondescript youth in Vienna, and (from 1913) in Munich, and after war service as corporal in the Bavarian List Regiment, adopted a political career, and from 1919 headed the National Socialist group in Munich, becoming its acknowledged leader in July 1921. Confined in Landsberg Castle 1924 following collapse of his Munich *Putsch*, November 1923. Built up Nazi Party from 1925 until it became second party in the State in 1930, and the largest party in 1932. Chancellor, 30th January 1933. On death of Hindenburg assumed Presidency, combining it with Chancellorship, and became Commander in Chief of the Army. Committed suicide 30th April 1945 after defeat in World War II.

HUGENBERG, Alfred (1865–1951). Industrialist and press 'lord', controlling also for a while the film complex, UFA. Founder of the Deutschnationale Volkspartei (Nationalists), and its leader until its dissolution in June 1933.

KAUFMANN, Karl (1900–71). Early organizer for the Nazi Party in Elberfeld, and Goebbels's first employer in the Party. Reichstag Deputy, appointed Hamburg Reichs-Statthalter in May 1933. One of Gregor Strasser's supporters, 1932.

KEPPLER, Wilhelm (1882–   ). Hitler's economic adviser 1932–6. Later served in Ministry of Economics.

LEIPART, Theodor (1867–1947). German Trade Union leader who for a while in 1932 considered possibility of forming alliance with Schleicher and Gregor Strasser until Social Democrat executive sternly forbade this.

MEISSNER, Otto (1880–1953). Chief of the President's Chancellery from 1919 to 1945.

NEURATH, Freiherr Constantin von (1873–1956). Hitler's Foreign Minister until 1938. Became Protector Bohemia-Moravia 1939–41. sentenced to fifteen years' imprisonment by the International Military Tribunal in 1946. Released from Spandau prison 1954.

PAPEN, Franz von (1879–1969). Reich Chancellor, 1932. Vice-Chancellor to Hitler, 1933–4. Later ambassador in Vienna until 1938 (the Anschluss), and in Ankara. Acquitted by the International Military Tribunal in 1946.

ROEHM, Ernst (1887–1934). Captain in the German Army, First World War. One of Hitler's earliest associates in the Nazi Party; played a prominent part in the Munich *Putsch*, 1923. After a period abroad, returned to become head of the SA, 1931–4. Cabinet Minister, December 1933, in Hitler's government. Principal victim of the Roehm purge, June–July 1934.

SCHACHT, Hjalmar (1877–1970). Minister for Economic Affairs for Hitler 1934–7, following his support for him among the industrialists in 1932. Minister without Portfolio until 1943. President of the Reichsbank until 1939. Although in touch with the resistance movement against Hitler, was not charged following the July attempt on Hitler's life, 1944. Acquitted by the International Military Tribunal in 1946.

SCHLEICHER, Kurt von (1882–1934). Principal political intriguer during the period preceding Hitler's appointment as Chancellor, 1932–3. Reich Chancellor for a brief period end 1932. Attempted to bring Gregor Strasser into prominence within the Party at Hitler's expense. Murdered during the Roehm purge 1934.

SCHWERIN VON KROSIGK, Graf Lutz (1887–   ). (Usually shortened to Schwerin-Krosigk.) Minister of Finance 1932, retained by Hitler until 1945.

SELDTE, Franz (1882–1947). Founder of the Stahlhelm (Steel Helmets) in November 1918, and co-leader of this ex-servicemen's movement with Düsterberg until its dissolution in 1933.

SEVERING, Carl (1875–1952). Prussian Minister of the Interior 1920–32, deposed by the 'Papen coup' of July 1932.

STRASSER, Gregor (1892–1934). Founder of the Berlin SA, and Hitler's deputy in Berlin. Differences in policy led to declining relations with Hitler from 1926. His association with Schleicher, which might have led to his being made Schleicher's Vice-Chancellor and gaining Party prominence at Hitler's expense to the point of splitting the Party, led to his murder during the Roehm purge, 1934.

STRASSER, Otto (1897–   ). Younger brother of Gregor. Left Nazi Party in 1930 to form his Black Front in Prague. Lived in Switzerland and Canada during the war.

STREICHER, Julius (1885–1946). Gauleiter of Franconia until 1940. Editor of *Der Stürmer*, the principal Nazi publication against the Jews. In spite of his rejection by Hitler in 1940, he was one of the principal defendants before the International Military Tribunal after the war, and he was executed in 1946.

THAELMANN, Ernst (1886–1944). Leader of the German Communist Party during the period of Hitler's seizure of power. Murdered in Buchenwald concentration camp in August 1944.

THYSSEN, Fritz (1875–1947). Multimillionaire industrialist and early benefactor of Hitler and Göring. Later broke with the Nazis.

TORGLER, Ernst (1893–1963). Leader in the German Communist Party, and prominent in the Reichstag 1932–3. Arrested after the Reichstag fire, charged with arson, but acquitted at the Leipzig fire trial. After the war, joined the Social Democrat party.

Part 1

Prelude:
Confrontation 1932

I

The factions which made up Germany's political life in the last years of
the Weimar Republic had by 1932 developed into a dangerous network
threatening the health of Germany's weakening democracy. Berlin had
become a centre of intrigue rather than a centre of true federal government. Debilitated by the traditional division of the nation into states
which were largely autonomous, with their own regional governments,
the Weimar assembly, with its democratic parliament housed in the
Reichstag, staggered on from coalition to coalition under the autocratic
but senile eye of President Hindenburg. During 1932 now one, now
another Chancellor was to keep in office for a few months at a time by
increasingly dubious moves which flouted decent principles of democratic statesmanship and responsible government. It was these last,
flagrant exercises of expediency by men such as Chancellors Franz von
Papen and Kurt von Schleicher which gave Hitler the opportunity he
needed to bring pressure to bear on the crumbling structure of the
Weimar Republic while scarcely hiding the naked power his Party
represented behind the cloak of pseudo-legality and loyalty to the
Constitution. At the same time he naturally played the game of intrigue
which the other contestants, including Hindenburg, thought they
understood by tradition far better than he did.

Hitler's negotiations with them in fact represented a confidence trick
played out on a giant scale. What he was planning, along with his
ablest colleagues, was a *coup d'état*, but a *coup d'état* conducted under
the mask of constitutional procedure. He had learnt his lesson some ten
years before during the abortive *Putsch* in Munich in November 1923,
when revolution staged with force on a purely regional scale in Bavaria
had brought him an ignominious defeat; it had put him in the dock,
and led to his confinement in Landsberg Castle, a confinement which,

however lenient, had cut him off from direct control of his scattered followers for virtually a year. Such failure must never occur again. He knew now that the way to power lay through internal conquest of the Reichstag itself, the heart of federal government, and the exploitation of such allies as he could bring together by the kind of intrigue fashionable in the various political party hierarchies. During the intervening years since 1925 he had reorganized the Nazi Party with such outstanding success that following the election in 1930 it stood second only to the Social Democrats in the Reichstag.

So the stage was reasonably well set for him by January 1932. But a great deal had to be taken into account as he sat brooding and calculating in his suite at the Berlin Kaiserhof hotel, in the Wilhelmstrasse, close to the Presidential Palace. The rooms were paid for out of Party funds, which to some extent were replenished from time to time by certain right-wing industrialists who at least preferred this somewhat doubtful demagogue to the Communists. They realized that the moderates, the Social Democrats, could exercise as little control in the streets over the growing number of Communist supporters as they could over the Nazi gangs of Storm Troopers.

Hitler, now gloomy and silent, now elated by some sudden outburst of instinctual energy, knew that he must bide his time to gather his potential strength, or fail utterly. In spite of the growing impatience of his supporters, there must be no second Munich. The readiness was all.

First he must watch the President, who favoured without question Hitler's more slippery rivals for the Chancellorship, the aristocratic Papen and the scheming untrustworthy Schleicher. Field Marshal Paul von Hindenburg, still stubbornly occupying the President's Palace at the age of eighty-five, was recalcitrant and difficult to handle, retaining power long after most men are retired from lesser occupations than that of being arbiter of the well-being of a State. Born in 1847, he had come of a Prussian military family and had served in the German army for some decades with no particular distinction. He had risen to a legendary kind of fame largely through having under him men of superior skill and intelligence, notably Hitler's future supporter in Munich, General Ludendorff, who had gained him victories in the First World War which had elevated him to the rank of General and Chief of the General Staff. It was he who had decided the terms of the severe treaty imposed on the Russians at Brest-Litovsk in March 1918, and he who had advised the Kaiser to leave Germany the same year when the offensive against the Allies had failed. Although a monarchist at heart, and a right-wing nationalist, he had allowed himself in April 1925 at the age of seventy-eight to become the President of the new Republic, believing in his own legend and no doubt seeing himself as some kind of temporary substitute for the exiled Kaiser. 'I am the trustee of the Emperor,' he said to Brüning in November 1931, when the Chancellor had broached the possible restoration of the monarchy, 'and can never give my consent to anyone succeeding to the throne except the Emperor himself.' Brüning had proposed at the time one of the sons of the Crown Prince, but Hindenburg had rejected this idea absolutely.

By 1930 Hindenburg had lost any real power of personal initiative, and the President's palace had become a centre of intrigue and reaction under the influence of the feudal land-owners and the military hierarchy. Any sign of constitutional difficulty led him to order temporary spells of authoritarian rule by emergency decree, using Article 48 of the German Constitution, which permitted the prorogation of the Cabinet and rule by decree.[1] Known as the 'Wooden Titan', he shuffled along the corridors like an aged automaton, or sat bolt upright before those who sought to influence him, a vast, impenetrable and cunning rather than intelligent figure. His hair clipped *en brosse*, he remained the stolid representative of the oldest power recognized in Germany, that of the Army. He loved money, insisting on a higher salary than normal as President, and accepting the estate of Neudeck on his eightieth birthday in 1927 from the militant Right-wing Stahlhelm movement and their industrialist supporters. Now, at eighty-five, Hindenburg looked like a bad statue of himself. His eyes were cold and lifeless, and everything about his head and body gave the impression of being square. Old as he was he still enjoyed good health; he ate, drank and slept well, and he had an old authoritarian's instinct which could, at moments, amount to perception. His chief virtue was that he hated and despised that 'corporal', Adolf Hitler, and his chief weakness was that he underestimated him.

Round him gathered his aides, the chief of whom was his son, Oskar von Hindenburg, the nominal owner of Neudeck in order to avoid the payment of state duties on Hindenburg's death. Born in 1883, Oskar Hindenburg in later years developed an overweening interest in politics and a dubious influence over his father. Any approach to Hindenburg became increasingly difficult except through his son and their close associate Otto Meissner, Hindenburg's Secretary of State, a career civil servant who was later to serve Hitler in the same capacity he had served Hindenburg and the latter's predecessor, President Ebert, a Social Democrat of working-class origin. Both men were to be deeply involved in Hitler's prolonged negotiations with Hindenburg.

Since the balance of political power between the rival parties in the Reichstag involved a constant shift of alliances between leaders whose associations, usually temporary, were only for the purpose of gaining

17

advantage for themselves, Hitler had to watch closely his day-to-day relations with those whose positions had brought them to the top as they jockeyed for the office of Chancellor. The Chancellor was, in effect, the German Federal Prime Minister, responsible for forming a governmental Cabinet, determining policy and exerting pressure to get laws through the Reichstag, in which he normally had to command a majority vote. Since the state of the parties in Germany in 1930 had precluded any one from enjoying a full working majority, the shifts of power had been made up of a whole series of uneasy alliances between groups where friendship was, at best, as suspect as it was temporary.

COMPOSITION OF THE REICHSTAG FROM SEPTEMBER 1930 TO JULY 1932

Parties	Leader	Votes (million)	Seats in Reichstag
SPD (Social Democratic Party)	Wels	8.5	143
*NSDAP (National Socialists)	Hitler	6.38	107
KPD (Communist)	Thaelmann	5.3	89
Catholic Centre	Brüning ⎱ Papen ⎰	4.6	76
Nationalists	Hugenberg	2.45	41
People's Party			
Agrarian (Landvolk)			
Economic Party		7.89	118
Democrats			
Bavarian Party	Fritz Schaffer		

Total voters 35 million out of potential 43 million.

The closest ally for Hitler was Alfred Hugenberg, a wealthy industrialist and formerly a leading man at Krupps, whose prime occupation had become the exploitation of Right-wing, nationalist politics, backed by a strong section of German industry. He controlled Germany's largest press and film organizations, and favoured the establishment of

---

* At the previous election (1928) the Nazis had polled only some 809,000 votes, representing 12 seats in the Reichstag.

an authoritarian government in order to control the Left. His party, the German Nationalists, had lost ground heavily in the Reichstag, in which following the 1928 election they had held seventy-eight seats, itself a decline from 103 in the previous House. In fact, until 1930 the German Nationalists had been the second party in the Reichstag; now with forty-one seats they were the fifth. According to Papen, Hugenberg was a good administrator but a poor leader, too narrow and preoccupied with finance to appreciate, as he put it, 'the spiritual values of true conservative policy'. But in Hitler's eyes, Hugenberg offered an invaluable political link with industry.

Nothing reveals more eloquently the fundamental dishonesty of Right-wing German political leadership at this period than the off-and-on relations which were to develop during the crucial months of 1932 between Hitler, Schleicher and Papen, each firmly playing his own hand. Papen's initial political associations were with the Catholic Centre. He was essentially the landed gentleman, handsome, smooth and charming, very much the professional diplomat with a military background. It was he who had organized the aristocratic group in Berlin known as the Herrenklub, and he enjoyed considerable influence in the circle surrounding Hindenburg. Born in 1879, he had seen long service in the Prussian army; an impoverished aristocrat, he had married advantageously into a wealthy family of industrialists. His initial approach to politics had been through service in the diplomatic corps as military attaché at the German Embassy in the United States, but he had been discredited in 1916 through involvement in sabotage in certain U.S. armament plants. He was a firm believer in a leader-class, holding that 'the man of good race and inner qualities is more highly suited to bear responsibility than the average man'. Needless to say, during the earlier months of 1932 Papen saw himself, and not Hitler, in this light. He was excellent company at a dinner party, a good and witty conversationalist, and he inspired further confidence in Right-wing society because he was known to be an excellent horseman. He was a political socialite, and he was, moreover, quite prepared to connive at the defeat of his nominal leader, Heinrich Brüning, in May 1932; Brüning, an able man with a thorough knowledge of economics and finance, was also one of the few honest men left in the forefront of German politics. This alone was sufficient to ensure his ultimate defeat at the hands of such opponents as Papen, Schleicher, and Hitler's representatives in the Reichstag. He had become Chancellor in March 1930, and was firmly opposed to Nazism. His enforced departure as Chancellor was a disaster, and the part played in it by both Papen and Schleicher was shameful.

Kurt von Schleicher was even less reputable than Papen. People never tired of the obvious joke that his very name meant 'intriguer', for this was precisely what he was. An able man, he had been born in 1882, and commissioned in 1900 in an exclusive regiment; he had become the friend of Oskar von Hindenburg, and had served on the General Staff during the war, working directly under Hindenburg; like Papen, he had charm and social pliability. He was also very much a ladies' man. He enjoyed power, achieving it unscrupulously. After the war he had been responsible, as Hindenburg's aide, for originating the idea of the Freikorps, the army groups established in 1919 to put down Communist uprisings in Germany and, with Allied approval, in 'border' territories such as Lithuania and Latvia. In 1928 he had become 'Chief of the Minister's Office' in the Defence Ministry (Reichswehr) serving under the Minister, Wilhelm Groener, Hindenburg's former Chief of Staff in the latter days of the war. Schleicher, who had been largely instrumental in achieving Brüning's initial appointment as Chancellor in 1930, was primarily responsible for his downfall in 1932.

These were the principal men whom Hitler had to take into account, either as opponents or as allies. But he had also to consider the position in his own Party, and the tensions which were developing now that some form of power in government seemed possible after the 1930 electoral landslide in his favour. Closest to him were Joseph Goebbels, Hermann Göring and Rudolf Hess, with all of whom he was in daily contact. Goebbels was the propagandist gadfly, Hitler's chief campaign manager, calculating but often impetuous with his advice to the Leader, concerned always with the day-to-day effect the Party was having and the organized strife in the Reichstag. He had a seat in the House and constantly attacked the Government in vitriolic speeches. Göring, a man of great ability hidden behind his mask of buccaneering bonhomie, was filled with his own self-importance and his capacity to deal with politicians, industrialists and the upper class, and the work of liaison with Hindenburg. Like Goebbels, he had been a troublesome Reichstag deputy since 1928. His concern was to see that Hitler, who remained outside the Reichstag, achieved the Chancellorship, if not the Presidency itself; 1932 was the year of the crucial Presidential elections. Hess remained in the background, Hitler's *alter ego*, his constant adviser and aide.

A more doubtful man in the Party was Ernst Roehm who had left the SA in 1925, and Germany itself in 1929, when he had departed on a military mission to Bolivia, from which he did not return until January 1931. He was well known as an extravert homosexual. At Hitler's invitation he rejoined the SA after six years' absence. Roehm, a professional soldier, had his own ideas of power. The SA and SS were virtually merged at this period, and by Brüning's orders during his Chancellorship they were disbanded and banned from wearing uniform in April 1932. The SS was made up at the time of some 30,000 men, while the SA numbered around 400,000. This represented the Party's power in the streets, and its forces of persuasion during election periods. Hitler had to balance in his mind the value of having this private army (in or out of uniform) with which to fight his opponents in the streets, and the degree to which the restless energy and crude violence of these men might cause scandal harmful to the Party during the delicate period of winning control of the State by 'legitimate means'. It was essential to retain the support of these roughnecks and their votes, though had Hitler done as they wanted he would by now have seized power in the State by force. The rise in recruitment of the nominally disbanded SA and SS was proportional to the rise of unemployment during these difficult days in Germany, as in the rest of Europe, following the economic recession. The figure for unemployment was in excess of five million in December 1931.

Worse still, the opposition to Hitler's principles, if not to Hitler himself, within the Party was evident enough early in 1932, and excites Goebbels's frequent exasperated comment in his published diaries of the period. This opposition centred upon Gregor Strasser, who was very active with his own propaganda; he was a prominent administrator in the Party and speaker in the Reichstag. While Hitler certainly did not fear Gregor Strasser, any open disloyalty could affect others and make Party management difficult when there was so much external business to watch, and so many elections to be fought—Presidential elections, Federal elections, and State elections—within the brief period of nine months, March to November 1932.

1932, therefore, could have been the year of Hitler's fall, defeated either by his opponents in other parties or by schism in his own. If his seeming hesitations and vacillations constantly drove Goebbels into a frenzy of frustration, it never strained his loyalty, nor that of Göring or Hess. They realized the reason for these calculations. They knew all along that they were dealing not with an able Party Leader, but with a new kind of political genius whose instinctual responses had to be obeyed because in them lay the secret of the Party's power. They had shared during the past year in the triumphant rise of the Party from its small, disreputable, back-street origins in the middle nineteen-twenties to the present powerful position in the State. Without Hitler's dedicated belief in himself, and through himself in the Party he created in such inauspicious circumstances, there would be no campaign to be fought, no potential seizure of control in Germany. They did not need Hitler to tell them that it was a process of attrition which they were conducting, and that, provided they stifled their impatience, the State could finally be theirs. But their dependence on Hitler's leadership was absolute.

The Strasser faction in the Party represented, as they saw it, a mere nuisance, to be stamped upon as soon as it became too openly manifest.

Outside the Party, Hitler was undoubtedly under-rated, alike in Germany and the rest of the world. The menace he stood for was virtually disregarded because few ever thought of him as a future leader in Germany. By the outside world he was even regarded as some kind of comic figure, the petty agitator who believed himself to be a prophet, but who in origin was little more than a social outcast. Nazism had developed at such speed that many thought, wishfully, that it would disappear just as quickly; nations concerned with their own dire economic and social problems left Germany to deal with hers, imagining that the Weimar Republic would survive its crises in much the same way as they could survive theirs, 'muddling through', as the British used to put it. Inside Germany, in spite of the obvious danger signs in the elections and the constant violence on the streets (blamed by the moderates as much on the Communists as on the Nazis), no one (the Nazis excepted) ever thought Hitler would be Chancellor. In any case, even if he did become Chancellor, for a few weeks or months, he would be hedged in (they imagined) by the powerful forces of the Right; it would be a case of the militarists and the industrialists making a momentary concession to the Nazi Party for their own political purposes.

Such thinking discounted the as yet barely revealed evil genius of the man. Hitler from his youth had developed an aggressive, non-conformist quality which had turned him into an entirely self-made, self-educated nationalist and racist fanatic. After war service, he had thought of nothing but the great national resurgence of which he was convinced he was born to be the leader. His discovery early in the 1920s of his great gift of oratory and hypnotic influence over audiences had deluded him too soon into undertaking the Munich *Putsch*, which was a disastrous failure, mistimed and badly planned. He was then thirty-four, and wholly inexperienced. Contrary to opinion, Hitler was always capable of learning, and after 1925 he gained a new, highly intuitive capacity to size up a situation and adjust himself to it. He believed himself to be a rationalist, considering all problems *ab initio*, without any concession to political or diplomatic convention or procedure. His immediate associates became used to his moods, his prolonged states of depression, his periods of sudden violent activity once he had decided on his policy. He poured his thought-processes, his instinctual reactions, his personal interpretation of history (in which he was widely read in a disorganized way), his prognostications and his bitter national and racial prejudices into *Mein Kampf*, his semi-autobiographical political testimony composed during his months of confinement following his failure in

Munich. This failure did not daunt him. He merely treated it as experience, and through it, and the weakly conducted trial which followed, he learned how to treat the seemingly powerful authorities. He learned what he taught his colleagues—authority is far more vulnerable than it seems, especially when treated with complete lack of respect and undermined by constant attack. This was the unalterable policy of Hitler, Göring and Goebbels both inside and outside the Reichstag.

II

Hitler was already experienced in facing Hindenburg, the ultimate authority in the State. Their first meeting had taken place on 10th October 1931, the month Hindenburg entered his eighty-fifth year. Hitler was by that time sufficiently prominent to be brought into the backroom discussions about Hindenburg's offering himself yet again for the office of President when the time for the Presidential election came in March of the following year. Hindenburg at first seemed unwilling; he was, he felt, far too old to continue with so many difficulties looming ahead. He had in fact suffered a brief mental breakdown a few months before. Vanity alone tempted him. Brüning, as Chancellor, was concerned that Hindenburg should remain in office in order to promote some sense of stability and continuity at the top, and he was anxious to win the support of others in bringing pressure to bear on the old man and securing the necessary legislation.[2] Consequently in September he had severally approached both Hitler and Hugenberg in order to urge their support, but neither had been prepared to respond, each trying to blame the other in order to cover his dissent. Brüning astutely used the occasion to emphasize these differences between his opponents. At the same time Brüning, working with Schleicher (who also began to see that Hitler and the Nazi Party should be brought into the picture, if only to control them), organized a formal meeting between Hindenburg and Hitler. Alarmed as he always was by anything which might place him in an embarrassing social position—there remained a streak of inferiority complex in Hitler in social matters involving special protocol and upper class behaviour—the Führer hurriedly summoned Göring back from Sweden. Göring was in Stockholm with his Swedish wife, who was dying after a prolonged period of ill health. Filled with remorse at leaving her at such a time, Göring none the less hastened to Hitler's side in order to support him at this important moment; he accompanied him to the President's palace. For Hitler, too, it was a difficult period in his private life; his niece, Geli Raubal, had killed herself three weeks before with her uncle's pistol in his flat in Munich, where she lived with her mother, Hitler's half-sister. Hitler's obsessive love for this over-sexed twenty-four year old girl was well known, and he was prostrated by her death which was, no doubt, caused partly by his unnaturally possessive attitude towards her.[3]

No record was kept of what was said at the meeting with Hindenburg; only a formal announcement followed:

> The President of the Reich today received Herr Adolf Hitler and Captain Hermann Göring, member of the Reichstag, and obtained from them a detailed account of the aims of the National Socialist movement. This was followed by a discussion of internal and external political questions.

However, it would seem that Hitler, dressed formally and therefore ill at ease, harangued the President about Nazi policy and so created a bad impression. Far from considering him suitable for high Cabinet office, Hindenburg made the celebrated comment to Schleicher that the best place for this oddity would be the Ministry of Posts.

Hitler went straight from this meeting to a demonstration of supposed Right-wing solidarity in Harzburg in the Harz mountains, where he felt equally out of place alongside Hugenberg, Franz Seldte and Theodor Düsterberg, the leaders of the Stahlhelm (Steel Helmet forces) and representatives of the Right in the Army and industry.[4] The frock-coats, the uniforms, the heel-clicking, all irritated him; his own men were under-represented and he felt himself outshone. Relations were at a low ebb. Hjalmar Schacht, the banker, who was present, gives his own account of the bad atmosphere which prevailed:

> It was already apparent that Hitler did not appreciate the fact that the initiative had originated with Hugenberg ... Hitler would spare no pains to avoid giving the impression that his adherents were marching under the German National banner. So it came about that during the march past of the non-National Socialist groups, Hitler was ostentatiously absent, which in turn meant that there was no competition when the National-Socialist march took place. There was much talk, later, of the 'Harzburg Front', but in reality this Front never existed. It was a 'get-together' in appearance only.[5]

Hitler restored his confidence by attending a vast rally of some 100,000 SA and SS men in Brunswick, while Göring returned to the Reichstag to belabour Brüning's attempts at forming a new Cabinet. A vote of confidence in the government was won by only twenty-five votes on 16th October; the following day Göring's wife died, and he hurried to Stockholm distraught with sorrow at having failed to be at her bedside.

He returned to Germany after the funeral wholly dedicated to work day and night for Hitler's success. Goebbels, on the other hand, had just married a divorcee, Magda Quandt, a woman of private means, and devoted personally to Hitler. Goebbels was to be unsparing in his efforts throughout the arduous campaigning of 1932 which was to bring success and make Hitler Chancellor.

Hitler had refused to accede to Brüning's request that Hindenburg should be returned as President unopposed and without the formality of elections, partly because he saw this as an attempt by Brüning to consolidate his own government. Hitler continued to conduct public warfare with Brüning in the effort to bring him down; this campaign took the form of open letters published on 14th October and again on 8th December attacking the 'ruinous character' of his plans, and issuing a challenge concerning the future of the Constitution once the Nazis had come to power:

> You refuse, as a 'statesman', to admit that if we come to power legally we could then break through legality. Herr Chancellor, the fundamental thesis of democracy runs, 'All power issues from the People'. The constitution lays down the ways by which a conception, an idea, and therefore an organization, must gain from the people the legitimation for the realization of its aims. But in the last resort, it is the People itself which determines its Constitution. Herr Chancellor, if the German nation once empowers the National Socialist Movement to introduce a Constitution other than that which we have today, then you cannot stop it.[6]

In the light of this and many other statements, made alike by Hitler and his Nazi lieutenants, no one can claim that Hitler did not tell the German people what was in store for them if they returned him to power.

Early in January 1932, when Hitler was in Munich, he received a telegram from General Groener, the Minister of Defence, which in his eyes represented a degree of recognition by 'authority' which advanced him considerably. Heiden describes his reception of this telegram:

> It was signed by Groener and requested his presence at a conference in Berlin. Hitler hastily read the wire, thrust the paper under the nose of all those present, and uttered a purr of triumph like a contented beast of prey. By turns, he brought his face close to Hess's, Rosenberg's . . . stared in their eyes, with little cries of 'Hey . . . hey . . . hey'—as if he wanted to say: 'You see? You see? . . . Here we are at last.' Then he brought down his fist on the telegram and cried: 'Now I have them in my pocket! They have recognized me as a partner in their negotiations.'[7]

25

Hitler, accompanied this time by Roehm as Chief of Staff of the Storm Troopers, was asked yet again to consent to the prolongation of Hindenburg's term of office. Meetings were held in the Ministry of the Interior, since this was the department concerned with such constitutional changes as the prolongation of the President's term of office. Hitler met Brüning and (for the first time) Schleicher at further conferences, but still withheld his consent, even attempting to communicate direct with Hindenburg by letter to offer him his support provided he would reject Brüning's proposal as 'unconstitutional'. He went further at a meeting with Meissner, offering support for Hindenburg as Presidential candidate if he would dismiss Brüning and hold new elections. Brüning in conversation with Hans Schaeffer in June 1932 gave an interesting first-hand account of Meissner's activity during this piece of negotiation:

> When we sounded out the Nazis on how to avoid the Presidential election altogether, Meissner first negotiated with Hugenberg and Hitler, and told me at first that everything would be all right. When both refused to play, Meissner did his damnedest to seduce Hitler. When they failed to agree about the wording of the press communiqué about the negotiations with the Nazis, Meissner went to see Hitler in the Kaiserhof three times in one single afternoon. In the end they produced a communiqué I couldn't possibly allow to go out. Meissner told me the Reich President had already approved the text, and wanted it published in that form. I made it clear I would resign that very evening. There was a meeting that same evening in my office attended by Groener, Meissner, Schleicher and Pünder. Groener tried to persuade me to stay, but Schleicher did not appear to like this at all. He looked at Groener in a manner which convinced me that he would in future intrigue against him. Finally, however, the communiqué was reworded as I wanted.[8]

As for Meissner, Brüning considered him, according to Schaeffer, as an opportunist, a weak but not unpleasant man.

Hitler assumed by now that he could not fail to make the Nazi Party the leading party in the Reichstag. Schleicher, meanwhile, was disenchanted with the Nazis, and in particular with his contact Roehm, from whom he expected support.[9] Roehm, however, advised Hitler against supporting Hindenburg. In short, in January 1932 everyone was at everyone's throat. Schleicher was overheard to claim at a fashionable restaurant in front of an admiring company of women that what Germany needed was a strong man—at the same time tapping himself on the chest. Brüning's days were numbered, and even Hindenburg was losing his taste for him during this period of intrigue concerning what seemed obvious to him—that Germany as a whole should be proud to prolong his term of office now that he had deigned to offer himself to the nation.

On 15th February Hindenburg announced his decision to stand as a candidate in open poll. Now that it was apparent the Presidential election would indeed have to be held, the question of Hitler's own candidacy exercised his intuitive judgment. Goebbels, who was to be responsible for the campaign, accepted Hitler's prolonged period of rumination with what patience he could muster; his diary is full of anxious expectation, as the time was growing short. His views are clear enough as he records the give-and-take during January. Of the meeting on 7th January he records:

> The Leader has been to see Groener. Groener tried to get his assent to parliamentary sanction for the prolongation of the term of office of the Reich President. That would be feasible, but in this case the Presidency is not really in question. Brüning only wants to stabilize his own position indefinitely and that of his Cabinet. The Leader has asked for time for reflection. The situation must be clarified from every viewpoint. For the moment a series of constitutional difficulties have first to be removed. No doubt Brüning is trying to bring off his big coup. And yet he will fail.
>
> The contest for power, the game of chess, has begun. It may last throughout the year. It will be a fast game, played with intelligence and skill.
>
> The main point is that we hold fast, and waive all compromise. We ought then, by all the rules, to come off victorious.[10]

After another session with Brüning on 10th January, he writes:

> Brüning's tactics were not good. He wants to turn the Presidentship into a mere business affair, and the price of our help is to be the acknowledgment of the legal constitution of our Party. The Leader rejected the proposition briefly and coldly. Brüning attempted to recall his suggestion, but it was too late. Now everyone is scuttling about in the Wilhelmstrasse like a lot of distracted hens. Brüning's position is seriously endangered. All sorts of pressure and countering forces are being brought to bear. But it is we who hold the ace of trumps.
>
> The Leader is going to bring about a dissolution of the Reichstag. This is the crux of the matter. The decision lies with the people. We alone can emerge victorious. This is perfectly well known to Brüning, and constitutes the reason why he wants to

avoid this issue. He will have to give in, or the struggle for the Presidentship will develop into a struggle between us and the System.

Great pity that the venerable Marshal von Hindenburg is being dragged into all this! But it is not our fault.

On 19th January Goebbels was with Hitler in Munich:

> Talked over the Reichspräsident question with the Leader. I report as to various conversations. No decision has as yet been reached. I strongly urge him to come forward as candidate himself.
>
> Nothing less can now be seriously considered. We scan the figures, but after all figures are not everything. It is his name that really signifies.
>
> Another SA man shot in Berlin. Public indignation is at boiling-point. Some time or other it will boil over.
>
> The Leader has made a marvellous reply to Brüning. His memoranda are always distinguished by logic, lucidity and consistency. It puts Brüning out of court.
>
> The Brown House is full of fight. Only the Defeatists of the Party are flagging. They fall back on Strasser.

The reference to Strasser is significant; he was advocating support of Hindenburg along the lines suggested by Brüning.

Hitler withheld his consent to be nominated for election as President until 19th February, four days after Hindenburg's announcement; this was partly, no doubt, showmanship, since everyone in the Party was palpitating to know whether or not he would stand. But it was also the result of Hitler's built-in sensitivity to any kind of public exposure which might lead to humiliation, and he was uncertain (and rightly so) whether he could conceivably win against the massive vote which Hindenburg was bound to attract, including all Leftists who were not Communist supporters. He had to consider whether the contest was indeed as essential to his present rising position as Goebbels, for example, kept insisting, and whether loss at the election with as high a poll as possible was not preferable to the anonymity of not standing at all and so allowing the Presidency to go to Hindenburg unchallenged for another term. The only other candidates were Ernst Thaelmann, the Communist leader, and Colonel Theodor Düsterberg, representing the Stahlhelm. It is significant that there was no candidate from the considerable 'moderate' wing in German politics; Brüning, of course, supported Hindenburg, who represented extreme Right-wing 'stability' rather than moderation, though he commanded the vote of all 'democrats' in Germany.

Goebbels entered the fortnight's election campaign with abandon—
'we must make up our minds to live dangerously . . . I hope to achieve
a masterpiece in the way of propaganda.' The campaign opened on
22nd February in the Sportpalast:

> Sportpalast packed. General meeting of the members of the
> northern, eastern and western districts. Immense ovations at the
> very onset. When after about an hour's preparation I publicly
> proclaim that the Leader will come forward as candidate for the
> Presidency, a storm of deafening applause rages for nearly ten
> minutes. Wild ovations for the Leader. The audience rises with
> shouts of joy. They nearly raise the roof. An overwhelming spectacle.

Hitler's Austrian nationality had not been overlooked. He was formally
made a German citizen on 25th February.[11] Hitler himself spoke
ceaselessly in places as various as Berlin, Breslau, Stuttgart, Godesberg
and Hanover. Goebbels spoke nineteen times in Berlin, and on nine
occasions in various other cities.

The only basic worry for the Party leadership had been lack of
finance in preparation for this sudden burst of activity, involving
massive printing commitments, propaganda films and gramophone
recordings, travel and the other manifold expenses occasioned by
election campaigning. This, however, was put right when Hitler visited
Düsseldorf on 27th January and addressed a meeting of industrialists
organized by Fritz Thyssen. He spoke with fervour for over two hours,
and with instinctive skill swayed this critical audience in his favour;
as a result, more money was made available to help the Party. But
Hitler was not the only one in financial straits at the time of the election.
Brüning suddenly discovered that the expenses for Hindenburg's
election campaign of 1925 had still not been paid, notably printing bills.
This time the money had to be found in advance for Hindenburg's
election literature. It came, according to Heiden, from such industrial·
ists as Siemens, Duisberg and Bosch.[12] Hitler certainly did not have
the support of the majority of the nation's industrialists, as is commonly
believed. Others again supported Düsterberg and the Stahlhelm.

The first ballot on 13th March just failed by 100,000 votes to give
Hindenburg his absolute majority:

Hindenburg	18,650,730	(49·6%)
Hitler	11,339,285	(30·1%)
Thaelmann	4,983,197	(13·2%)
Düsterberg	2,557,590	(6·8%)

Hitler had plainly lost the election but, as Goebbels put it, 'it is better to lose a battle than fight shy of it'. Hitler's vote, however, was substantial, and he was 'entirely composed' and ready to face the second round.[13] Goebbels hit on the brilliant idea of sending Hitler this time round Germany by air, with the symbolic sense of a great leader descending from the skies to implant his urgent political message in every part of the nation. This was to initiate a permanent policy of electioneering by air throughout the rest of the year. Although Hindenburg achieved his majority in the second round, Hitler raised his poll by over two million votes, while the Communist candidate, Thaelmann, lost over a million and a quarter. Düsterberg had withdrawn from the contest. The results of the ballot of 10th April were:

Hindenburg	19,359,533	(53%)
Hitler	13,418,051	(36·8%)
Thaelmann	3,706,655	(10·2%)

Had Hitler actually won the Presidency, there was some suspicion but no evidence that the SA and SS were in readiness to conduct a *coup d'état* and seize control of the Army, the Reichswehr (which they greatly outnumbered) and therefore of the State. Schleicher (having gathered some hints of this from Roehm, who was the enthusiastic author of these advance plans, which included putting SA forces in a ring round Berlin) instigated, along with the Defence Minister Groener, a police raid on National Socialist headquarters; this was carried out on the order of Carl Severing, the Social Democrat Minister of the Interior in Prussia.[14] Severing alleged that his men had found documentary evidence of the plans for a *coup d'état*, including Roehm's orders. However, Hitler's absolute determination to maintain in public his mask of 'legality' is evidenced in his statement on 11th March 1932 to Sefton Delmer, the distinguished correspondent of the London *Daily Express*, in response to Delmer's query whether he would, if appointed Chancellor, continue the system of government by emergency decree. Hitler replied: 'No, I consider that government by emergency decree is a crime against democracy. It is absolutely illegal. Emergency decrees are only justified in rare emergencies', such as 'a Polish invasion of Germany'.

Hermann Rauschning, the member of the Danzig Senate who was in touch with Hitler during this period, records the mood of the Party at the time:

> Hitler's followers reproached him with the charge that he had missed the most favourable moment to strike. And in truth the economic crisis began in 1932 to ease a little. The influx into the Party fell off. Hitler's opponents began to draw together, and

seemed well in the running. Driven to the wall, outflanked in all his chances of action, Hitler saw his plans to capture power melting away. The Reich presidential election was a heavy defeat for his party.[15]

Goebbels sought what consolation he could:

> The second election has enormously enhanced our chances. There is no occasion for despair. The Conservative parties have been beaten all along the line.
> The public will stand for anything except cowardly giving in.[16]

Although they had lost the Presidential election, the Nazis were greatly heartened by the great leap upwards in the votes cast for them. Now they could proceed with the next phase in the year's election—that for the Diets in a number of States, and notably the State of Prussia.

To appreciate the widely differing importance of the provincial elections (which ran parallel to those for the Presidency and the Reichstag) it is necessary to realize the difference in size and relative strength of the States listed under the Federal system. The German Republic was composed of seventeen States with the following populations:

Larger States (*over a million*)		Smaller States (*under a million*)	
Prussia	38 million	Mecklenburg-	⎫ Over half
Bavaria	7 million	Schwerin	⎭ million each
Saxony	5 million	Oldenburg	⎫
Württemberg over	2 million	Brunswick	⎬ 0·5 m
Baden over	2 million	Anhalt	⎫ One-third
Thuringia	1·5 million	Bremen	⎭ million each
Hesse	1·5 million	Mecklenburg-	⎫ Around
Hamburg	1·5 million	Strelitz	⎪
		Lippe	⎬ 100,000
		Lübeck	⎪ each
		Schaumberg-	⎭
		Lippe	0·05 m

Among these States it is clear that the dominant one was Prussia, all the more so because its centre of government was in Berlin, side by side with the federal administration of the Reich.

The day-to-day regional administration of Germany was conducted through the State Diets or Parliaments, each controlling its individual

Ministries. Above all, control of the police of Germany was invested in these States through their Ministry of the Interior. They were therefore much concerned with the civil strife caused by the Nazis and Communists; Prussia in particular was bringing pressure to bear on Groener to exercise control by Federal decree on the vast army of Storm Troopers whom the Nazis were deploying in the streets.

The all-important elections in Prussia, which contained some two-thirds of the population of Germany (total 65 million in 1932), had been timed by Carl Severing to follow immediately after the Presidential elections in order to exploit what had been calculated as Hitler's likely defeat at the polls. The election was to be held on 24th April, parallel with that in Bavaria, Württemberg and other States. The Prussian government, in particular, was firmly set against Hitler's strong-arm policy, however much it might be masked by 'legality'; as soon as it was clear which way the Presidential elections were going, Otto Braun (the Prussian Premier) and Severing brought the fullest pressure to bear on Groener at the Defence Ministry to have Hitler's forces disbanded.[17] They were successful, and in spite of Brüning's misgivings that the action might boomerang, the SA and SS were demobilized by government decree on 14th April on the grounds that they 'form a private army whose very existence constitutes a state within the State, and represent a permanent source of trouble for the civil population'. This put a great strain on the relations between Roehm and Hitler; Roehm, prone always to maintain his own line of thought about 'his' army of 400,000, was not above conducting independent discussions with Schleicher or (since his forces outnumbered those of the official Army four to one) considering taking independent action to seize the State, ostensibly on behalf of Hitler.[18] At the back of Roehm's mind was his own ultimate emergence as head of the combined forces of the SA and the State Army, the last thing Hitler would ever wish to see.

At this moment of internal crisis, ten days before the State elections, Hitler's authority held. The miracle, he claimed, would be wrought on 24th April, and the SA and SS must meanwhile become full-time Party workers obediently discarding their uniforms and their street parades and rallies. Hitler resumed his propaganda 'whistle-stop' flights the day after the prohibition had been placed on the SA. The *deus ex nimbo* flew down like a bird of prey, speaking in twenty-six centres during the nine days prior to the election. Goebbels describes them:

> The Leader is planning a new 'plane campaign for the Prussian elections. He intends to start on Sunday. His perseverance is admirable, and it is amazing how he stands the continual strain.

At work again organizing his great 'plane trips. Now we have quite a lot of experience in these matters.

An important problem is how to make use of the Leader's propaganda flights for the Press. Everything has to be minutely prepared and organized beforehand.[19]

Goebbels himself had to conduct the campaign largely from a sickbed; but he enjoyed nothing better than to dramatize each moment of 'supreme' effort. His diary entries reflect the hectic energy with which the Nazis conducted their campaign at a period when peak results were essential to their future survival:

I give an address in each of the two halls. The audience has no idea how bad I feel. And at last we get home, where I drop into bed. Am in high fever all night.

On Friday morning I am still very ill, and to make matters worse, I am not allowed a moment's rest; the telephone is going all the time, I am wild at being checkmated in bed, just when things are at the climax.

The Leader passes through Berlin on his trip by air. From Tempelhof he goes on directly to Neuruppin. In the evening, when he comes to see me, I am feeling a little better. He gives a wonderful description of his tour, which has really become very extensive. In East Prussia the people have risen as a whole.

Now he is speaking in the Sportpalast. The Berliners are quite beside themselves with enthusiasm, and are eager for the fray. I feel slightly better and manage to get some sleep for the first time for three days. On Saturday morning I am more or less myself again.

The Leader flies to Schleswig-Holstein.

At noon I hold a last big conference from my bed. Everything is in perfect working order. The flags of the Parties bedeck the streets. The Swastika is victorious.

The concentration of energy from Nazi headquarters bore fruit, in Prussia especially. The results of the various provincial elections were as follows:

Prussia	National Socialists	162 seats (previously 9 only) 36 per cent of vote (8 million votes cast)

In comparison the Communists won 56 seats.

(Although this did not give the Nazis absolute control, their position as the strongest Party in the Diet meant that the coalition in the previous government which had supported Brüning was now powerless.)

Bavaria	National Socialists	43 seats (previously 9)
		32·5 per cent of vote
Hamburg	National Socialists	31·00 per cent of vote
Württemberg	National Socialists	26·4 per cent of vote

The following month the Nazis obtained a clear majority in the State of Oldenburg, with its half-million population, achieving a poll of some 48 per cent. Goebbels was the last person to despise successes in the lesser States, where it was possible to bring the full force of Nazi persuasion to bear on comparatively small communities, boosting such results as foretastes of greater victories to come:

> Good news late in the evening: we have carried off an absolute majority in Oldenburg. We have obtained twenty-four of the forty-six mandates. That is the first coup! If it goes on like this all over the country, there will be no stopping us. . . . The Poll! The Poll! It's the people we want. We are all entirely satisfied.[20]

This minute victory ran parallel with important movements on the Federal level.

III

After his election in April, Hindenburg—disgruntled by the considerable measure of support Hitler had achieved and the difficulties in which he was being placed by the advice and counter-advice of Brüning, Schleicher, and Groener [21]—found himself in a dangerous position. Hitler had to be reckoned with, however distasteful this might be to the Field Marshal. He had been committed by Groener (who was now a sick man and unreliable) to prohibiting the SA and SS on 14th April, but what of the Marxist Reichsbanner and the Right-wing Stahlhelm, of which Hindenburg himself was President? At Schleicher's instigation he had been led to commit himself in a letter to Groener demanding an investigation of the Reichsbanner. This letter was published in the press, as was Groener's reply implying that the President's allegations were exaggerated. The Nazis naturally had made the most of the 'defence' of the Marxist forces by the government during their Prussian election campaign. Schleicher, meanwhile, was able to undermine still further the influence of Brüning and Groener in the Presidential circle, helped by both Oskar and Meissner. He had his eye firmly on acquiring the Chancellorship for himself, and the powerful advances gained by the Nazis in the provincial election made it clear to Hindenburg that Brüning should no longer remain Chancellor. Certain projected land reforms made him unpopular with the landowning class with whom

Hindenburg was identified.[22] His credit on the State was being over-drawn. All that was left to Brüning now was to secure some notable victory for Germany in the field of foreign relations, primarily clearing Germany, if at all possible, of the obligation to pay further reparations, and achieving some revision of the worst elements in the Treaty of Versailles affecting Germany's military situation and her parity with the other principal European nations. But the Reparation Conference at Lausanne had been postponed till July, and Brüning's efforts at Geneva were, it would seem, frustrated to a degree through Schleicher's influence with the French Ambassador in Berlin. Could Brüning hold out against both his enemies and his critics (who now included Hindenburg himself) for long enough to achieve a notable victory in the international field? Meanwhile, the Nazis kept up a constant bombardment against him in the Reichstag and in the press.

By the time Brüning returned on 1st May, empty-handed and despondent, from Geneva, where the French had refused to endorse his very fair plan for German parity with the other nations alike in armament or disarmament, the forces gathering against him at the Presidential Palace and in the Reichstag were soon to prove insuperable. Hindenburg wavered between his traditional respect for Brüning and his response to Schleicher's evil influence.

The first blow was the enforced resignation of Groener as Minister of Defence (but not as Minister of the Interior, his other ministerial position) on 12th May. Groener had rallied to defend the Reichsbanner, which he did not consider a sufficiently subversive organization to ban, and had in consequence come under merciless attack in the House from Göring. It was his own man in the Ministry of Defence, Schleicher, however, whom he had always trusted and regarded as a son, who coldly informed him he had lost the confidence of the Army and must resign; his demise had been prepared by Schleicher and backed by General Hammerstein, the Commander-in-Chief of the Reichswehr.[23]

Schleicher was now fully engaged in secret discussions with the Nazi leaders, though Hitler kept as much in the background as possible. Both sides were debating how power should be divided. Hitler's unerring instinct at this time was to keep matters in the balance, not to compromise, not to come to power half-cock. These interesting and informative efforts at compromise should be left to the others; even Brüning was forced to consider how to bring the Nazis into some pattern of coalition government in Prussia without yielding his own authority. Hitler wisely held off, sensing the tide was moving in his direction. Goebbels's comment at the time (9th May) reinforces this:

A colourless temporary Cabinet will make way for us. Its composition must not be too strong, so that it can readily be dissolved. It is of capital importance that our liberty of action be restored.

It would pay not to rush precipitately into any form of government office which might prove unstable. It mattered far more at the moment to get the ban of the SA lifted.

Schleicher's position was that he sought the goodwill of the Nazis by appearing fervently to oppose the ban, and proposing a new short-lived Cabinet under Papen which would enact this. Certainly Brüning would never yield on this point, and in a long overnight interview with Schleicher, in which he offered him the post of Minister of Defence (which Schleicher refused), Brüning prophesied that one day he would become caught up in the toils of an intrigue. The nature of these intrigues was revealed in a meeting at Schleicher's house on 8th May, which is described by Heiden dramatically as follows:

> On May 8, in Schleicher's home, Hitler met Oskar von Hindenburg, the President's son, and State Secretary Otto Meissner, his adviser. These figures, little known or entirely unknown to the general public, now concluded an agreement for the salvation of Parliamentary democracy with the best-known, most-voiced and photographed demagogue of the day. In order that Hitler might help to provide a 'functioning Reichstag', the present Reichstag must be dissolved and new elections held—which lay within the sphere of the Reich President's power. Then the National Socialists would return with twice their strength; but in order that they might fully develop their strength, the stirring tramp of the Brown SA must once more be heard in the streets. Hitler again had an opportunity to make it clear to doubting minds that the SA was no army for civil war, but a propagandist organization for the election campaign. The salvation of Parliamentarian democracy demanded that the SA must again enjoy freedom—this was the gist of the pact of May 8. For Hitler promised at the same time to 'tolerate' the Cabinet which the President would appoint after Brüning's fall—this meant not to attack it, hence actually to support it.[24]

This paved the way for the temporary Papen government planned by Schleicher, in which he would hold office as Minister of Defence, and power behind the throne. Goebbels's comment is eloquent:

> The Leader has an important interview with Schleicher in the presence of a few gentlemen of the President's immediate circle. All goes well. The Leader has spoken decisively. Brüning's fall

is expected shortly. The President of the Reich will withdraw his confidence in him.

The plan is to constitute a Presidential Cabinet. The Reichstag will be dissolved. Repressive enactments are to be cancelled. We shall be free to go ahead as we like, and mean to outdo ourselves in regard to propaganda.[25]

Hindenburg, meanwhile, had been withdrawn at the end of April by his circle to Neudeck so that he be kept as free as possible from Brüning's influence. He did not return to Berlin until a month later, at the end of May, and not before Schleicher had paid him a visit to try to secure the immediate downfall of Brüning as soon as the President returned to Berlin. Hindenburg, as usual, was vacillating according to his mood and the most recent influence brought to bear upon him. Finally, on Sunday, 29th May, he summoned Brüning to the palace and, in a state of unease, his hands shaking, began to read him a set statement from a sheaf of notes. He permitted no interruption until he had finished. The upshot of his accusation was that Brüning's government no longer commanded the nation's confidence. He did not, however, directly demand his resignation. The Cabinet met later in the day and decided resignation was their only choice. At noon the following day Brüning was summoned to the presence again, and before Hindenburg could utter any further comment he tendered the resignation of himself and his Cabinet. It is ironic that only that morning he had heard through the American Ambassador that France was now willing to negotiate disarmament terms if Brüning could return to Geneva. The last honest man and last democratic statesman of stature in Germany had been out-manœuvred and driven from power, and a clearway for Hitler to realize his ambitions was opening up. Worn out, Brüning went home to bed, and slept for twenty-four hours.[26]

There is an interesting sidelight on Schleicher's character in Hans Schaeffer's unpublished diary, recording a conversation he had with Brüning on 7th June, a few days after his loss of the Chancellorship. Schaeffer asked Brüning whether Schleicher was really strong, or the type of senior officer who thrives on success, but panicked when things went wrong. Brüning replied, 'I should think, the latter. He's a very energetic man, but very moody. He changes his mind repeatedly. At times he has stood up for me quite vehemently, and then again he would intrigue against me with the Old Man [*Alte Herr*: Hindenburg].' Later in the same month, Schaeffer noted Groener's observations on Schleicher. He was, Groener said, 'resolute, but he frequently changes his aims'. As for Schleicher's relations with Hitler, Groener observed shrewdly, 'He wants to stop Hitler getting to power on his own. He wants to "tame" him by obtaining some minority share in the government for the movement.'

Brüning also made interesting observations on Oskar von Hindenburg, and on the influence of the women in the Hindenburg circle. Schaeffer asked Brüning who in his entourage really influenced the President:

> BRÜNING: His son, more than anyone else.
>
> SCHAEFFER: And what about him?
>
> BRÜNING: He's a fairly simple man, not really malicious, but obsessed by the historical image of the family name. For that to be cursed by the Right and held up by the Left, for the Social Democrats to provide his father's electors—that's the anomaly he can't stomach. His wife, incidentally, is a very intelligent and sensible woman, and a moderating influence.
>
> SCHAEFFER: Schleicher's wife's intelligent and sensible too.
>
> BRÜNING: I agree. I was impressed by her. The women incidentally have played some part in these matters, particularly since Groener's recent marriage.

Goebbels was naturally beside himself with glee at Brüning's fall:

> The bomb has exploded. Brüning has presented the resignation of the entire Cabinet to the President, at noon. The System has begun to crumble. The President has accepted the resignation. I at once ring up the Leader. Now he must immediately return to Berlin. . . . The news of Brüning's downfall came through just as I was dictating the last article against him. So I could bid him farewell at once.
>
> Meet the Leader at Nauen. The President wishes to see him in the course of the afternoon. I get into his car and give him a good all-round summary. We are enormously delighted. The whole country is relieved.[27]

The second meeting between Hitler and Hindenburg took place on 30th May at four in the afternoon, with Göring present. The interview was entirely formal, and they were not even invited by Hindenburg to sit down. The President informed them he intended to appoint Herr von Papen Chancellor, and that he had gathered Herr Hitler was prepared to support him. Hitler answered 'yes', and that was all. Behind Hitler's affirmation was the understanding that the SA ban would be lifted. Goebbels gave an advance view of the appointment at Party Headquarters: 'Von Papen is likely to be appointed Chancellor, but that is neither here nor there.' All they wanted was the SA back in force, and new Reichstag elections. Papen's days were numbered before he began to take control.[28]

In a sense, Papen, who was virtually unknown to the German people, and was a member only of the Prussian Diet, not of the Reichstag, was initially at least Schleicher's puppet.[29] He was aged fifty-three. His charm soon commended him to Hindenburg and his circle, where he became known as 'Fränzchen'. Papen's arrival moved the government markedly to the Right, since it was made up largely from the nobility or from the industrialists; neither Brüning nor any of his former colleagues would join the new government, though Papen had originally belonged to the same Catholic Centre Party as Brüning. The Centre Party had repudiated Papen, remaining loyal to Brüning in his defeat. Among the Ministers whom Hindenburg virtually dragooned into office were Konstantin von Neurath (Foreign Minister), Count Schwerin von Krosigk (Finance Minister), while the Minister of Justice, Franz Guertner, was virtually a pro-Hitlerite, having in the past favoured him when Minister of Justice in Bavaria.

But what really mattered was the presence of the *éminence grise*, Schleicher, who took over the Ministry of Defence. Since Papen's government depended entirely on the goodwill of the Nazis, the game of who was going to betray whom first could now proceed. The British Ambassador wrote the following dispatch to London on 14th June 1932: 'The present Cabinet is a Cabinet of mutual deception. Herr von Papen thinks he has scored off General von Schleicher and Hitler, General Schleicher thinks he has scored off Hitler, and Hitler, for his part, believes he has scored off both.'

Papen's government was to last just over six months, from 2nd June until early December.[30] In accordance with Schleicher's various agreements, Papen's first actions were to dissolve the Reichstag on 4th June, ordering new elections to be held on 31st July, and to rescind the ban on the SA and SS on 15th June. Immediately the street battles between Nazis and opposing factions of the Left began with renewed vigour, in spite of the President's order accompanying the withdrawal of the ban:

> I have met the Government's request for the present regulations to be relaxed in the expectation that political activity throughout the country will become more orderly, and that all acts of violence will cease. I am determined, if these expectations are not realized, to use every means in my power to halt abuses, and I authorize you to make known my intention in this respect.

Papen's own account of his first meeting with Hitler is not without interest, considering their later relationship:

I met Hitler for the first time on June 9, 1932. The initiative had come from me. I wanted to hear his version of his arrangement with Schleicher and to try to gauge what attitude the Nazis would adopt to my Government. We met in a flat belonging to Herr von Alvensleben, a friend of Schleicher. I found him curiously unimpressive. Press pictures had conveyed no idea of a dominating personality and I could detect no inner quality which might explain his extraordinary hold on the masses. He was wearing a dark blue suit and seemed the complete *petit-bourgeois*. He had an unhealthy complexion, and with his little moustache and curious hair style had an indefinable bohemian quality. His demeanour was modest and polite, and although I had heard much about the magnetic quality of his eyes, I do not remember being impressed by them.

After a few polite formalities I asked him for his views on the possibility of supporting my Government. He brought up his usual list of complaints—previous governments had shown a lamentable lack of statesmanship in excluding a political party with such wide support from its due share in the affairs of the State at a time when an attempt should be made to correct the errors of the Versailles Treaty and restore full German sovereignty. This struck me as a most important point, and as he talked about his party's aims I was struck by the fanatical insistence with which he presented his arguments. I realized that the fate of my Government would depend to a large extent on the willingness of this man and his followers to back me up, and that this would be the most difficult problem with which I should have to deal. He made it clear that he would not be content for long with a subordinate role and intended in due course to demand plenary powers for himself. 'I regard your Cabinet only as a temporary solution, and will continue my efforts to make my party the strongest in the country. The Chancellorship will then devolve on me,' he said.[31]

It was clear that Hitler was using his technique of good behaviour on this occasion, though the sting was in the tail. Actually there had been some discussion of making Hitler Vice-Chancellor, but, as Göring put it fourteen years later when on trial at Nuremberg: 'I remember that I told Herr von Papen that Hitler could become any number of things, but never as a "Vice". Whatever he was to become, he would naturally have to be in the highest position.'

On 20th July, eleven days before the Reichstag elections, Papen (recently back from the Lausanne conference where he had been forced to agree, nominally at least, to final reparation payments of three thousand million marks) dismissed the Prussian government and, under Article 48 of the Constitution, appointed himself Reich Commissioner for Prussia. This was necessary, in his view (with which the President concurred), because of the rising disorder on both the Left and the Right, and the party impasse in the Prussian Diet itself.[32] The position in Berlin was anomalous because the security of the Federal Ministry buildings and personnel came under the Prussian police administration, not the central Federal government. The Prussian police force was very large, numbering some 90,000 men. The Prime Minister of Prussia, Otto Braun, was ill, but Carl Severing, Prussian Minister of the Interior, declared to Papen, face to face in Berlin, that he would yield only to force. This he formally did, as did his police chiefs when they too were confronted by Lieutenant-General von Rundstedt (the future Field-Marshal) representing the military authority assigned the task by Papen.[33] Broadcasting to the nation, and on the external services to the rest of the world, Papen declared that civil war was imminent, and that he had been forced to take these measures. His words had been anticipated by Goebbels himself almost a month earlier in the security of his private diary:

> To Munich by night train with Helldorf and Heines. We talk over the serious situation in Berlin. Civil war smoulders there. At any moment it might burst out. We must be on the *qui vive* and watch over the safety of the Party with the utmost vigilance and, in a given case, seize the power.[34]

Democratically minded heads in the Prussian administration were replaced by men of the Right. It was a *coup d'état* of a State within the State, and a full dress-rehearsal for Göring's action the following year.

Once again the election fever was at its height. The Nazis at least had youth on their side—Hitler was forty-three, Göring thirty-eight, and Goebbels thirty-five. Hitler undertook a third series of propaganda flights. As Goebbels described it:

> Once more eternally on the move. Work has to be done standing, walking, driving, flying. The most urgent conferences are held on the stairs, in the hall, at the door, or on the way to the station. It nearly drives one out of one's senses. One is carried by train, motor car and aeroplane criss-cross through Germany. One arrives at a town half an hour before the beginning of a meeting or sometimes even later, goes up to the platform and speaks.[35]

But they were happy—'A National Socialist only feels himself when he is at liberty to make a fight of it. . . . Our boys are quite beside themselves. One could go horse-stealing with them'. Speech-making and street fights went alongside each other. Within a month ninety-nine were killed in the streets, and 1,125 were reported wounded. The Altona riots of Sunday, 17th July near Hamburg were among the worst: thirteen (some say nineteen) were reported to have been killed and about 300 injured.

The election of July gave Hitler the highest vote he was ever to achieve in a national ballot conducted under a free system of polling. The principal results were as follows:

Nazis	13,745,781 votes	37·33% of votes	230 seats in Reichstag
Social Democrats	7,959,712 votes	21·6% of votes	133 seats in Reichstag
Communists	5,282,626	14·3% of votes	89 seats in Reichstag
Catholic Centre	5,782,019 votes	15·7% of votes	75 seats in Reichstag
German Nationalists	2,177,414 votes	5·9% of votes	37 seats in Reichstag

The total votes cast were some 36·9 millions.

Although their vote was now almost double that of the Social Democrats, the second party, this still did not give the Nazis a working majority against their various opponents, even when the parties of the extreme Right aligned themselves with Hitler. In spite of the record figures, Goebbels's comment is subdued:

> The situation seems to show that we can only achieve anything under the parliamentary system in union with the Zentrum. This party would be the touchstone. They would handcuff us and try to tame us down. We will have to be extremely wary and trust no one but ourselves. Things will not be made easy for us. . . . We do not intend to be content with mere apportionment of power.[36]

Hitler was, after all, by far the most powerful single political figure in Germany, and the Party, reeling with its electoral increases, expected something dramatic from him. But Hitler kept his head. He was far from being in power; the combined forces poised against him, though made up of parties which were much smaller individually, amounted collectively to a formidable opposition. Indeed, whatever bombast they might utter in public, or even among themselves to hearten their flagging spirits, the Nazi leaders must have known that they had achieved the peak of their genuine support from the German nation. After this, the only change they could anticipate would be a gradually declining vote in any free and secret ballot. This accounts for the note approaching despair which is recurrent in Goebbels's published diaries, even though edited to give the utmost favourable impression of himself and Hitler.

There followed now a succession of meetings at which hard bargaining took place behind the scenes, while the SA stood in a state of excited readiness, anxious to take part in a *coup d'état* and enjoy licensed blood-letting in the streets. Meanwhile Hitler met Schleicher (not Papen) on 5th August at Fürstenberg, near Berlin, and put his demands for office on the table. These were:

Hitler:	Chancellor
Other Nazi leaders:	Prime Minister of Prussia
	Reich and Prussian Ministers of the Interior (controlling the police)
	Minister of Justice
Minister of Defence:	Schleicher
Minister of Popular Enlightenment and Propaganda: Goebbels.	

Hitler then left it to Schleicher to arrange this with Hindenburg and Papen (whose name was absent from the list), and departed for his mountain retreat at Berchtesgaden, there to await the President's summons.

But the days went by. Nothing happened for a week.[37]

Both Hindenburg and Papen dug in their heels. The President, who remained in Neudeck until 10th August, would not hear of a single Nazi on the government benches, while Papen, blandly happy to be Chancellor with the President's if no one else's support, refused to budge. At a Cabinet meeting on 10th August Papen declared to his colleagues that he thought it imperative to draw Hitler into a position of 'responsibility' commensurate with the 37 per cent of the electorate which he now commanded. The powers and functions of the leadership must be clearly defined, and then this vociferous Nazi movement, with certain of its leaders in the Cabinet, must no longer be allowed to interfere from the streets with the business of government. The Minister of Finance (Schwerin-Krosigk) thought it preferable to have the Nazis in the government than to continue in this state of uncertainty; with the SA at Hitler's disposal, it would be better to 'make the poacher act as gamekeeper'. Baron von Braun considered that Strasser, as representing the 'more staid and reasonable strata of the Party', might be given the Ministry of the Interior.

Eventually the summons came to a third meeting with the President, on 13th August. Hitler was in a state of uncertainty, as Goebbels describes:

> He paces up and down the room and the terrace the whole evening. Visibly a struggle is going on within him. The decision which has to be arrived at on the morrow is of immense importance; it must be deeply considered from all points of view. Further develop-ments will depend on his visit to the President of the Reich. Is the fruit of ten years' work ripe at last? None of us dare hope so. One has to be prepared for anything.

As a preliminary, on 12th August he had met Papen, who calmly offered him the position of Vice-Chancellor, with the Prussian Ministry of the Interior as make-weight. Papen has given his own account of this preliminary confrontation:

> I soon realized that I was dealing with a very different man from the one I had met two months earlier. The modest air of deference had gone, and I was faced by a demanding politician who had just won a resounding electoral success. 'The President,' I told him, 'is not prepared to offer you the post of Chancellor, as he feels that he does not yet know you well enough.' I urged upon him the necessity of joining in a coalition government as proof that he and his party were willing to accept their share of responsibility for governing the country. . . .
>
> I told him he must not think that because I was not prepared to vacate the Chancellorship in his favour, I wanted to exclude his party from their share of responsibility in the affairs of state. I had no great wish to retain the post, but I suggested that for the time being he should join the Government as Vice-Chancellor and that some of his more trusted party colleagues should become ministers. I was prepared to give him my word that if our co-operation in the Cabinet was successful, I would resign the Chancellorship in his favour, once the President had got to know him better.
>
> I had tried to be as serious and straightforward as possible, and I had clearly given Hitler food for thought. But he still tried to convince me how impossible it would be for the leader of such a large movement to play second fiddle to another Chancellor. His movement expected to see him at the head of affairs. . . .
>
> I used every possible argument to convince him that for the moment there was no other practical way of granting him a share of the responsibilities of state. He could not afford to maintain his party in opposition; if he did, their campaign must begin to flag. It was in his own interest to act now.

It was all no use, and I resigned myself to the unpredictable consequences of my failure to reach some understanding.[38]

The next day Hitler, furious at Papen's 'betrayal', as he saw it, went to see the President at four o'clock in the afternoon. It was an angry session. Meissner, who was present, has given his own account of what was said:

> This meeting was held in Hindenburg's study, and, aside from Hindenburg and Hitler, only Goering and myself were present. Hitler outlined in a long speech his general ideas and his political aims, emphasizing that he wanted to come to power by legal means, discussing at length the domestic reforms he hoped to achieve, as well as declaring a desire to regain Germany's sovereignty in the military field and over the whole extent of German territory. At this conference he stressed explicitly that he wanted to achieve all these aims only by pacific means, through negotiation and persuasion. He stressed repeatedly that in order to achieve these aims and to work successfully he needed to have full power, that he would be unable to carry out these plans with coalitions and promises by rival groups. He therefore rejected any division of power with other parties. Hindenburg stated that because of the tense situation he could not in good conscience risk transferring the power of government to a new party, such as the National Socialists, which did not command a majority and which was intolerant, noisy, and undisciplined.
>
> At this point, Hindenburg, with a certain show of excitement, referred to several recent occurrences—clashes between the Nazis and the police, acts of violence committed by Hitler's followers against those who were of a different opinion, excesses against Jews and other illegal acts. All these incidents had strengthened him in his conviction that there were numerous wild elements in the Party beyond effective control. With regard to foreign policy, Hindenburg stated that conflicts with other states had to be avoided under all circumstances. After extended discussion, Hindenburg proposed to Hitler that he should declare himself ready to co-operate with the other parties, in particular with the right and centre and that he should give up the one-sided idea that he must have complete power. In co-operating with other parties, Hindenburg declared, he would be able to show what he could achieve and improve upon. If he could show positive results, he would acquire increasing and even dominating influence even in a coalition government. Hindenburg stated that this also would be the best way to eliminate the widespread fear that a National

45

Socialist government would make ill use of its power and would suppress all other viewpoints and gradually eliminate them. Hindenburg stated that he was ready to accept Hitler and the representatives of his movement in a coalition government, the precise combination to be a matter of negotiation, but that he could not take the responsibility of giving exclusive power to Hitler alone. In his reply, Hitler stated that it was not his intention to place party members in all ministerial jobs and leading positions, but that he would take in experts and experienced civil servants. He was adamant, however, in refusing to put himself in the position of bargaining with the leaders of the other parties and in such manner to form a coalition government. As was announced in the communiqué following this meeting, Hindenburg and Hitler failed to reach any agreement concerning participation in the government by the Nazis.[39]

'The atmosphere was icy when Hitler took his leave,' wrote Papen, who was also present.

The official communiqué describing the meeting in severe terms was published at such speed that even Goebbels was caught out. It read:

> The President inquired of Hitler whether he, either alone or in the company of other appropriate members of the NSDAP, were prepared to join a government under the direction of Chancellor Papen. Hitler said he was not prepared to join in such a government, demanding of the President, instead, that he (Hitler) be granted direction of the new government, with full government powers in his hands. President von Hindenburg refused this demand most emphatically, arguing that neither his private conscience nor his public obligations would permit him to transfer full government powers to the National Socialist movement, which intended to use these powers to further its private ends.

Hitler, angry and deeply disappointed because he had thought victory was his, retired to Berchtesgaden. 'Deep despondency besets the Party,' wrote Goebbels on 14th August.

In his report of this meeting between Hitler and Hindenburg to his Cabinet on 15th August, in which he said the session actually lasted ninety minutes, Papen made the point that Hitler had said the three million additional votes of the Marxist parties were dangerous, and that it was his aim in life (*Lebensziel*) to destroy these parties completely, and that it must be done 'by fire and sword', with no regard for the bloodshed involved. Papen added that in offering Hitler the Vice-Chancellorship he had exceeded what the President had authorized.

In refusing the office, Hitler, said Papen, had claimed that after the March on Rome the King of Italy had given Mussolini full power, and not a Vice-Chancellorship.

During the remaining period in August certain uneasy attempts were made to secure some common ground with the Centre Party. It may seem strange that the Party most closely associated with Brüning should consent, out of its antipathy to Papen, to hold discussions with the Nazis. The reason is given by Brüning himself in a letter written to a friend of Schacht, Paul Rohrbach, a journalist and politician, who gave the text of the letter to Schacht:

> For weeks past I have been urged by persons who do not belong to my Party not to refuse a discussion with the National-Socialist leaders. As long as negotiations were pending between the National-Socialists and the Government I could not bring myself to engage in such discussions for fear of upsetting these negotiations. Since, however, the Government subsequently failed to come to an agreement with the NSDAP (a situation clearly foreseen by knowledgeable politicians at the time of the dissolution of the Reichstag), and following renewed petitions by patriotically minded people, I have signified my readiness to seek contact with them.
>
> Such a discussion would serve to determine whether it were anyhow possible to form a constitutional Government, and I considered it my bounden duty to attempt it. I feel it is incumbent upon me now as heretofore, vis-à-vis all those who elected the President of the Reich, to spare no effort to consolidate the President's authority and prevent any straying along an unconstitutional path. You will see from this that my action is determined, not by any bitterness but by anxiety for my country.
>
> I am in entire agreement with you in your condemnation of the events at Beuthen and also of Herr Hitler's statements in this connection. If, nevertheless, you still raise objections to my having discussions with leaders of the National-Socialist Party you will have meanwhile gathered from the newspapers that even the Government does not refuse to have dealings with Herr Hitler after his above-mentioned statements. As a matter of fact, my activities in this matter are confined to this discussion. The actual negotiations are in the hands of persons connected with the Central Party who have been expressly nominated by the Party committees to conduct such negotiations.[40]

In the light of this letter it cannot be claimed that Germans, or at any rate those alert in politics, were unaware of the threat Nazism repre-

47

sented under its mask of legality. Hitler himself, as well as his chief propagandist, was frank enough; they were already forecasting the notorious Enabling Act which, once they achieved office, would give them the absolute power they needed. The real culprits were the German electorate who, in the face of a corrupt form of 'democratic' authority, increased Hitler's strength in the State till it was impossible for those in authority to disregard him. The only temporizing measure either the moderates or the Right could think of was to build Hitler into their administration, and by these means control or restrain him. Hitler, however, was wise enough to realize he should enter the government only in the highest office available to him, the Chancellorship, where he would be in the ascendant to conduct the ultimate struggle for power. Goebbels expressed the point clearly in his Diary note for 16th September:

> The Leader is great just because he follows out one sole end with dauntless tenacity, and is ready to sacrifice everything for it. It is this which especially distinguishes him from those *bourgeois* politicians who maintain that they think and aim as he does. Without Hitler, Germany would long ago have been extinguished in a maelstrom of anarchy.

When the Reichstag assembled on 30th August it was witness to an odd scene. By tradition the oldest member of the House always presided at the opening session. This duty fell by right to Clara Zetkin, an eighty-four year old Communist, a Party relic who had been included among the Communist deputies (elected on the basis of proportional representation) solely to gain publicity by taking the floor in this way. She staggered through a long speech on Marxism which the House tolerated more out of astonishment and amusement than anything else, especially as the old lady had for a long time lived in Moscow and had come specially to Berlin to play the part. Torgler, the Party Leader in the House, got her through the speech by standing beside her and prompting her. The Nazis no doubt thoroughly enjoyed the attack on the Papen government which had been put in her mouth. Shouting began only after she had finished, and had been helped down from the rostrum. In the uproar, Göring, as had been prearranged, was nominated for President of the Assembly, amid shouts from supporters and opposition alike.

Göring had been nominated by the Nazi deputies in alliance with the Zentrum (Centre) and the Bavarian People's Party. He won 367 votes; his rivals, Loebe the Socialist and Torgler the Communist, received only 135 and 80 respectively. 'I assert to the entire German nation,' he proclaimed to the Reichstag (and through it to Hindenburg) 'that my election as President . . . has clearly demonstrated that the . . . Reichstag enjoys a large, workable majority and that therefore absolutely no legal state of emergency can be said to exist.' It was a remarkable achievement for a man who only five years previously had been an unemployed exile returning to Germany from Sweden. No one knew that seven years previously the new President, who was entitled to reside in a Presidential palace situated opposite the Reichstag, had been confined in a strait-jacket during his cure for drug addiction in Langbro mental institution in Stockholm. Göring, Goebbels, Roehm and other top Nazis were by now fully fledged members of the exclusive Herrenklub, and could hobnob with the gentry and the generals. Only Hitler, as befitted his image of prophet leader, kept aloof.

Göring explained when on trial at Nuremberg in 1946 what his new position entailed:

> If, for instance, a government resigned in the Reichstag or was brought to fall by a vote of no confidence, it was my duty . . . to suggest to the Reich President, after having negotiated with the Parties, what the possibilities were in my opinion for a new coalition government. Thus the Reich President was always bound to receive me in this capacity with regard to these matters. Therefore I could bring about a rather close connection between the Reich President and myself.[41]

What the Nazis wanted to achieve at this stage above all else was the defeat of Papen, not the dissolution of the Reichstag. With the Centre Party so antipathetic to the Chancellor, they had high hopes of using their new-found alliance with the Centrists to win a vote of no confidence in his government. On the afternoon of 10th September, Göring's Presidential palace, decorated in gilt and plush, was the scene of a lengthy discussion between Hitler, with his aides, and leaders of the Centre Party, including Monsignor Ludwig Kaas and Brüning. His aim was to use them to obtain the Chancellorship. Goebbels reports on this exploratory meeting:

> The Leader's arguments are strong and clear as usual and his statements are logically marshalled. The gentlemen of the Zentrum who meet him for the first time are obviously impressed by the force of his personality. Nothing decisive results, but general overtures are made.[42]

The House reassembled on 12th September, and it was there that the celebrated incident took place in which Göring attempted to outmanœuvre Papen and secure the fall of his government. Papen, however, had already called on the President at Neudeck late in August and secured the necessary dissolution order for use in self-defence if this should seem necessary. It was, in effect, an insurance policy, since it meant that Papen could step in and dissolve the Chamber if it appeared at all probable that his new government was unlikely to secure the necessary vote of confidence. He would then, with Hindenburg's backing, rule by emergency decree. At a Cabinet meeting on 31st August he had reported that the President was determined to keep the present Government, his 'Presidential Cabinet', in being as long as possible, and had given him, Papen, a blank authority to dissolve the Reichstag if and when it should prove necessary, but that he would use this authority only if it was quite unavoidable. If the Reichstag could stay dissolved for six months or so, which Papen would have preferred, then the Government, working by emergency decree, might be able to make some progress, especially in the economic field and in the battle to resolve unemployment. However, it would in fact be a breach of the Constitution to postpone elections beyond sixty days following a dissolution. To keep the Reichstag in a state of dissolution for so long was against the Constitution, and could involve Hindenburg, who tended to be strict in these matters, in breaking the letter of his oath of office.

However, there was another factor which affected the session on 12th September. On 4th September a Presidential order of considerable importance 'for the revival of the economy' had been promulgated; its aim was to take steps to overcome the depression, and it included a form of 'tax voucher' to encourage business credit and turnover, while employers were to be permitted to lower wages in proportion to their employment of extra labour. This greatly angered the Communist and Socialist parties, and built up a further stiff reaction against Papen in the Reichstag.

When Papen arrived in the Reichstag at three o'clock in the after-noon of 12th September he was apparently expecting ample time to place his programme for the alleviation of the economy, as well as other important matters such as foreign affairs, before the House for debate. The House was overflowing; the Visitors' Gallery was filled, with many of the Diplomatic Corps present. Papen noticed that numbers of the Nazi delegates were in brown-shirt uniform. The agenda had been agreed on 30th August, and in Papen's view the debate on his pro-posals might well last a matter of days. He did not therefore bring the dissolution decree with him, which since Bismarck's day had always been prominently displayed in a red portfolio. It would, to say the least, have appeared out of place in his hands at this initial session. Under Göring's presidency, Papen as head of government should have been called upon to speak first. Instead, Torgler, the principal Communist deputy, intervened on a point of order to demand that the agenda be altered, and that a vote be taken immediately repealing the emergency decree of 4th September, followed by a vote of censure on the government.

Such a proposal would have been constitutionally acceptable provided no delegate rose to object. At a preliminary meeting of the House Steering Committee, however, the Nationalists had declared they would raise an objection to such a proposal. However, no one rose up from their ranks. The Nationalists, it seemed, had been instructed not to oppose Torgler's proposal because they knew Papen's safety measures, and therefore imagined he would step in and dissolve the House before any vote was taken. This they would have favoured, or, as Goebbels put it, they did it 'to annoy us'. But Papen did not have the dissolution order with him, and so was in a grave dilemma. It was Frick, however, of all people, who unconsciously came to Papen's rescue, by proposing there should be a 30-minute recess. As leader of the National Socialists in the House, he felt the need for Hitler's advice. The Centrists supported him, and the motion was carried. So the deputies trooped out to consult in Party Groups about what should be done.[43]

The half-hour's grace was used to the full. Papen sent for the missing red portfolio; there would now be no mistaking his intentions. Göring and the Nazi leaders conferred hastily with the representatives of the Centre Party, who wanted to oppose Torgler's resolution. Göring challenged this: he welcomed the vote of censure. Hitler had been sent for, and hurrying over to Göring's Presidential Palace, opposite the Reichstag, approved the decision to go along with the Communists' resolution. Göring went back to the session chamber determined at all costs to put Torgler's proposal to the vote, and so displace Papen on a combined Nazi-Centrist-Communist count. The red portfolio would then go by default, since Papen would technically no longer be Chancellor and a dissolution signed and presented by him would be invalid. Or so Göring was prepared to gamble.

Göring once again achieved his ends by sheer buccaneering, refusing even to look at Papen, who was carrying the prominent red folder with the dissolution order. Papen demanded the hearing which was his right (by Article 33, paragraph 3 of the Weimar Constitution) amid a wild hubbub of voices. Göring resolutely turned a deaf ear, studiously looking away from the Chancellor, and put the Communist resolution to the vote. Papen slapped the dissolution order down on Göring's desk, but he brushed it aside and the vote of no confidence was put and carried 513 to 42, with 5 abstentions. Only then did Göring deign to notice the dissolution order, and immediately declared it to be void because it carried the signature, he claimed, of a Chancellor who was no longer in office. Papen meanwhile had left the House in a rage, followed by his Cabinet. His exit was, as he put it, accompanied by a 'positive howl of derision'.

Papen knew that, legally speaking, he was still Chancellor, and acrimonious exchanges between him and Göring followed in the form of written memoranda. Göring also knew perfectly well that what he had done was *ultra vires*, and that by the action of placing the dissolution order on Göring's desk *before* the vote had been taken, it was the vote of no confidence that was invalid, not the order of dissolution. The President upheld this, as he was bound to do. The Reichstag was therefore dissolved, while Papen remained Chancellor. It was perhaps ironic that through Göring's action Papen, throughout his six months' tenure of office as Chancellor, was never to have an opportunity to address the Reichstag. Moreover, the country had had a chance to see something of Nazi tactics in the crude action of Göring, and of Nazi violence once again in the horrifying Potempa murder, which had received nationwide publicity. The new campaign had to be fought in the atmosphere of gathering criticism of the Nazis.* Papen was convinced that the longer he played for time, the greater were the chances that popular support for the Nazis would wane. He would have preferred, if possible, to postpone the election indefinitely, but this was against the Constitution and the conscience of the President.

The challenge to Hitler's strength was opened.

* This was one more reason for the utter lack of realism in Schleicher's pet idea of splitting the Party by getting Strasser and Leipart, the trade union leader, to link up in a Schleicher administration. Apart from much other evidence we have statements by Fritz Heine and Professor J. Caspari (prominent SDP members at the time) that while the fact of Leipart's having had informal talks with Schleicher was known (and disapproved of), the SDP leaders, both in the Party and in the Reichstag, made it clear to Leipart that 'under no circumstances could any co-operation with Schleicher be tolerated'.

Part 2

The Hundred Days:
Approach and Climax

I. From the 1932 November election to Hitler's appointment as Chancellor, January 1933

i

The election date was set for 6th November, the latest allowable under the Constitution. The Nazis were desperately short of money; as Goebbels put it on 20th September: 'The election campaign costs money, and money, at present, is very difficult to obtain.'[1]

The election proved that Papen was right. The Nazis lost over two million votes, and thirty-four seats in the House, whereas the Communists gained ground, increasing their seats from eighty-nine to a hundred. The principal results were as follows (with comparative numbers for the July election in parenthesis), the total number of deputies in the new House being 584 (608 in the previous House).

	Votes	Per cent of votes	Deputies
Nazis	11,737,010 (13,745,781)	33·1 (37·33)	196 (230)
Social Democrats	7,247,956 (7,959,712)	20·4 (21·6)	121 (133)
Communists	5,980,102 (5,282,626)	16·85 (14·3)	100 (89)
Centre Party	4,230,500 (4,589,400)	11·9 (12·5)	70 (75)
German Nationalists	3,019,099 (2,177,414)	8·5 (5·9)	52 (37)

Thus the German Nationalists and Communists had gained substantially, and largely at the expense of the Nazis and to a lesser extent the

Social Democrats, who had lost over half a million votes. The Catholic Centre, opposed to Papen, lost almost half a million votes. Nevertheless, Papen took some courage from the Nazi losses, so far as they went, which was scarcely far enough. They were still by far the largest single Party in the House, and so had to be reckoned with. No possible coalition could consistently outvote them. Papen's instinctive feeling that time was on his side and that Hitler's influence in Germany was passing its zenith was now directly opposed to Hitler's instinctive calculation that he could certainly win if only he could hold out until the vacillating opposition was forced to seek stability in his leadership, and so enable him to keep his restive supporters calm.[2]

Papen had hoped to maintain a Presidential (or Presidial) Cabinet, as he put it, 'free from and above party political ties', gaining a majority vote of confidence in the House. At Nuremberg he maintained it was 'a cabinet independent of the parties, directed by experts'. The weakness of this position was, as the British Ambassador had put it in his Report of 19th September, that 'persons wishing to support the Papen Government, and they are in increasing numbers, will not know how to vote'.

At Nuremberg in 1946 Papen gave Germany's 1932 unemployment figures as 1·5 million unemployed young people, 6 to 7 million chronically unemployed, and 12–13 million only partly employed. Papen's analysis of Germany's economic position was as follows:

> There seemed to be no reason why Germany should not still solve her economic difficulties. In purely mathematical terms, her national debt was one of the lowest in Europe, barely a third that of Great Britain, not an eighth that of France, and only half the pre-war debt. Our main problem was psychological. During the whole of the reparations period, and as a result of inflation, economic pessimism had become endemic. The workers were so bemused by unemployment, and by Communist, Socialist and Nazi propaganda, that they had lost confidence in the power of government to relieve their lot. We had to convince both capital and labour that the solution was largely a matter of confidence.
>
> Our chief instrument was a system of interest-bearing tax-bonds, intended to provide industry with working capital and encourage it to take on workers and increase production. Each new worker employed ensured the employer a reduction of 400 marks in his tax assessment. Other alterations in the tax scale encouraged the introduction of a forty-hour five-day week by the employment of as many workers as possible. We hoped to provide, by the back door, so to speak, not only a powerful impetus to industry, but to

combine it with measures of social reform. In spite of this, the Socialist parties opposed every aspect of the plan.

The financial position was desperate enough. It was calculated that 23,500,000 Germans—about 36 per cent of the population—were dependent on public funds. That included the Civil Service, the Army, pensioners, and the unemployed. Such a burden made the free interplay of economic forces almost impossible, but we had made a start. Our 2·2 milliard marks had been provided out of our own resources, without having to apply again for an international loan. It made a call on our last reserves, and the success of our plan depended on whether the sums expended in unemployment pay could now be devoted to more productive enterprises. The first month raised our hopes high, with a reduction during October in the number of unemployed by 123,000.[3]

In the days following the election, Papen cast about for supporters. The Centre (Zentrum) Party still refused to co-operate; they preferred to try to make some deal with Hitler. Papen therefore felt forced to deal with him himself, and wrote on 13th November:

Dear Herr Hitler,
When the President of the Reich appointed me to be leader of the Government on 1 June, he gave orders that the Presidential Cabinet, which I was to form, should represent the strongest possible concentration of all nationalist elements. You warmly welcomed this decision of the Reich President at the time and you pledged your support of such a Presidential cabinet. When after the election of 31 July we tried to establish that concentration within the Presidential cabinet, you took the attitude that such concentration of all national elements was only possible under your leadership. You know how much I, in a series of conferences, tried to find a solution which would profit the country best. But for reasons which are well known to you, the Reich President considered he had to refuse your claims for the Chancellor's office.

Since then a position has arisen, owing to the political antagonism of the nationalist elements amongst themselves, which can only be considered regrettable from a patriotic point of view.

A new situation has arisen through the election of 6 November and at the same time a new opportunity for all nationalist elements to be concentrated anew. The Reich President has instructed me to find out by conversations with the leaders of the individual parties concerned, whether and how far they would be prepared to support the carrying out of the political and economic programme on which the Reich government has embarked. In spite of the national-socialist press calling it a naïve attempt for Reich Chancellor von Papen to confer with the people concerned in the nationalist concentration, and that there can be only one answer, namely, 'No negotiations with Papen', I should consider it neglecting my duties and I would be unable to justify it to my own conscience, if I did not approach you in this matter. I am quite aware from the papers, that you are maintaining your demands to be entrusted with the Chancellor's office, and I am equally aware of the continued existence of the reason for the decision of 13 August. I need not assure you again that I myself do not come into this matter at all. All the same I feel that *the leader of so great a national movement, the merits of which for people and country I have always recognized, in spite of necessary criticism*, should not refuse to enter into discussions on the situation and the decisions required with *that German politician*, who at present bears the full responsibility. We must attempt to forget the bitterness of the elections and *to place the welfare of the country, which we both of us serve, above all other considerations.*[4]

But Hitler refused to budge by moving one step to meet Papen, who he was convinced must inevitably lose his hollow Chancellorship.[5] He wrote a lengthy and uncompromising letter in reply on 16th November:

Dear Reich Chancellor,
After a full consideration of your request dated 13 November for a conference on the situation and the decisions required, I have to give the following reply:
In spite of misgivings, I share your opinion that as leader of a large party one should not refuse to enter into negotiations on the situation and the decisions required with that German politician who at present bears the full responsibility. However, the nation expects more from such a conference than a *theoretical* approach to the difficulties and problems which occupy them at present. Besides, I have so often in my writing and speeches explained my attitude concerning this, that you, Herr Reich Chancellor, must be aware of same. Small as appear to be the advantages of such a general discussion, as large may be damaging consequences derived therefrom, because millions of our fellow countrymen expect *positive* results from negotiations if they take place at the present moment and if they become generally known. And quite rightly so! Discussions of the position by themselves won't help anybody. Therefore I consider negotiations at this very moment only advisable if their negative outcome is not established from the onset. I am therefore

obliged, dear Reich Chancellor, to name four conditions under which such an exchange of ideas might take place.

Item 1. *I am unable to attend a verbal discussion,* but would ask that, if ideas are to be exchanged, this should be done *in writing.* The experience of the verbal discussions which have taken place so far and in the presence of witnesses, proves that the recollecting powers of the two parties do not yield an identical reproduction of the text and context of the negotiations. You yourself, Herr Reich Chancellor, state right in the beginning of your letter, that you had at one time been assured of the support by the national-socialist party of the Presidential cabinet to enable you to carry out your instruction 'to effect the strongest possible concentration of all nationalist elements'. The facts are that I stated in the presence of Hauptmann Goering, when I was informed that the cabinet was to be reshuffled after the elections, that I would not insist on this, provided the government would fulfil its nationalist duties. I instantly refused a request made to me about the same time to issue in writing a declaration of support, and stressed that this was quite out of the question. One could not possibly ask me to give a blank cheque to men who were partly personally and in any event politically unknown to me. The economic and political measures taken by this cabinet during its first six weeks in office, have justified this reserved attitude of mine.

Your contention, Herr Reich Chancellor, that I had demanded total powers, whilst in fact I only asked for the leadership, prove how far verbal discussions may lead to erroneous conceptions. You yourself were to be a member of the new cabinet in the capacity of foreign secretary; General Schleicher, enjoying the special confidence of the Reich President, was to be minister in charge of the Reichswehr and agent from the Home Office, and two, or at the very most three, ministries of no political significance, all positions were to be staffed by personnel who were either already in office or were to be agreed upon in negotiations between the parties concerned. You, Herr Reich Chancellor, have interpreted our demands, which at that time were more than modest, in such an erroneous light, that wise through experience, I am no longer willing to deviate from the only safe method, that is, to deal with such questions in writing, all the more, since I am obviously powerless against so-called official communiqués. You, Herr Reich Chancellor, are not only able to submit your interpretation to the German people through the officially inspired broadcasting system, but you can also force it on to the readers of my own party newspapers by means of the publications regulation [*Auflagever-*

fahren]. I have no defence against such methods. *If therefore, Herr Reich Chancellor, you intend to enter into a discussion, under observance of the other three conditions, I would ask you to let me know your attitude and/or your questions in writing when I shall similarly let you have my written replies.*

Item 2. There is no point in starting discussions, unless you, Herr Reich Chancellor, let me know in advance how far you do in fact feel and regard yourself as fully responsible in your capacity as the leading German politician. Under no circumstances am I prepared to expose myself again to the methods used on 13 August. For in my opinion it is inadmissible for the 'German politician bearing the full responsibility', to share out his responsibility at a given moment when responsible action is required. I refer here to a passage of your letter in which you now speak of reasons leading to the decision of 13 August, reasons which continued to apply, though at the same time you remark that you yourself do not come into this discussion at all! Herr Reich Chancellor, once and for all I should like to state: Just as I regard myself as basically responsible for the political decisions of the national-socialist party, as long as I am the leader of that party, so are you responsible for the political decisions of the Reich government, as long as you are Reich Chancellor. For that reason I asked you on 13 August to take the responsibility for the breaking-off of our negotiations yourself, instead of setting it on the Reich President. I told you that since, as you assured me, our demands could not be met owing to reasons connected with the Reich President, I had obviously to refuse to call on him in the circumstances. I told you that, as long as a Reich Chancellor bore the political responsibility, it was his duty to cover his sovereign, be he king or a president. When you asked me what ideas I had on this subject, I suggested you should issue an official communiqué to the effect that negotiations concerning the Reich Government reshuffle had taken place between you, Herr Reich Chancellor, and me in my capacity as leader of the national-socialist movement; these negotiations had been unsuccessful and had therefore been broken off. For since I had previously been a presidential candidate, it seemed to me inadvisable toward the millions of my adherents to let the Reich President appear as being in any way connected with my being turned down, which was now to be expected. You were the politician bearing full responsibility for the Reich, and in my opinion it was up to you, especially in this case, to shoulder the responsibility, except if your conscience would have prevented you, in which case it would have been your duty to resign. Unfortunately you could not be prevailed upon to shoulder the due proportion of your responsibility; I carried mine all right. Your chancellery, however, succeeded by means of a subterfuge, against my wishes and in spite of the declaration which you had made, to involve me in a discussion with the Reich President. The outcome, which to you was a foregone conclusion, may have relieved you of the responsibility in your own eyes; it did not destroy me, but it dragged the Reich President, at the age of 85 years, into a common squabble and settled him with a heavy responsibility. I do not wish to see a repetition of this game. *I am therefore only prepared to enter into a correspondence on the situation in Germany and the alleviation of our difficulties, if you, Herr Reich Chancellor, are first prepared to admit unambiguously your full responsibility for the future.*

Item 3. I would ask you, Herr Reich Chancellor, to inform me to what purpose an inclusion of the national-socialist movement is desired. If you intend to get me and the national-socialist movement to subscribe to the political and economic program, on which, as you state in your letter, the Reich government has embarked, any correspondence in this matter would be irrelevant, nay superfluous. I am unwilling and unable to give an opinion on what the government regards as the program of its own violation, since, in spite of the closest consideration, I have never quite understood the program. *However, if it is a question of continuing those internal, foreign and economic-political measures which are being carried out at present, I shall have to refuse any support on the part of the national-socialist movement, since I consider these measures partly as inadequate, partly as insufficiently planned, partly as completely useless, even as dangerous.* I know that you, Herr Reich Chancellor, have a different opinion, but I consider that the practical activities of your Government have already been proven to be at least *unsuccessful.*

Item 4. You say in your letter that as a result of 6 November 'a new opportunity for the concentration of all national elements' had arisen. I must confess that I am quite unable to understand the purport of this remark. I am of the opinion that that possibility has obviously only deteriorated through the dissolution of the diet in September, because the result is on the one hand an immeasurable strengthening of Communism and on the other a revival of the small splinter parties, which are without the slightest practical political value. The formation of a politically practicable block within the German people is thereby, from a party point of view, only imaginable by the inclusion of the Nationalist [*Deutschnationale*] and German people's party [DVP], because I have to decline a prior suggestion, which you seem to have in your mind, to include the Socialist party [SDP]. As you know yourself, the leader of the Nationalist party [*Deutschnationale*] has, prior to the elections, most unambiguously branded any co-operation with the Catholic center party [*Zentrum*] as treason and a crime against the nation. I do not believe that all of a sudden Geheimrat Hugenberg would prove himself so lacking in character that he would do after the elections what he had so strongly condemned before the elections. *Your endeavors, Herr Reich Chancellor, appear to me vague and thereby as much a waste of time as they are useless, as long as you are unable to inform me that Herr Hugenberg has changed his mind after all.*

These four points, Herr Reich Chancellor, I regard as my conditions for an exchange of ideas and/or correspondence. Approval or disapproval depends on you.

In conclusion I should like to assure you, Herr Reich Chancellor, that I am nursing no bitterness on account of the elections. During the 13 years of my struggle for Germany I had to suffer so much persecution and so many personal attacks, that I have learned in time to place the big task which I serve above my own miserable self. What embitters me is merely, to have to observe how, under your somewhat unfortunate statecraft, Herr Reich Chancellor, day after day some of the national wealth, in the creation of which, within the framework of German history, I participated to the best of my ability, is being squandered. *This wastage of the hope, faith and trust of the nation in a German future is what fills me with sorrow and pain but at the same time confirms me in my unswerving resolution, to insist on my demands, which in my opinion can alone overcome our danger.*

Yours faithfully (etc.)

(sgd) Adolf Hitler.

PS. Since I understand that General von Schleicher has been informed of the contents of your letter, Herr Reich Chancellor, I take the liberty of forwarding on my part a copy of this reply.[6]

Papen and his Cabinet finally decided on resignation on 17th November. This placed President Hindenburg in a dilemma. Papen is reputed to have suggested to the President initially that Hitler be invited to try to form a coalition government which commanded a majority vote, so that his certain failure to be able to do so would further expose the weakness of his position in the Reichstag.

Hitler, summoned by telegram, was received once more by Hindenburg on 19th November; after calming himself by listening to music with Goebbels the night before, he went to the Wilhelmstrasse at noon to see the President, who received him and Göring (hurriedly returned by plane from Rome where he had been meeting Mussolini) somewhat more politely than on previous occasions. The meeting was summarized as follows by Meissner:

> By request of Herr Hitler, approved by the President, the first part of the meeting was 'under four eyes'. The second part was attended by signatory Meissner. The Herr Reich President summed up the relevant points of the personal talk like this:
>
> Herr Hitler claimed to have the strongest popular movement in Germany behind him. It was impossible to govern without popular support; hence he, the leader of the movement, should head the new Government.
>
> I answered that I must stick to the principle of a supra-party Government. A Cabinet led by Herr Hitler would be Party Government. Surely Herr Hitler and National-Socialism could further their aims by being assigned some ministerial posts in the Government led by a supra-party man. I would ask you, Herr Hitler, to reconsider matters with your friends and other party leaders. I do not want to give you a definite answer now, nor do I want a definite answer from you. Let us consider the matter and meet again in a few days.
>
> A.H. I respect the sincerity of your convictions. But I can only enter a cabinet in political leadership. I certainly do not intend to have National-Socialists in all ministerial posts. But the political leadership must be uniform. After all, I invest not only my name but my movement. If that perishes Germany would be in dire peril, what with 18 million Marxists and maybe 14 to 15 million Communists. Hence it is in the nation's interest to preserve my movement, and that means leadership. I repeat: my movement does not want the entire power, just the leadership. I would try to let others share in the Cabinet, and I think a basis for co-operation can be found.
>
> When asked by the President why the NSDAP joined the Berlin traffic strike:
>
> A.H. People are bitter. Had I forbidden my men to join, the strike would have happened anyway, and I would have lost support in the working class which would have been bad for Germany. I know the task of forming a Government is far from easy and the country's misery is immense. Even so I would shoulder the task, hoping to bring the country out of this crisis.
>
> REICH PRESIDENT: I can only repeat my request: help me.

I appreciate the greatness of your movement and your own sincerity, but I cannot accept a party cabinet.

When asked whether he was contacting other parties with a view to co-operation:

A.H. I can only do that once the Herr Reich President has instructed me to form a Government. Then, I am sure, we will find a basis for an Enabling Law of such a kind that the Reichstag would only agree to give to myself.

The President concluded by saying that he would reconsider the matter, and he appealed to Herr Hitler's soldierly sense of duty and comradeship.

Length of meeting one hour, 5 minutes, signed, Meissner.[7]

The meeting, which was still abortive from Hitler's point of view, was followed by another on 21st November. This time Hindenburg and Hitler addressed each other through written documents, which they read and interchanged on the spot. The nature of these interchanges was of the greatest importance, for through them both Hitler and Hindenburg came to know each other far better, and so reach a stage where some form of negotiation, at least, was possible. It paved the way to the Chancellorship which was to come in the following January.

There followed then the celebrated interchange of letters between Hitler and Meissner, writing on behalf of Hindenburg. The first exchange, however, took place at the second meeting held at the President's palace on 21st November. Meissner wrote:

The Herr Reich President received Herr Hitler in the presence of the signatory and said initially that he appreciated Herr Hitler personally, and certain of his ideas. After the last meeting he had further pondered the question of the manner in which the National Socialist movement could co-operate in the Government:

REICH PRESIDENT: You know that *I* represent the ideas of a presidial cabinet, meaning one that is led not by a party leader but by a supra-party personality who enjoys my confidence. *You* have stated that your movement would only be available for a cabinet headed by you, the Party leader. If I were to go along with this I would have to demand that such a cabinet commands a Parliamentary majority. Hence I request you, as leader of the largest party, to ascertain whether and on what conditions you could obtain a working majority for a Cabinet led by you with a firm programme. I would like your answer by Thursday evening. (The Herr Reich President hands this over in writing.)

Herr Hitler states that in view of the importance of the matter he too had put down his thoughts in form of a letter which he handed to the Herr Reich President.

A.H.: From press accounts and a confirmation handed to me by Herr Staats-Sekretär Meissner, I learned of Your Excellency's intention officially to request me to enter into negotiations with the other parties, without the previous formation of a new presidential cabinet. This request seems to me so important that, in the interest of your Excellency's great name as well as in the interest of the German people, I wish to state my position in writing.

For 13 years by now I have been fighting the parliamentary system, which I consider to be useless alike in forming or expressing the will of the nation. This conviction, thanks to my own and my collaborators' tireless propaganda, has become the common philosophy of many millions of German men and women. Hence, they all welcomed what seemed to be Your Excellency's decision to recognise new ideas and to initiate new ways in the leadership of the state. If this new leadership is not to end in catastrophe, it must find a constitutionally acceptable point of departure and, as quickly as possible, become the genuine representative of the will of the nation. This means forming a living relationship with that substantial part of the German people who are already our supporters. What matters is to increase the proportion of this support so that it may, in due course, involve the entire nation. Failing this, the result would be a dictatorship supported by and dependent on bayonets. That sort of Government would surely break down when facing its first real test, internally or externally; and the consequence of this could only be Bolshevism. Hence—since I foresaw the failure of the Papen administration after its first six weeks—I emphasized on 13 August that the task could only be faced by entrusting the National Socialist movement with this mission.

For reasons which need not be mentioned here, Your Excellency felt obliged at the time to reject my suggestions.

After governing for six months the Papen cabinet—as I had predicted—has now got itself, and thereby the nation, into hopeless isolation. There have been attempts to save our economy and to deal with unemployment, but the results are either nugatory or unsatisfactory. The general misery is terrible and the nation's confidence has vanished almost completely. The Bolshevisation of the masses proceeds rapidly.

If a new Government is to take over this heritage, equally terrible politically, economically and financially, it has no chance of success unless strong authority from above is linked with great strength from below.

Having been called to Berlin again by Your Excellency to help alleviate our people's greatest crisis I can only do it if my movement and I are granted the position required for fulfilling the task—a position, incidentally, which is owed the movement by the nature of its strength within the nation. The hard necessity to put Germany above Party will only be appreciated when the strongest movement, a priori, is given the powers which, up to now, Your Excellency has never denied the leaders of presidial cabinets. It would, too, be a basic requirement in all fairness, considering that my movement, with its 196 deputies in the Reichstag, already commands two-thirds of the number of seats needed for a Parliamentary majority and constitutionally legal Government.

I can promise Your Excellency that I am determined to provide the constitutionally required basis of long and fruitful work for a Presidial Cabinet, led by me and approved by Your Excellency; my only request is that you grant me the same kind of authority and power you have given my predecessors, who could not bring to the great authority of Your Excellency's name as much as I can. Even though, in fulfilling the constitution in respect of the legal activities of the forthcoming Government, I have to enlist the co-operation of other parties; after all, Herr Reich President, I have the support of by far the greatest of all parties. My own name and the existence of my great movement would be destroyed if our effort should end in failure. The alternative, Herr Reich President, would not be a military dictatorship but sheer Bolshevik chaos.

Should you, nevertheless, intend to return to the old parliamentary form of Government, Your Excellency, you should plainly say so. I for one would deeply regret it.

In summing up, may I ask Your Excellency to appreciate my reasons and to abstain from any attempt of that kind in seeking a solution to the crisis.

(sgd) A. Hitler

Verbally Herr Hitler added that, so far, unofficial contacts with the Zentrum had shown that they would create what would seem to be insuperable difficulties over the question Reich-Prussia.[8] Herr Hitler then asked the President which 'presidial conditions' would arise for the formation of a Government. The Herr Reich President answered:

1. A program for the economy. No return to the dualism Prussia-Reich. No negotiations with the *Länder* demanding special privileges. No limitation of Art. 48.

2. I reserve to myself in person the final word in approving the

list of ministers. The appointment of the Foreign Secretary and the Minister of Defence is to be my prerogative.

This formulation was also handed to Herr Hitler in writing.

Herr Hitler then declared that he would give the Herr Reich President his answer in writing this very afternoon. The signatory then informed Herr Hitler that the Herr Reich President intended to issue a press communiqué, the gist of which he read out. Herr Hitler had no objections.

The Herr Reich President concluded the meeting with these words:

However this matter and the negotiations may end only God knows. We do not. But one thing I wish to emphasize: whatever the end of our negotiations, my door will always be open to you.

Length of meeting about 20 minutes.

(sgd) Meissner

Letter from Hitler to Meissner, dated 21.11.32.

Well aware of my great responsibility in these grave times, I gave much thought to the Herr President's instruction received earlier today, and, having thoroughly discussed it with leaders in my movement and in public life, have come to these conclusions:

When I compare the two documents containing the Herr Reich President's instructions on the one hand and his underlying conditions on the other, there appear to be some insoluble contradictions. But before explaining my view of this and my ensuing ultimate decision, may I ask you, Herr Secretary of State, to ascertain the views of the Herr Reich President and to let me know which form of Government the Herr Reich President desires and, indeed, envisages in this particular case. Does he envisage a presidial cabinet involving the parliamentary toleration constitutionally required? Or is His Excellency thinking of a Parliamentary cabinet with conditions and restrictions involving the need for an authoritarian leadership? When comparing the two documents, Herr Secretary of State, you will admit the need for clarification. I would like to add that Chancellor Brüning was and remained the party political leader of the Zentrum and yet was a Presidial Chancellor in his second administration. As for myself, I did not feel myself to be a party leader, but simply a German; mainly to relieve Germany from the pressure of Marxism, I have created and organized a movement which is alive and effective way beyond the borders of the German Reich. We only entered parliament because the Constitution forced us to take that legal path. Myself, I have deliberately abstained from any parliamentary activity. The difference between my view of authoritarian leadership and the views of the Papen Cabinet is simply this, that I would insist on any such leadership being deeply anchored in the will of the nation. My ardent and solemn aim is to bring this about by lawful means for the benefit of the nation.

(sgd) Adolf Hitler

Letter from Meissner to Hitler, dated 22.11.32.

In answer to your letter of yesterday, I have this to say following instructions by the Herr Reich President:

The Herr Reich President sees the difference between a Presidial Cabinet and a Parliamentary Government as follows:

1. The presidial cabinet—due to the grave times and the failure of Parliament—will usually initiate the required governmental measures by means of Art. 48 of the Reich Constitution and without Parliamentary approval. Its power primarily derives from the President, and Parliament is usually required merely for sanctioning or tolerating such measures. A Parliamentary Government on the other hand has to submit its bills, edicts and decrees to the discussion and approval of Parliament, and derives its power from a Parliamentary majority.

Hence, the leader of a presidial cabinet must enjoy the special confidence of the President.

2. The presidial cabinet must be composed and conducted on supra-party lines and must pursue the supra-party program approved by the President. A Parliamentary Government is usually based on a coalition enjoying a parliamentary majority, the President's influence being minimal and indirect. Hence, a party leader cannot be the leader of a presidial cabinet, least of all one who insists on the exclusiveness of his movement.

3. Reich Chancellor Brüning's first administration was clearly a parliamentary one based on a majority of a coalition of parties; but it gradually changed into a presidial cabinet when the Reichstag could no longer sustain its legislative duties, though Herr Brüning had gained the full confidence of the Herr Reich President. The various reshuffles in the second Brüning Cabinet were usually prompted by the Herr Reich President in order to avoid even the suggestion of any dominance by the Catholic Center Party. Similarly, of course, a Parliamentary Government under your leadership could, in the course of time, change into a presidial cabinet.

4. The Papen Cabinet was a presidial one which had to resign because it could no longer find a parliamentary majority to sanction

or tolerate its legislative measures. Hence, a new presidial cabinet would be an improvement only if it could find such a majority and, at the same time, had the qualities of the Papen Government, such as supra-party leadership and the special confidence of the Herr Reich President.

5. Hence, the Herr Reich President's invitation to you, my dear Herr Hitler, can only mean the formation of a *Parliamentary majority cabinet*. The Herr Reich President has decided to try this out, since the meetings with other party leaders seemed to reveal the possibility of a parliamentary majority for a cabinet under your leadership with an Enabling Law to follow. The 'conditions' mentioned by the Herr Reich President do not preclude a parliamentary solution. It has been the practice of the Herr Reich President as well as that of his predecessor to lay down certain principles for every newly appointed cabinet, and meetings with all relevant party leaders have not revealed any objections in principle. If, however, one or the other of the President's conditions for your formation of a Government would seem to you to impede the achievement of a safe parliamentary majority, the Herr Reich President would expect you to report to him.

(sgd) Meissner

Letter from Hitler to Meissner dated 23.11.32.

In answer to your letter of yesterday I venture to raise three points.

a. As for your definition of a presidial cabinet I have this to say in contradiction:

The claim that a presidial cabinet can enjoy a status which is more supra-party than a parliamentary one contradicts itself, partly because of the very genesis of such a cabinet and partly because of its limitations. When a presidial cabinet is forced to govern by dint of Art. 48 it requires—as you admit yourself—parliamentary majority approval. True enough, it is not required *before* the bill is passed, but it *can* be demanded later.[9]

Such a parliamentary majority must, inevitably, be expressed by parties. Hence a presidial cabinet really depends just as much on a parliamentary majority as a parliamentary cabinet. Thus, the leader of such a cabinet must either possess or acquire the confidence of a parliamentary majority no less than the confidence of the President. Moreover, the Supreme Court has recently ruled that Art. 48 is to apply to certain limited cases and periods only. Hence, the next Chancellor, in order to cope with a great many urgent measures, will have to secure a majority for an Enabling Law, however limited in scope and time. The chances of success will largely depend on the authority of the person concerned, and on the parliamentary voting power already under his control.

Whether a Government program would seem to be based on party or supra-party considerations is immaterial. What matters is success. I protest against the notion that I would refuse to carry through a sensible program merely because it happens to be created by a Party and as a result should be ruled out by a presidial cabinet which sternly maintains its supra-party character. Programs exist to attract human beings who are usually united by the bond of a party. A 'supra-party' programme is likely to be devoid of supporters; how on earth it is to procure a parliamentary majority to approve or tolerate its measures would seem to me an insoluble dilemma. In trying to solve it Herr v. Papen failed utterly.

I resolutely decline that sort of leadership because, inevitably, it leads nowhere, unless propped up by bayonets. I have suggested that, provided I enjoy the confidence of the Herr Reich President, I would be more likely than anybody else to avoid such a catastrophe since, after all, two-thirds of the deputies required are already in my party. The step from 200 to 300 should be easier than the one from 50 or 60 to 200.

b. You tell me, Herr Secretary of State, that the Herr Reich President now desires a 100 per cent parliamentary solution. Which means that I should first agree with the other parties on a program, seek a majority for it, and then form a government based on that majority. May I say that had I been set such a task before 12th September 1932 it might have been easier to accomplish.

It cannot be achieved at all if the task is inhibited by conditions which make its accomplishment impossible. For in case of purely parliamentary procedure we would have to adhere strictly to the Weimar Constitution which requires (Art. 54) a parliamentary majority for the formation of the Government, the selection of the cabinet, and the formulation of the program.

Since the President appoints the Chancellor and the ministers, he reserves, of course, the final decision on the list of ministers. But the supposition that the appointment of the Foreign Secretary and the Minister of Defense should remain the personal prerogative of the President would be incompatible with Art. 53 of the Constitution. These two ministers must be proposed by the Chancellor, for how else could he determine the direction of foreign and home policies for which, according to Art. 56 of the Constitution, he is responsible to the Reichstag. This is not altered by the fact that the President represents the Reich when signing treaties with other states, receiving their Ambassadors (Art. 45) and being the supreme commander of the armed forces (Art. 47). For all orders of the President, including those affecting the Army, require the countersignature of the Chancellor or the Minister concerned (Art. 50).

The economic program, no return of the Dualism Reich-Prussia, no restriction of Article 48—all these are matters in which the President can influence a parliamentary majority cabinet only by Articles 68 and following.

Since you, Herr Secretary of State, tell me that the Herr Reich President, like his predecessor, has laid down certain principles for every newly appointed Government, my answer to this is:

1. Never with conditions on such a scale.

2. Never have we had a situation as catastrophic politically and particularly economically as just now, which means that never was the Chancellor's full authority more needed than it is now.

3. May I remind you that the system of parliamentary Government has never been interfered with as drastically as by Herr v. Papen's presidial cabinet; it would be my responsibility as his successor to submit all this for Parliamentary approval and toleration—submit it, mind you, to parties which have strongly opposed most of these measures! And all that at a time when the position of these parties is strengthened by declaring, first, that I do not enjoy the special confidence of the Herr Reich President, and secondly, that I had been instructed to proceed on the lines of a parliamentary majority coalition.

c. You tell me that the other relevant party leaders are in agreement. Well, they have not stated so in writing, and the very opposite is more than likely. As a matter of fact, the Bavarian People's Party (indispensable for a majority coalition) has clearly said so in official statements. It is all very well to tell me that, in case of unsuccessful negotiations, I could acquaint the Herr Reich President with the reasons; but that would not alter the fact that one could rightfully state I had failed to live up to my instructions.

The consequences for my movement, and hence for the entire German people, would be obvious. I have come to the conclusion, shared by all my collaborators, that the instruction is unworkable in view of its inner contradictions. Hence, I have refrained from contacting other parties during these ensuing days, and I would ask you, Herr Secretary of State, to convey to His Excellency the Herr Reich President this most respectful message:

The instructions given me by the Herr Reich President on Monday, 21st of this month, cannot be fulfilled in view of their inner contradictions, I consider them unworkable and return them to the Herr Reich President.

Yet, in view of the catastrophic situation which confronts our fatherland, it is everyone's duty to do his best to prevent the nation sinking into chaos. Hence, I am still prepared to put our movement and the faith and strength of our youngsters at the disposal of the Herr Reich President and Marshal of the World War who is revered by us all. These are the practical steps I propose:

1. The President asks me to submit within 48 hours a brief program of the most urgent measures to be taken in domestic and foreign policy and in the economy.

2. If this is approved, I should then submit a list of ministers within 24 hours.

3. Apart from other ministers to be taken over from the present cabinet, my suggestions will include General v. Schleicher for Defence and Herr v. Neurath for the Foreign Office.

4. The President appoints me as Chancellor and approves the list of ministers.

5. The President instructs me to provide the constitutional basis for our work and gives me the powers never denied to previous Chancellors.

6. I promise that with the full weight of my person and my movement I will do my utmost to save our fatherland.

Thanking you, Herr Secretary of State, for conveying this message. Yours etc.

(sgd) Adolf Hitler

Meissner to Hitler, dated 24.11.32.

In answer to your letter of yesterday, the Herr Reich President instructs me to reply as follows.

1. The Herr Reich President notes that you consider the attempt to form a parliamentary majority Government as not likely to succeed, and that in consequence you decline the invitation. As for the reasons given by you, the Herr Reich President wishes to observe that, according to statements of party leaders, such as the Zentrum and the Bavarian People's Party, as well as your own statements in the meeting of 19 November, he considered a Reichstag majority quite possible. He cannot recognize an 'inner contradiction', more especially since in my note of 22 November further discussions were envisaged in case one of the President's conditions would appear to provide a stumbling-block in your negotiations.

2. The Herr Reich President thanks you for your readiness to

accept the leadership of a presidial cabinet. But he feels that, in his responsibility to the German nation, he cannot give presidial power to the leader of a party which, over and over again, has stressed viewpoints not approved of by the Herr Reich President. He cannot but fear that a presidial cabinet under your leadership would automatically lead to a Party dictatorship, causing increased and bitter strife within the nation. He cannot be responsible on his oath and conscience for such eventualities.

3. The Herr Reich President regrets that in recent exchanges—including the occasion when General v. Schleicher met you yesterday with the President's approval—you categorically refused collaboration in any shape or form, within or without a new Government. In these circumstances the Herr Reich President can see little point in further written or verbal exchanges.

But the Herr Reich President would like you to know that he is ready at all times to listen to what you have to say about pending questions.

He asked me to tell you that his door is always open to you, and he still hopes that, in due time, it will be possible to persuade you and your movement to collaborate with constructive forces in the nation.

Yours etc.

(sgd) Meissner

Hitler to Meissner, dated 24.11.32

Confirming receipt of your letter containing the President's rejection of my suggestions for resolving the crisis, I would like to make a few additional, concluding points.

1. I did not call the attempt to form a parliamentary majority Government hopeless. I merely said that in view of the conditions attached it was impossible.

2. I pointed out that whatever conditions are made must be constitutionally justified.

3. I did not request the leadership of a presidial cabinet. I merely submitted some independent suggestions for solving the crisis.

4. Unlike others, I have emphasized at all times the need for some constitutionally justified collaboration with Parliament; and I made it quite clear that such were the only conditions in which I was prepared to work.

5. I never asked for party dictatorship; indeed, even now no less than in August I was prepared to negotiate with all other relevant parties in order to find a basis for Government. These negotiations

were doomed to failure because of the preconceived intention to maintain the Papen administration, come what may, as a presidial cabinet. Hence, there is no need to win me over to collaboration with other constructive forces since, in spite of many calumnies, I have done my utmost in this direction all through the summer. I must decline, though, to see this presidial cabinet as 'a constructive force'. Events have proved me right in my negative assessment of this cabinet.

6. It was this assessment which made me issue warnings at all times against an experiment bound to lead to brute force and thereby to failure.

7. Above all, I was never prepared and I never shall be to put the movement I created in the service of interests other than those of the German people. I feel responsible for this to my conscience, to the honour of my movement, and to the very existence of millions of German men and women who have been driven into more and more wretched misery by the recent political experiments.

Regardless of all this, will you please convey to His Excellency the Herr Reich President the expression of my sincere and unchanging devotion.

(sgd) Adolf Hitler

On 24th November Göring held a press conference in order to ensure that the published exchanges between Hitler and the President should be fully understood from the Party's point of view.

The press had received copies of the written exchanges between Hitler and the President, and Göring declared that he wanted to ensure they had what he called a coherent survey of the position. This was necessary in view of what had happened after the conference on 13 August. Pressmen should be well aware that versions containing the very opposite of what, in fact, has occurred could be circulated as an official account.

The decisive point, continued Göring, was why Hitler had not been asked to form a government on 13 August. The manner in which the other side negotiated must needs lead to grave doubts whether they took the negotiations seriously and meant them to succeed, or whether their sole concern was to prove a so-called emergency existed, with the consequence that it was necessary to retain the Papen cabinet. The President's condition that any government must command a majority was impossible. That could easily be proved, said Göring.

It was demonstrably untrue, as Meissner claimed, that the previous week's sessions with the party leaders had led to agreement in principle between them and the President. For instance, there had been no agreement over the question of the amalgamation of the Reich and Prussia. Anyone checking the statements of the Zentrum and the Bavarian People's Party would see that these two parties would never approve of the offices of Prussian Premier and Reich Chancellor being merged.

As for the President's claim that he should appoint the Minister of Defence and the Foreign Secretary (because he was Supreme Commander of the Army and the Reich's signatory for foreign treaties) this would be a breach of the Constitution. The Chancellor is in charge of both Defence and Foreign Policy, and he is responsible to the Reichstag.

Göring claimed that Hitler's suggestion to Meissner on 23 November had been completely misinterpreted. He had not requested the Chancellorship in a Presidial cabinet, and had, in fact, refrained from differentiating between Presidial and Parliamentary Government. He had merely suggested that he should be appointed Chancellor with the requisite powers to create a viable Government with a parliamentary majority. This had been rejected by the President. There can be no question of Adolf Hitler having been offered a chance this time. They had not offered him a chance; they had just 'thrown a spanner in the works'.

Göring hinted that he suspected a certain clique around the President (which he need hardly specify) had done their damnedest to sabotage any possibility of Hitler forming a Government.

Summing up, Göring said that there were only two possibilities open to Hitler. Either, he could have been invited to form a Government, based on parliamentary majority; in which case no special conditions should have been made; or, Hitler should have been entrusted with the Chancellorship, along with all the requisite powers needed to bring pressure to bear on the parties and the Reichstag and, if need be, to appeal to the nation against an 'obnoxious' Reichstag. This would have given Hitler a proper chance: it would have been a fair instruction.

It was never in Hitler's mind to govern in despite of the Reichstag. That was one of the points in which he differed absolutely from Herr von Papen. But he should have been given a chance to acquire a parliamentary majority.

Göring concluded by observing that, while both sides had not irrevocably banged the door, the Führer and his movement would not, in any circumstances, deviate from their clear-cut policy. They would not (repeat *not*) support or even tolerate any Presidial Cabinet. They would make short shrift of any such cabinet, as in the case of the Papen cabinet. It was only Hitler who could save the German people. Finally Göring mentioned an interview Dr. Schacht had given in which the banker had said: 'If Hitler isn't made Chancellor now we'll be forced to send for him four months from now.'[10]

On 25th November Schleicher reported to Papen's Cabinet, which was still nominally in existence, on five specific questions he had put to Hitler. First, Schleicher had asked him if he was prepared to enter a new, re-shuffled Cabinet as a member. Hitler had said directly, 'No'. Secondly, would he oppose a Cabinet led by Schleicher himself. Hitler had replied, 'Yes, even though regretfully.' Thirdly, would Hitler permit any other member of his Party to serve in a Cabinet of which he, Hitler, was not the leader. Hitler said 'No' to this. Fourthly, would he permit a Party member to act as an 'observer' or as 'liaison' in any Cabinet. Hitler replied again, 'No'. Schleicher had asked finally if Hitler were prepared to maintain contact with either the present Reich Government and with the President. Hitler had refused to make any contact with the Government; as for the President, he would always be welcome to Hitler's advice should he seek it. Hitler had added that the first duty of any new government would be to dissolve the Reichstag. Schleicher told his colleagues that the President was determined not to appoint Hitler head of an authoritarian government, or to permit any change in the Constitution. While the Reichstag was in abeyance he regarded himself as the sole guarantor of the Constitution.

Hindenburg, meanwhile, was under pressure from a group of prominent industrialists to reform the Cabinet with the Nazi Party represented. Their ideas were embodied in a memorandum sent to the President late in November:

> Your Excellency:
> Much Esteemed Herr Reich President:
> Filled, like your Excellency, with profound love for the German people and the fatherland, the undersigned welcome hopefully the fundamental change which your Excellency has initiated in the conduct of state affairs. We agree with your Excellency on the necessity of a government run independently from parliamentary party matters; the ideas which your Excellency formulated with regard to a Presidial Cabinet bring this thought into the open.
> The outcome of the Reichstag elections of November 6 of this year had demonstrated that the former cabinet, whose sincere intentions no one among the German people doubted, did not find adequate support within the German people for the pursuit of its

course; it also demonstrated that the goal at which your Excellency is aiming has the support of a full majority of the German people if we—as we should—exclude the Communist party whose attitude is negative to the State. Not only the Black-White-Red party and its related smaller groups, but the National Socialist German Workers Party as well are fundamentally opposed to the former parliamentary party régime; thereby they have agreed to the aim of your Excellency. We consider this result extremely gratifying and cannot imagine that the realization of the goal should now founder at the maintenance of ineffective methods.

It is evident that an oft-repeated dissolution of the Reichstag with increasingly frequent and sharpening elections would not only be detrimental to a political pacification and solidity but to an economic one as well. It is equally clear, however, that any constitutional change which is not supported by the broad masses would elicit even worse economic, political, and psychological results. We therefore consider it a moral duty to ask your Excellency respectfully that, in order to attain the goals of your Excellency which all of us support, the reorganisation of the Reich Cabinet be carried out in a manner which would line up the greatest possible popular force behind it.

We confess to be free of any narrow party-political attitude. We recognize in the national movement which penetrates our people the promising beginning of an era which, through overcoming of class contrasts, only now creates the essential basis for a rebirth of German economy. We know that this rebirth will claim many sacrifices yet. We believe that these sacrifices can be made willingly only when the largest group of this national movement receives a leading share in government.

Entrusting the leader of the largest national group with the responsible leadership of a Presidial Cabinet which harbours the best technical and personal forces will eliminate the blemishes and mistakes with which any mass movement is perforce afflicted; it will incite millions of people, who today are still standing apart, to a positive effort.

With full confidence in the wisdom of your Excellency and your Excellency's feeling of solidarity with the people, we greet your Excellency with the most profound respect.[11]

The many prominent signatories included Schacht, Schroeder, Thyssen, Krupp, Siemens and Robert Bosch.

On 30th November Hitler sent a further brief letter to Meissner, writing from Weimar where he was electioneering. He had just heard through Göring that the President had wanted to see him again in Berlin the following day, 1st December. Hitler wrote to Meissner:

> I have just received your invitation to see the Herr Reich President tomorrow with a view to discussing the political situation and the measures to be taken. Since I have made my position perfectly clear, in writing and by word of mouth to the Herr Reich President, and to the public, and since I was available in Berlin for a week to elucidate whatever point might be doubtful, I have really nothing relevant to add, less so since the political situation has not materially altered.
>
> Moreover I have respectfully submitted to the Herr Reich President the only positive suggestions which I consider feasible for solving the crisis; but these suggestions, as you have let me know, Herr Secretary of State, are *not* to be a basis of tomorrow's discussion. Hence, I cannot be answerable to public opinion by raising new hopes which are bound to be dashed. Moreover, as I happen to be in the middle of the Thuringian election campaign, a merely informative visit to Berlin would seem to be difficult. So I would respectfully ask the Herr Reich President to refrain from inviting me at this juncture.

The events of 1st–2nd December leading up to the abortive attempt to split the Nazi Party were summarized at the Nuremberg Trial by Papen from his standpoint and with the benefit of hindsight:

> PAPEN: The Field Marshal, on 1st December, asked General von Schleicher and me to meet him for a conference. I should like to remark that previously no conversation between Herr von Schleicher and myself about the possibilities for the formation of a future government had taken place.
>
> Herr von Hindenburg asked us about our attitude; I set forth the following:
>
> The attempt to include the Nazi movement into the Presidential Cabinet of Hindenburg had twice failed. Hitler equally refuses to form a majority government. On the other hand, he is exercising a tremendous amount of opposition and is trying to have all my decrees rescinded by the Reichstag. If therefore there is no possibility to form a parliamentary government or to include Hitler into our government without making him Chancellor, then a state of emergency has arisen which requires extraordinary measures. Therefore, I proposed recess of parliament for several months, immediate preparation of a constitutional reform bill later to be

presented to the Reichstag or to a national assembly. This proposal involves a violation of the Constitution.

I emphasize that I know how the great soldier and statesman cherishes the sacredness of his oath, but my conscience leads me to believe that a violation of the Constitution seems to be justified in view of the extraordinary situation, for which the German Constitution provides no remedy.

Then Herr von Schleicher spoke. He said:

'Field Marshal, I have a plan which will make it unnecessary for you to break your oath to the Constitution, if you are willing to put the government into my hands. I hope that I will be able to obtain a parliamentary majority in the Reichstag by splitting the National Socialist Party.'

During the discussion of this plan, I said that it was doubtful to me whether a splitting of the Party, which had sworn loyalty to Hitler, could be achieved. I reminded the Field Marshal of the fact that he should free himself of weak parliamentary majorities through a basic reform. However, the proposals were thrown overboard through the solution offered by Schleicher. The solution offered by Schleicher was only a provisional matter, and a very doubtful one.

KUBUSCHOK (for the defence): What was the decision of the Reich President?

PAPEN: The decision of the Field Marshal was perhaps the most difficult that he had to make in his long life. Without giving any further reasons he told me:

'I have decided in favour of the solution of Herr von Papen, and I request you to start immediately negotiations for the formation of a government to which I can give the instructions in accordance with your proposals.'

The conference was over.

KUBUSCHOK: What did Herr von Schleicher do then?

PAPEN: I exchanged only a few brief words with Herr von Schleicher and tried to persuade him to recognize the decision that the Reich President had made. Herr von Schleicher said 'no'.

Then the same evening, I started discussions with several ministers with regard to the formation of a new government. These ministers told me, 'The plan is excellent, but Herr von Schleicher has told us that we will have a civil war and in that case the Reichswehr will not be in a position to keep law and order in the country.'

I interrupted the discussion; called the cabinet together the next morning and presented to it the situation and informed them of Hindenburg's decision. Then I asked Herr von Schleicher to tell the cabinet now why he believed that there would be a civil war, and why the Reichswehr would not be in a position to keep law and order in the country. Herr von Schleicher called on one of his general staff officers to tell the cabinet that this case had been considered from a practical and theoretical point of view and that they had come to the decision that the Reichswehr and police were not in a position to keep law and order in the country.

Then I said to the gentlemen, 'This is a new situation which I have to report to the Reich President.'

I went to Hindenburg and reported to him. Herr von Hindenburg, deeply stirred about my report, said to me, 'I am an old man, and I cannot face a civil war of any sort in my country. If Herr von Schleicher is of this opinion, then I must—as much as I regret it—withdraw the task with which I charged you last night.'

With that, Herr von Schleicher was appointed Chancellor on the conditions which he had offered to the Reich President at this meeting.[12]

Thus Schleicher's idea, which seemed a possibility at the time, to attempt to break the Nazi Party up into two opposing factions, was put into action. Gregor Strasser was regarded by a section in the Party as a possible alternative to Hitler, especially by those who for some while would have preferred to take a less uncompromising line and see the Party join in some form of coalition government of the kind which had been offered to Hitler.

Gregor Strasser was one of the pioneers in the Nazi Party, and had been for some while the leader in the North while Hitler was re-asserting his authority in Bavaria after his release from Landsberg Castle. Gregor Strasser, through Kaufmann, had been the original employer of Goebbels, who came to him at the same period, in 1925, as an impoverished young academic claiming he could win the working classes for the movement. Strasser, who with his brother Otto had employed Goebbels to sub-edit their party journal and act as party agent and agitator in the Ruhr, was a pharmacist by trade; he had money, and his true interest lay in politics. Goebbels, soon seeing that Hitler was the born leader of the movement, deserted Gregor for him, and became in 1926 Hitler's Gauleiter, or Party leader, in Berlin, his notable successes there soon earning him his position as head of Party propaganda in 1928, as well as a Party deputy's seat in the Reichstag. Gregor Strasser's views lay far more in the direction of socialism than Hitler's, but their differences were more academic than acrimonious during the early years. Strasser was an educated man of some integrity, and had always been accorded a high place in the Party hierarchy; he became one of the twelve Nazi deputies in the 1928 Reichstag. Goebbels owed his own socialistic leanings and sound approach as an orator who appealed to the working class to his initial training under Strasser. Hitler's attitude was essentially opportunistic and certainly non-socialistic, and in January 1926 Strasser had staged a conference in Hanover which was his first challenge to be the leading figure in the Party. Goebbels had then spoken against Hitler. At the answering conference organized in February at Bamberg (where Goebbels recorded in his private diary his shock at what he then regarded as Hitler's reactionary views) Goebbels said nothing in public in support of Strasser, for he was rapidly developing the instinctive opportunism which was to be the foundation of his career in Hitler's service.

Differences had existed between Goebbels, Hitler and the Strassers in Berlin during the period in the late 1920s and early 1930s, when the Strassers became more concerned with revolution among the unemployed, while Hitler was endeavouring to win and retain the support of the Right, and specifically as many industrialists as possible.[13] The Strassers controlled their own wing of the Nazi press, and Otto had already broken away from the Party in 1930 to found his own ineffective movement, the Black Front. Gregor, however, at this stage stood by Hitler at the time of the great electoral successes in 1930.

It was during the period 1931–2 that Gregor Strasser's essential difference in policy from Hitler came finally to the forefront in the Party. During the period when Brüning's Chancellorship was in the balance, Strasser was among the small minority who had favoured coalition with him. Goebbels's published diary for 1932 is full of critical references to him as the clever defeatist in the movement, but it should always be stressed that Goebbels edited his diaries carefully for publication and was interested to denigrate Strasser throughout the year.

March 14th (during the Presidential election):

> With the exception of Strasser we all look at things from the same point of view. We must go on with the fight.

May 10th:

> Reichstag is sitting. Strasser speaks. A little too long and without any special effect. Queer, how little opposition he meets with in the house. Of us all he is the most popular with the enemy. That tells strongly against him.

(This was a reference to Strasser's notoriously 'socialist' speech, in which he spoke of the great 'anti-capitalistic yearning' of the German workers.[14])

May 18th–19th:

> From the Strasser side a sort of guerrilla warfare is in process. But we lay counter-mines. ... I accidentally and indirectly hear that Strasser intends to have a word with Brüning. That would be quite like him. We succeed in scotching the possibility! ... The Strasser clique is double-crossing us through the Parties and Trade Unions.

June 14th:

> Strasser broadcasts. To my notion not aggressively enough.

June 27th:

> Strasser has adroitly managed to finesse the Party. He believes he can direct things into a new course by changes in the organization. But all this is too clever to be successful. Every attempt to disintegrate the Party, or to remodel its structure, will be frustrated by the loyalty to the Leader of all its members. Nevertheless, it is our duty to keep watch. In any case, the Leader can rely upon us all.
>
> Strasser delivers an address to the District Leaders in the afternoon. He takes up the attitude of a 'good fellow'.

August 31st:

> The Leader is very courageous. For the first time he openly speaks of the doings of the Strasser clique. Here, also, he has kept his eyes open; and if he has so far observed silence it was not because he had not noticed anything.

September 3rd:

> Admitted to the Leader all that was on my mind. He mistrusts Strasser very strongly. This is why he will wrest the authority he has in the Party from his hands.

It is a matter of speculation if the course of European history could have been changed had Strasser proved a strong enough character effectively to frustrate Hitler at this delicate period in the Party's progress. The impasse into which German political life had entered induced the leaders in other parties to turn to Strasser as a possible alternative to Hitler, and as one who might split the Party by leading away a substantial splinter group of malcontents prepared to compromise in a way Hitler was not. Nevertheless, Hitler himself made use of Strasser to explore contacts with the other parties, knowing that this man could never become an effective opponent to himself within the Party. Strasser's position, however, was strong in the Party organization, since he was, in effect, its administrator, with contacts through the Party Gauleiters in every area in the country. From July 1932 he dissociated himself more and more from Hitler's 'all or nothing' policy, and during the uneasy period of discussion between the Centre Parties and the Nazis, there were many who would have preferred Strasser to Hitler as the principal representative of Nazism. He was not a lone fanatic, but a man of normal pliability like themselves, a politician of the kind they could understand.

During the middle months of 1932 Strasser was frequently speaking on behalf of the Party but was, apparently, still loyal in public to Hitler. At a mass meeting held in the Circus Krone at Munich, he specifically disclaimed that it was ever the Party's intention to join in some form of coalition government, adding significantly that it made no sense to mention his name in connection with this or that ministerial post. He then declared categorically:

> In the NSDAP it is the Führer who makes the decisions. We do not hanker after ministerial posts. And I resent having my name connected with alleged factions within the Party. There are no such factions—there is one Party only, its leader Adolf Hitler, and we his followers [*Gefolgsleute*]. What we strive for is merely the welfare of the German people, work and bread for every German.[15]

At an election conference of Nazi Gauleiters and other Party representatives in the regions (*Gaue*) held in Berlin on 9th June, Strasser, as Party organizer at headquarters, said to the assembled officials that organization must be strengthened in such a way that 'no power on earth could snatch victory from the Party'. A couple of weeks later at a mass meeting in Frankfurt he claimed that the 'Hitler movement was on the eve of power', while on the following day (14th June) in a radio speech which was banned in the States of Bavaria and Württemberg, he declared that the National Socialist State could only be established by National Socialists. On 20th June, speaking in Cologne, he declared that Hitler had the confidence of the majority in the nation, and this gave him the right to govern. He will live up to this and restore the people's faith in justice, while in the same period in Hamburg he said: 'Give Adolf Hitler power, and he will give you work and bread and freedom. . . .'

On 14th August Strasser began to make strenuous efforts to meet Brüning, sending emissaries in search of him on the train in which he knew he was that day travelling to Munich. Brüning, after consulting other Centre leaders, agreed, and met him in a private house in Tübingen three days later. Strasser was very forthcoming, suggesting Hitler might not insist on his immediate appointment as Reich Chancellor if some effective agreement could be reached right away. He suggested a further meeting in Berlin as soon as possible, if Hitler were agreeable. At this later meeting, which took place in the house of an industrialist who favoured Hitler, Wollmann, Hitler was accompanied by Strasser, Goebbels, Göring, Roehm, and Frick. Brüning did not want office himself, and nothing came of this encounter other than an exchange of views. According to the Gauleiter Hinrich Lohse, Strasser met Brüning again on 23rd August.

Now, when things were in the balance once again concerning who was to be Chancellor and what form of Cabinet was to be set up, Schwerin-Krosigk records in his published observations of the period that a private meeting with Strasser in a 'neutral place' on 13th November was cancelled because Hitler had now forbidden further discussions unless they turned on the 'Führer' being considered as Chancellor. However, they met informally for lunch on 20th November at the house of Fritz von Zitzewitz. Schwerin-Krosigk admits himself impressed by Strasser's 'sanity and sincerity'. Strasser, however, said that unless Hitler was given office soon the radical Nazi rank and file would quite possibly start a civil war.[16]

Strasser's speech at the Sportpalast on 22nd October, in which, according to Goebbels, 'he makes conspicuous overtures of friendship to the Nationalists', and in which, quoting both Hugenberg and Theodor Leipart, the trade union leader, he declared the Party should be ready to co-operate with 'anybody who says "yes" to Germany and is prepared to save Germany with us', led to comment in the opposition press that the Party was facing division and disagreement.[17]

Up to the actual resignation of Papen, who had proved such a favourite with the President, Schleicher had been forced to remain satisfied with his strong influence in the Cabinet as Minister of Defence. With the resignation of Papen, Schleicher's intrigues led him to fall into the trap which he had always preferred to prepare for others—a difficult or impossible Chancellorship. He was easing Papen out by claiming in advance to Hindenburg's circle that the Chancellor no longer commanded the respect of the Army, the Reichswehr—always a strong card with the President. He had also according to Papen planned to split the Nazi Party in two, as we have already seen:

> If he took over the Government himself, he thought he could bring a split in the National Socialist Party which would ensure a parliamentary majority in the present Reichstag. He then gave a detailed explanation of the differences of opinion within the Nazi movement which made it more than likely that he would be able to attract the support of Gregor Strasser and about sixty Nazi

members of the Reichstag. Strasser and one or two of his close supporters would be offered posts in the Government, which would be based upon the support of the Trade Unions, the Social Democrats and the bourgeois parties. This would provide a majority which would make it possible to put through the economic and social programme of the Papen Government.

Schleicher had at last cast himself for the role of Chancellor, and his appointment was announced on 2nd December. 'It is high time,' Hindenburg is reported to have said, 'that the people were talked to in plain German; for that reason we must have a General as Chancellor of the Reich.' The previous day, 1st December, Hitler had held a conference of Nazi leaders at Weimar, at which Strasser had urged cooperation with Schleicher should he become Chancellor.

Schleicher was realistic enough to attempt to widen the range of members for his proposed Cabinet. He was already talking with Theodor Leipart, President of the Association of German Trade Unions, who in October had made a speech, like that of Strasser in the Sportpalast, insisting on the need for collaboration, a speech which Strasser had praised.[18] Then he approached Strasser himself, alarmed at the possible rapprochement between the Nationalists and the Nazis which was being fostered at the Herrenklub. In a confidential talk on 3rd December, he offered Strasser the Vice-Chancellorship and, if he could win the necessary votes in the Prussian Diet, the Premiership of Prussia. He considered at least sixty Nazi deputies in the Reichstag would support Strasser, and split away from Hitler. However, when on the same day the Nazis suffered a catastrophic drop of 40 per cent in the State election in Thuringia, Hitler sent Göring to Schleicher to discuss whether he (Göring) could be appointed Premier of Prussia. Schleicher told him only Strasser was acceptable to the Centre.[19]

This led directly to the often-described confrontation of the Nazi Party leaders—Hitler and Strasser. The first took place at a meeting of party leaders on 5th December in the Kaiserhof; among those present were Goebbels, Göring, Roehm and Frick (who ostensibly supported Strasser, and was himself Party leader in the House). This conference is described by Goebbels as follows:

> At the Kaiserhof we hold a long conference with the Leader. We discuss our attitude to the von Schleicher Cabinet. Strasser's standpoint is that we ought to tolerate Von Schleicher. The Leader retorts upon him in the sharpest possible way. Strasser, as usual with him lately, paints a black picture of the situation in the Party, and takes a gloomy view of everything. But even if he were right, we must never capitulate because of the apathy of the masses.

Quite by chance we learn the true reason for Strasser's private willingness to scuttle the Party. On Saturday he met General von Schleicher, who offered him the Vice-Chancellorship. Strasser has not only not rejected this offer, but has also declared his intention to draw up a list of his own at a new election. That is the worst bit of treachery the Leader and the Party have yet experienced. It did not surprise me, for I never expected anything else of Strasser.

We are now only waiting the moment in which he will proclaim his treacherous attitude in public.

A man shows what he is made of in a crisis. He who fails now, proves he is not made for great things. Everything depends, at a crisis, more on character than on intelligence. Strasser is doing everything in his power to get those present at an assembly of Party Leaders over to his side, but all stand by the Leader so firmly that nothing comes of it. . . .

. . . Faction session: the Leader castigates the growing inclination to compromise. There can be no idea of it. It is not he, but the honour of the Party which is concerned. He who would do anything treasonable now only shows that he has never conceived the greatness of the Movement.

Strasser's face turns stony. The Faction itself unanimously agrees to a continuation of the struggle. A dissolution of the Reichstag is to be avoided if possible, since we have no good jumping-off place at the present moment.

A long time we sit drawing up the terms to be proposed to von Schleicher. Göring and Frick are submitting them.

This was followed the next day by a further policy conference preparatory to the Reichstag assembly.

Hitler was by now determined to expose the man who from the earliest days in the Party had been his principal opponent in thought and policy. Strasser had all along maintained such radical principles as he possessed in the face of Hitler's manifest control of the Party; nevertheless, he had managed to maintain at least an outward show of loyalty until the final months of 1932, when he believed Hitler was deliberately throwing away the first and only chance the Party had of obtaining a firm footing in the Government. At this delicate stage in Hitler's strategy, Strasser's tentative negotiations with Schleicher appeared to the Führer like an act of treason. He was therefore determined to defeat and humiliate him, once and for all.

The whole Nazi assembly in the Reichstag, 196 deputies, was summoned by telegram to meet Hitler on 7th December. At this meeting, which took place in the Reichstag itself, Hitler turned on

Strasser, accusing him of treachery in his dealings with Schleicher. As his voice rose in denunciation, no one, not even Strasser, who was pale with shock and mounting anger, dared to interrupt. Such dealings behind his back, Hitler shouted, were sabotage, aimed at cheating him, the Party leader, out of the Chancellorship which was his right as head of the largest Party in the Reichstag. Strasser, he alleged, was trying to split the Party wide open. His actions amounted to the grossest disloyalty.

Strasser could never have been Hitler's equal in such a scene as this. Hitler's rage, whether real or assumed for the purpose of annihilating Strasser before the rest of the parliamentary party, was overwhelming once it descended on the heads of the assembled deputies. Strasser endured it for as long as it lasted and then summoned the courage to speak.

'Herr Hitler, ist das Ihr Ernst? Do you really mean this?' was all he said.

'Ja,' Hitler shouted at him.

Strasser had no more to say.[20] Seizing his briefcase, he left the assembly abruptly, banging the chamber door. He went back to his hotel, the Excelsior, near the Anhalt station, there to ponder and write the letter of resignation from the Party which was to reach Hitler at the Kaiserhof the following day.

On 8th December all senior Gauleiters (*Inspekteure*) who favoured Strasser's point of view and who happened to be still in Berlin, were summoned at very short notice to meet Strasser during the morning at the Reichstag. Lohse, who was among those who responded, records in his unpublished notes on the period, that no one knew what the meeting was for. Strasser was accompanied by his closest aide, Paul Schulz.[21]

He looked very serious. In addition to Lohse, those present included Robert Ley, Bernhard Rust, Heinrich Haake, Jakob Sprenger, Martin Mutschmann, and Wilhelm Leoper. Goebbels was absent; had he been invited? Lohse wondered. Strasser spoke with emotion: 'I have asked you here to tell you that for some while now I have been through a severe conflict in my mind which, at least to some extent, I have now resolved. This morning I have sent the Führer a letter resigning from all the positions I hold in the Party. I have invited you here so that I can give you my reasons for this, which has been the most difficult decision I have had to make in my life.'

He then explained that there were two ways to power, the legal and the illegal. He had been, he said, prepared to follow the Führer along either way, provided there was a clear line of action and no shifting and delay such as they had been experiencing month after month. If one wanted to follow the legal path to power, in his view Hindenburg's offer of the Vice-Chancellorship should have been accepted in August. That, he thought, was the right way to get things done, rather than continue with this eternal talk about power. Hitler as Vice-Chancellor should have been able to handle the situation. If not, too bad. As for the illegal way, that was certainly a possibility also; in history, it is not the way or the means which matter, but a successful outcome. The illegal way would be costly and bloody, but, had it been taken, Strasser said he would have been prepared to 'do his bit'; what he could no longer tolerate was doing neither one thing nor the other.

He then turned to what he called the 'personal aspect', the 'intrigues within the Führer's inner entourage', the 'personal slights and insults which, in my position, I simply could not tolerate any longer'. He continued: 'Of course I felt the need from time to time to see the Führer and have some words with him. But when you go to the Kaiserhof or the Braunhaus in Munich you always see the same people hanging around, and you learn nothing precise about the problems of the day. I'm tired of playing second fiddle to Göring, Goebbels, Roehm and the others. If they are invited by Hitler, then I should be invited too. But this has never happened. I am simply not prepared to stand this sort of thing any longer. I'm at the end of my tether; my nerves are in pieces. I have to get away to the mountains to recuperate. As for you all, please don't take, any of you, any independent action. Just go on doing your duties.'

Lohse describes the emotion everyone felt at this moment. Some of these Nazi officials, it would seem, could hardly restrain their tears, feeling (says Lohse) like children who had lost a father; they kept on begging him to change his mind. The only one who appeared quite untouched was Paul Schulz, who sat apart watching.

Meanwhile, Goebbels describes in his diary the consternation Strasser's 'defection' had caused at Party headquarters when the letter had arrived on 8th December at noon. Strasser's resignation was already being announced in the opposition press, although Hitler had wanted the matter to be kept strictly secret.

> At midday the bomb explodes: Strasser has written a letter to the Leader informing him that he resigns all his posts in the Party, but gives very poor reasons for doing so. The moment, he considered, had arrived to lead the Party to the State, to give in; the Party was ruining itself by useless opposition. He could not any longer approve of this course, and was obliged to decline responsibility.
>
> These reasons, of course, were not sound. But they prove that

with Strasser the ambition to be a Minister is stronger than his loyalty to the Leader of the Party.

It is not difficult to recognize von Schleicher in this letter. All the leaders of the Party are with the Leader. They all look gloomy; their rage and indignation are vented against Strasser and his adjutant, Captain Schulz.

In the evening the Leader comes to us. It is difficult to be cheerful. We are all rather downcast, especially in view of the danger of the whole Party's falling to pieces, and of all our work being in vain. We are confronted with the great test. Every Movement which desires power must be proved, and this proving generally comes shortly before the victory, which decides everything. This testing-point is a question of nerve-endurance.

We must not be downhearted now; we shall surely find a way out of this desperate situation. The essential thing is not to give ourselves up.

'Phone call from Dr. Ley: The situation in the Party is getting worse from hour to hour. The Leader must immediately return to the Kaiserhof.

At two o'clock in the morning I am called up from the Kaiserhof. I go down at once and meet Chief of Staff Roehm, and Himmler. The morning edition of the *Tägliche Rundschau* is publishing an article about Strasser's hitherto secret resignation. This can only be Strasser's own doing. Here he is proclaimed as the great man of the Party, who alone is in a position to steer the Movement through its disastrous confusion. The article, of course, ends by claiming that Strasser ought to be appointed Head of the Party, instead of Hitler. Strasser publicly announces that he has gone away on leave. His letter to the Leader is a masterpiece of rhetorical pettifoggery. We are all dumbfounded at such baseness.

Treachery, treachery, treachery!

... For hours the Leader paces up and down the room in the hotel. It is obvious that he is thinking very hard. He is embittered and deeply wounded by this unfaithfulness. Suddenly he stops and says: 'If the Party once falls to pieces, I shall shoot myself without more ado.'

A dreadful threat, and most depressing.[22]

After Strasser's meeting at the Reichstag, Rust of Hanover went straight to Hitler at the Kaiserhof to confer with him about Strasser's position. Hitler ordered all those who had attended Strasser's meeting (except Strasser himself and Schulz) to come over to the Kaiserhof that afternoon. He received them all in his suite standing, and by some instinctual gesture to emphasize the emotion and gravity of the meeting, continued to stand himself and keep them on their feet before him in a semicircle for some two hours. He started with great reserve and seriousness, eyeing them all intently. Lohse reconstructed the effect of what he said:

'Since I got Strasser's resignation this morning without any detailed reason or justification we have to see where we are, gentlemen, for you are among the pillars of the movement. If just one or two pillars break, the edifice needn't collapse; if just one of my collaborators breaks faith with me in the most crucial hour of the Party, the movement can survive; but if you *all* want to leave me, the movement collapses and my life's work loses every meaning. Apart from this movement and the task it means for me, I have nothing that would keep me on this earth'—here he paused a while, and cast a soulful glance at Geli's bust on the mantelpiece— 'I would then take the consequences and my last and only request would be to cover my body and my coffin with the flag which I have created for the movement and as a symbol for a new Germany.'

Since Strasser had not seen fit to give any valid reasons in his letter of resignation, Hitler asked them to report what he told them this morning. Ley gave a pretty accurate account of what Strasser had said, Hitler reacting with vivid gestures. His first response was that he would have considered Strasser more intelligent than such behaviour seemed to reveal; why on earth did he not have it out with him personally, instead of making that brusque and ill-considered rupture? Hitler then went on to 'answer point by point'.

Whether or not he (Hitler) should accept the Vice-Chancellorship? Well obviously, within the first week there would have been insuperable differences with Chancellor Papen, who would have told him with a smile that if he did not like it he could go. What then could he report to their great Party and movement, which would break asunder giving the Communists their chance? He could not and would not enter the Government except as Chancellor; and that would happen soon enough. Everything else was as unrealistic as the 'illegal' measures envisaged by Strasser. 'After all, the Army's oath of loyalty is Hindenburg's, not mine.' He quoted General Reichenau, who had complimented him on his and the Party's self-discipline and told him that if his storm-troops did 'march against law and order' the Army, albeit 'with a bleeding heart', would obey orders and shoot. 'I wouldn't chase the flower of our nation and our youth into the machinegun fire of the Police and Reichswehr, gentlemen; I'm not that irresponsible, and Gregor Strasser will have to wait for that in vain.'

He then added that it was incompatible with Party discipline and strategy for someone like Strasser to conduct 'independent' negotiations. 'While I am away from Berlin, Göring is my authorized representative and he can always reach me at a moment's notice.'

Finally he came to Strasser's complaint of being 'neglected'. 'Gentlemen, I haven't known "private life" for years. Wherever I am, I am surrounded by masses or by persons. I can't issue personal invitations and I never do. Whoever comes to see me is welcome. Whoever wants to see me on this or that matter is received as soon as I can make time for him. As for Strasser I have noticed for some time that he avoids me and is reticent and aloof whenever we do meet. But is that my fault? Can I help it if Göring and Goebbels though not 'invited' come to see me more often than Strasser? Have I ever refused to see any of you gentlemen whenever you wished to see me? Haven't I asked you and others to share my table when you happened to be there, and whenever I had time for you? What sort of reason is this for one of my oldest and closest collaborators to turn his back on the movement?'

Hitler deliberately kept his manner throughout quiet, reasonable, convincing. His aim was to win over these 'Strasserites' to his point of view, his irrefutable policy of all or nothing in the State. In the end they all assured him of their inviolable loyalty.

That same evening, 8th December, Rust went back to Hitler and managed to get his permission to seek out Strasser in the hope that matters might be mended. It is evident that Hitler had taken the affair deeply to heart; he was either exaggerating its real importance to the Party, or exploiting it to develop still more fervent loyalty to himself. Rust hurried off to a restaurant which he knew was a favourite place for Strasser to dine, and found him there. Strasser proved very reserved; he had made up his mind, and he refused to see Hitler again, or reconsider what he had done. He paid his bill, and went straight to the station to catch the night train to Munich.[23]

Strasser had taken himself off home to Munich with the intention of fetching his wife and children and leaving with them for Italy. The Party seemed about to fall apart, and news from the regions was depressing. But Hitler's reserves of energy were soon restored when he saw his aides and colleagues stupefied by the situation. With one of his characteristic resurgences of leadership, he dismissed the absent Strasser from his organization, turning the defector's administrative work over to Ley. Later, on 15th December, Hess was to be given full responsibility for co-ordinating the Party.

On 9th December Hitler summoned his Party leaders and all the regional Gauleiters to a conference in Göring's luxurious palace, where he appealed to them directly to support him in this personal crisis. Goebbels describes this highly emotional scene:

> In the palace of the President of the Reichstag the District Leaders and Inspectors, together with the deputies, are assembled. The Leader first addresses the District Leaders on such a self-confident and strong personal note, it goes straight to the heart. He strongly arraigns Strasser and the sabotage he has worked in the Party. Old Nazis, who have fought for years in the Party, have tears in their eyes, tears of anger, pain and shame. The evening is a great success for the unity of the Movement. At the end, the District Leaders and deputies present burst into spontaneous ovations for the Leader. All shake hands with him, promising to carry on until the very end and not to renounce the great Idea, come what may.
>
> Strasser now is completely isolated, a dead man.
>
> A small circle of us remain with the Leader, who is quite cheerful and elated again. The feeling that the whole Party is standing by him, with a loyalty never hitherto so displayed, has raised his spirits and invigorated him.
>
> He has now, personally, done with Strasser.

Everyone in the assembly, led by Frick, swore loyalty to Hitler; the Strasser faction finally dissolved before the heat of Hitler's indignation. Hitler then inserted in the Nazi press on 9th December his own, brief official account of what had happened in order to clamp down rumour and dissension:

> Party member Gregor Strasser has taken three weeks' sick-leave with the Führer's approval. All rumours and speculation surrounding this subject are untrue and devoid of foundation.[24]

The error in Schleicher's calculations arose from his belief that Strasser had been strong enough openly to deprive Hitler of the support of a section of the Party which he, and not Strasser, had built through the magnetism of his personality. Strasser, though a good Party organizer, did not possess this magnetism, or the degree of courage which went beyond the ability to argue his point of view in closed session or from the public platform. He could not outface Hitler when it came to direct confrontation.[25] Undoubtedly Hitler's own strength and self-assurance had grown with the phenomenal rise of the Party during the past three years; his eye was firmly fixed on the goal of the Chancellorship, which he was convinced would be his in a few weeks, or at the worst months. His whole being turned instinctively against any member of the Party who threatened his inspired progress to high office. Strasser had no chance against the firmly rooted belief which Hitler possessed in his divinely appointed leadership of the Party, and ultimately of the German people as a whole. Faced by the full force of this belief he simply crumpled, wrote his letter of resignation, packed his bags and left.[26] Although he was to return soon to Germany and remain a shadow in the political background, he was never to oppose Hitler again to his face. But Hitler was never to forget or forgive this 'injury', the most serious and personally shocking 'defection' among the Party hierarchy until Roehm's alleged 'conspiracy' in 1934 and Hess's alleged 'betrayal of trust' in 1942. The customary term of address 'Mein Führer', and the salute 'Heil Hitler' now became standing orders for the Party.

The Abwehr (Military Intelligence) at this time 'tapped' a report dated 9th December and sent from Berlin by the Italian Ambassador, Vittorio Cerruti, to the Foreign Office in Rome. It dealt with a visit paid to Göring that day in the Reichstag by Marshal Italo Balbo, the Minister-Head of the Italian Air Force, who was Göring's guest. This gave Göring's observations on the current situation as expressed to representatives of a Power considered friendly to the Nazis, especially since his visit the previous month to Mussolini:

His Excellency Balbo has arrived in Berlin and joined me today in attending a meeting of the Reichstag. We had hardly arrived when Göring came to the diplomatic box to pay his respects in his capacity of Reichstag President. During an interval he took us to his private room and informed us that he was negotiating to take over the Prussian Premiership and the Prussian Home Office, his condition being that the Reich Government must no longer entrust the Reich Chancellor with the office of Reich Commissar for Prussia. Göring told us quite candidly that he would continue opposing the Reich Government if they should try to hamper him as Prussian Premier. He added that Schleicher, so far, had not agreed. He would rather have Strasser appointed Prussian Premier and Vice-Chancellor in the Reich. Incidentally, the latest news about Strasser is that he has asked for and obtained three weeks leave. But this, of course, is merely a subterfuge to hush up the differences between him and Hitler. I asked Göring if, apart from the Prussian Premiership, he would accept the Vice-Chancellery in the Reich. He said, certainly not (being quite emphatic about it), but added he would have no objections against one of the Prussian Ministers becoming a member of the Reich Government.

As for the general political situation and the immediate parliamentary programme, he said that, even tomorrow, the Reichstag would probably be prorogued till the second half of January. And soon thereafter Parliament would be dissolved once again with a view to new elections in the spring, this time no longer peaceful ones. They would not be afraid to use force which, in the long run, he considers inevitable.[27]

In fact, when the Reichstag had reassembled on 6th December, Göring had been re-elected President (with a greatly reduced vote of 279 out of 545) and had then used his commanding position in the House to blackmail it into acquiescence in its own demise. He had said outright that its life would be short, and had proceeded during the details which followed to study the faces of the deputies through binoculars, checking upon anyone who appeared unfamiliar against a file of photographs on the desk before him. His huge bulk towered over the assembly like an avenger; he had stared at Strasser, the deep suspect; and he had stared at those among the Party's deputies whom he believed to be Strasser's supporters. The house had gone into recess on 9th December, with the intention of re-assembly early in the New Year, though this in fact was not to happen.

A letter survives,[28] dated 13th December and addressed to the Crown Prince, in which Strasser is alleged to have telephoned the writer, General von Hörauf, from Rome, saying he would be back in Germany before Christmas. Hörauf goes on to say that he has spoken to Frick, who remained a whole-hearted supporter of Strasser's policy of collaboration in a coalition government, saying that he and Strasser would 'assemble behind them all the best elements in the Party'. Strasser added that he would be willing to meet the Crown Prince and Schleicher for further discussions, if they wished it.

A further letter, written by Hörauf to the Crown Prince on 27th December, after Strasser's return home to Munich, claims that Strasser, with whom he had had a long talk, 'has in his heart completely broken with Hitler', and that his judgment remains 'cool and clear'. 'The man's career is by no means finished,' he adds. Hörauf considered the number of Strasser's supporters still to be 'very large'. These letters show that at least in some quarters Strasser's potential usefulness was still worth discussing.

Strasser's movements are not now too difficult to trace. He had left for Italy with his wife Else after having cleared his desk and files at the Braunhaus; he had returned to Munich before Christmas, and was in Berlin at least by 4th January, when he was due to have a further meeting with Schleicher. But it would appear that Strasser's supporters,[29] who believed with him that Hitler should compromise and bargain with those Parties who would offer him the best terms in a share-out of governmental powers, had by now disintegrated like mist before the rising sun. Hitler had realized that the Party was at its lowest ebb since its period of ascendancy earlier in the year, and that all now depended on him and on him alone to summon every vestige of support he could. Goebbels's admiring eye had been on him throughout December, 'At heart the Leader is a sensitive, astute man. His instinct quickly grasps any situation ... the von Schleicher cabinet will have no chance against him,' he had written on 6th December before the 'bomb' was dropped by Strasser. 'The feeling in the Party is still divided,' he had noted on 11th December; and again on the 15th, 'If we succeed in holding the Movement, we shall also succeed in saving the situation.' Hitler, having faced the Gauleiters on 9th December, had realized that personal contact in the regions was the only real solution; once again he had undertaken a speaking tour, along with other leaders, including Goebbels and Göring, to reinvigorate his lagging followers.

Heiden describes Hitler's tactics at one of these assemblies:

> On December 17 Hitler had addressed his functionaries in Halle. Only his will counted in the party, he shouted: then he bade each one of them give him his hand and swear loyalty. While those in the front rows were giving him their hands, fighting broke out in the back of the room; men were knocked down, rebellious SA and SS men shouted that the comedy should be stopped. In these speeches Hitler did not strike a very convincing tone: 'Perhaps our enemies did give us a numerical set-back in the last Reichstag elections, but next year we shall pay them back with interest and compound interest. . . .' In three months the catastrophe would be at hand: 'I think that in March we shall again face these gentry in open battle. By then we shall have created the necessary conditions and the guarantee that our blade will be sharp.'[30]

This makes it clear that the nadir in the Party's current fortunes had been reached. Goebbels admits constantly the Party's 'troubles and worries. . . . This sort of thing always follows an internal crisis.' 'The two brothers Strasser have done us great harm,' he adds. The sentimental season of Christmas, which always meant so much to him, even though he was essentially a pagan, was blotted out—'The Feast of Divine Love is drawing nearer,' he writes hypocritically. His wife was ill in hospital. 'I am overwhelmed by a feeling of dreadful solitude, and morose desolation.' 'The year 1932 has brought us eternal ill-luck ... I am at home alone, pondering over my life. The past was sad, and the future looks dark and gloomy; all opportunities and hopes have quite disappeared.'[31]

The Party finances were also at a level any normally responsible organization would have regarded as catastrophic, with debts estimated (by Heiden) as at least 12 million marks. The SA were sent out on the streets to beg with money-boxes which they shook under people's noses.[32]

Meanwhile, Schleicher had broadcast to the nation on 15th December, in lieu of speaking to the Reichstag. 'I bring not a sword, but peace,' he declared. He proclaimed the right to parity in arms with the other nations of Western Europe, but at the same time declared that Germany was not re-arming. However, the Fatherland had no intention of remaining unprotected, unarmed, or in a situation where the German people could have 'their throats cut'. He alienated the big landowners (and incidentally Hindenburg) by saying that some 800,000 acres of the large estates in North Germany and East Prussia would be re-distributed, as the Papen Government had intended, so that some 25,000 small and medium farms could be established. Hitler and Goebbels were not slow to see possible allies here against Schleicher. Heiden quotes Schleicher as saying that the 'settlement of peasants must proceed more rapidly than before. . . . My heretical view is that I am a supporter neither of capitalism nor of socialism. For me concepts like private economy or planned economy have lost their terrors.'

Goebbels spent Christmas planning the provincial election campaign for the Diet of the minute State of Lippe-Detmold in north-west Germany, with its population of little more than 160,000, and an electorate of some 100,000. It was not the almost absurd size of the petty State which affected Goebbels; it was that its election results if favourable (and favourable they *must* be), could be represented as a symbolic turning-point in the fortunes of the Party. From the national point of view, Lippe was to be a propaganda election of high significance. Meeting Hitler again among the mountains of Berchtesgaden on New Year's Eve, Goebbels records, 'I shake hands with the Leader and say nothing but: "I wish you Power!"'

There were still some slight repercussions from the Strasser incident. In Goebbels's diary, the echoes persist that Schleicher still wanted him in the Government, and Strasser is recorded as having met Brüning at Freudenstadt on 28th December. According to Brüning, Strasser stayed until well after midnight, and told him of the meeting between Hitler and Papen which was being arranged in Cologne early in January. Brüning, however, advised Strasser to make his peace with Hitler. They agreed to meet again.[33]

It appears that Strasser was still maintaining some degree of liaison with Schleicher.[34] Strasser even reached the stage of being received by Hindenburg on 11th January; Hindenburg wanted to assess Strasser's worth at first hand. There were indeed press reports about a possible reshuffle of the Cabinet, with a National-Socialist as Vice-Chancellor. But nothing now could come out of the original proposal that he should join the Schleicher Cabinet. However, it would appear that Strasser impressed Hindenburg favourably. According to Meissner, who was in the best position to know, Hindenburg found Strasser quite suitable 'material' for a ministerial post, or even the Vice-Chancellorship. He did not find 'anything revolutionary' about him.

Brüning was to have a further, final, meeting with Strasser in January. He found Strasser 'very insecure', and he took the opportunity of warning him that Schleicher, in his opinion, was on the way out, and that in any case Hindenburg's mental condition now was such that his word could no longer be relied upon.[35]

That Strasser was not, in the Party's view, quite disposed of [36] is clear enough from Goebbels's statements in his diary on 13th–14th January, when he and the other leaders were away from Berlin conducting the campaign for the Lippe election on 15th January.

> The Leader comes to see us at Vinsebeck. We sit by the fireside, making plans for the future.
>
> Speak twice at Detmold in the evening, and afterwards in a small village nearby.
>
> At midnight Göring also comes to Vinsebeck. Strasser is the eternal subject of our discussion.
>
> ... The Berlin Press says that he is going to be appointed Vice-Chancellor next week.
>
> ... We have definite news that Strasser is prepared to enter the Cabinet as Vice-Chancellor. Only a great success in the Lippe contest can get us out of this dangerous situation.

This is confirmed in Otto Braun's account of his meetings with Schleicher, the first shortly after Schleicher's appointment as Chancellor, and the second early in January. On the first occasion, Braun writes, Schleicher had said: 'This time my policy will pay off. Strasser's choice as Prussian Premier is well under way and his appointment as Vice-Chancellor will follow. Strasser is sharply opposed to Hitler. Once he and the really useful and valuable elements in the Party shy off Hitler, the Party will be split and the section of it that remains with Hitler will have no appreciable influence.' Braun had warned Schleicher that Hitler was not to be disposed of so easily. At the second meeting, on 6th January, Braun had found Schleicher to be far less confident, and already wishing he were back at the Defence Ministry. He had not quite given up the idea of splitting the Nazi Party, but Strasser's name was far less in evidence in the conversation.[37]

So, it would seem, Strasser went into political retirement, living quietly until Hitler chose to have his sudden and bloody revenge on him the following year. Meanwhile, new efforts were being made behind the façade of government to overthrow Schleicher and create a situation in which it could be impossible any longer to keep Hitler out of leadership in the government.

ii

On 4th January 1933 the celebrated meeting had taken place between Papen and Hitler at the house in Cologne of the banker Baron Kurt von Schroeder, a supporter of Hitler, and all of the signatories of the memorandum sent to Hindenburg in November supporting Hitler for Chancellor. That it took place at all, ostensibly in secret, was already a sign that Schleicher's brief and abortive reign was coming to a close. The President's palace was inundated with demands from the Junkers for Schleicher's dismissal. Papen, who had never been out of favour with Hindenburg, knew that the President would be only too happy to bring him back as Chancellor in preference to Schleicher if he could resolve the deep dilemma posed by the Nazis. Papen also knew, as everyone did, that the Nazis lacked money, and he felt that the most practical way to circumvent them would be to attempt to settle their present financial discontents in order to prevent the civil war, which everyone so much feared, from breaking out. He therefore consented to take part in this meeting, promoted initially by Hitler's friend and financial adviser, Wilhelm Keppler.

Speaking in his defence at Nuremberg in 1946, Papen claimed:

> This conference on 4th January, on the occasion of which the prosecution asserts that I pledged myself to National Socialism, was a conference which took place on the initiative of Hitler. At this conference, nothing was said about the overthrow of the government of von Schleicher; and there was nothing said about the formation of a government by Hitler, as it later actually took place on 30th January. We merely discussed the necessity for Hitler to decide to take a responsible part, not as Chancellor, but with his Party. And, my Lord, that I did not engineer or cause this conference to be called may be seen clearly from the statement of Herr von Schroeder, at whose home this conference took place. ... Immediately after ..., I wrote a letter to Herr von Schleicher, which must have reached him the next morning. And after I had

returned to Berlin, I went at once to Herr von Schleicher and told him just what had been discussed at this conference. Thereupon, Herr von Schleicher caused an official communiqué to be issued. . . : 'The conversation revealed the complete lack of foundation for the assertions deduced from this meeting by the Press about controversies between the Reich Chancellor von Schleicher and Herr von Papen.'[38]

The statement by Schroeder referred to by Papen was made for use at the Nuremberg Trial, and reads as follows:

On January 4, 1933, Hitler, von Papen, Hess, Himmler and Keppler came to my house in Cologne. Hitler, von Papen and I went to my den where we were closeted in a discussion lasting about two hours. Hess, Himmler and Keppler did not participate in this discussion but were in the next room. Keppler, who had helped arrange this meeting, came from Berlin; von Papen came alone from his home in the Saar; and Hitler brought Hess and Himmler with him, as they were travelling with him to Lippe in connection with the election campaign. The discussion was only between Hitler and Papen; I personally had nothing to say in the discussion. The meeting started about 11.30 a.m., and the first question raised by Hitler was why it was necessary to punish the two Nazis who had killed the Communist in Silesia. Von Papen explained to Hitler that it had been necessary to punish these two Nazis, although they had not been put to death, because the laws were on the books and all political offenders under the law must have some punishment. He further explained to Hitler that it might be possible to get a pardon from President Hindenburg; and to persuade the President to give serious consideration to making Hitler the Chancellor at the time that Hindenburg met with Hitler and von Papen and that he had understood that Hindenburg was perfectly willing to discuss this matter with Hitler at that time. He said that it came as a great surprise and shock to him when Hindenburg was unwilling to do so and he felt that someone, probably von Schleicher, was responsible for the change in Hindenburg's point of view. Next, von Papen told Hitler that it seemed to him the best thing to have the conservatives and nationalists who had supported him join with the Nazis to form a government. He proposed that this new government should, if possible, be headed by Hitler and von Papen on the same level. Then Hitler made a long speech in which he said if he were made Chancellor, it would be necessary for him to be head of the government but that supporters of Papen could go into his

[Hitler's] government as ministers when they were willing to go along with him in his policy of changing many things. These changes he outlined at this time included elimination of Social Democrats, Communists and Jews from leading positions in Germany and the restoration of order in public life. Von Papen and Hitler reached an agreement in principle so that many of the points which had brought them in conflict could be eliminated and they could find a way to get together. They agreed that further details would have to be worked out and that this could be done in Berlin or some other convenient place.

I understand they met later with von Ribbentrop and worked out further details.

The meeting broke up about 1.30 and the three of us joined Hess, Himmler and Keppler at lunch, during which there was general conversation which lasted until about four o'clock when they, all the guests, departed.[39]

Although the main conference at Cologne took place solely between Papen and Hitler, Hess, Himmler and Keppler accompanied Hitler, although they stayed outside the key discussion. Sir David Maxwell-Fyfe's cross-examination of Papen during the Trial is illuminating as a further gloss on this notorious meeting.

MAXWELL-FYFE: Do you say that von Schroeder was not present?

PAPEN: Schroeder may have been present for parts of the conversation. I recall that in the main I talked to Hitler alone.

MAXWELL-FYFE: The meeting started at about 11.30 in the morning, did it not? The meeting between you and Hitler?

PAPEN: Yes.

MAXWELL-FYFE: And the first thing you did was to explain to Hitler that, although you had not been able to release the two Nazis who had been condemned for killing a communist you had tried to get President von Hindenburg to pardon them. Is that not right?

PAPEN: I recall that Hitler strongly reproached me because of the death sentence against the National Socialists.

MAXWELL-FYFE: And then you explained to Hitler that it was not through any intrigue or machinations of yours that President von Hindenburg had refused to discuss with Hitler the question of the latter becoming Chancellor. Was that not the second matter dealt with, that it was not you who had caused von Hindenburg to refuse the discussion?

PAPEN: Yes. I explained that my offer to him of 13 August 1932 had been meant absolutely honestly.

THE PRESIDENT: I do not think that was an answer to your question.

MAXWELL-FYFE: Did you not explain to Hitler that it was not your fault that von Hindenburg had refused to discuss the question of making Hitler Chancellor in August of 1932—

PAPEN: No.

MAXWELL-FYFE:—when Hitler had met von Hindenburg?

PAPEN: No, that cannot be right, for according to the evidence of historical documents Hitler had a talk with von Hindenburg on 13th August, and Hindenburg explained to him the reasons why he did not agree to Hitler's Chancellorship.

MAXWELL-FYFE: What I am putting to you is that you told Hitler on 4th January, with reference to his meeting with von Hindenburg: 'I want you to understand it was not my fault that von Hindenburg was not ready to discuss the question of your being Chancellor.' Did you not tell him that, that it was not your fault, that you thought von Hindenburg would have been ready?

PAPEN: No, Mr Prosecutor, that is what Herr von Schroeder says, but that is not right.

MAXWELL-FYFE: Well, now, what do you say was said about this matter? If you do not accept what I suggest to you, what do you say?

PAPEN: What Hindenburg told Hitler can be read in all the books; that is a well-known matter of history.

MAXWELL-FYFE: No, no. What we want to know—if I may say so, with great respect to the Tribunal—is what you told Hitler on 4th January. What did you tell him, if you told him anything, about the position between President von Hindenburg and himself?

PAPEN: If you had permitted me to make an explanation of the course of the conference, I would already have explained that.

In the course of this talk I did nothing but call Hitler's attention to the fact of how necessary it was to reach an agreement with Herr von Schleicher, how necessary it was to enter his government. In other words, I continued those efforts, which I had made in 1932, to induce the Nazi Party to co-operate.

MAXWELL-FYFE: Are you seriously telling the Tribunal that you told Hitler that he should not go into a Schleicher cabinet?

PAPEN: On the contrary, I told him he should enter a Schleicher cabinet.

MAXWELL-FYFE: That is what I put to you. I am suggesting that is entirely wrong. What you suggested to Hitler was that it would be a sound thing for the conservatives and nationalists, whose political views coincided with yours, to join with Hitler in forming a government; you suggested to him at this meeting what, in fact, actually happened on 30th January. Do you say that is untrue?

PAPEN: Not one word is true; that is absolutely false. As proof of this I state the following:

Immediately after the conversation I wrote a letter to Schleicher, on 4th January, in the afternoon. He probably received the letter on the morning of the 5th. However, even before Herr von Schleicher received this letter of mine giving an account of the meeting, the morning papers of 5th January started a tremendous campaign against me, asserting that this talk with Hitler showed disloyalty to Schleicher. Returning to Berlin, I went to see Herr von Schleicher immediately, and I gave him full particulars of the conversation I had had with Hitler. Herr von Schleicher then published a communiqué on this subject. This communiqué—

MAXWELL-FYFE: But he was not the only person, you know, who published a communiqué. You and Hitler published a communiqué.

I want you to remember, defendant, I put to you that the suggestion from you was that you and Hitler would form a coalition with the conservative forces behind you and the National Socialist forces behind Hitler. Now just look at the communiqué which you and Hitler issued. Look at the foot of it, defendant, the end of the document:

'Adolf Hitler and Herr von Papen publish the following joint declaration: "In answer to false deductions which have in many cases been circulated in the Press regarding Adolf Hitler's meeting with the former Reich Chancellor von Papen, the undersigned declare that the conversation dealt exclusively with the question of the possibility of a great national political united front and that, in particular, the opinions of both parties on the present Reich Cabinet were not touched upon at all in this general discussion."'

Now, defendant, when you have been reminded of what you published yourself, is it not correct what I have put to you, that you suggested to Hitler that you should form this coalition of conservatives and nationalists who agreed with you, and the Nazi Party under Hitler?

PAPEN: No, Mr Prosecutor, this communiqué states two things: In the first place, I point out that we did not speak at all about overthrowing the Schleicher cabinet or replacing it by another government, as the Press generally assumed. Then I state that it is necessary to create 'a great national political united front'. Herr von Schleicher headed the same cabinet that I had headed, with the same political forces. So if I called on Hitler to enter this cabinet, then that is exactly the same political combination as if I had asked him to join my cabinet.

MAXWELL-FYFE: Defendant, I am not going to argue with you. If you say that communiqué is your way of expressing that you had asked Hitler to take the Nazis into von Schleicher's government, and that you had not discussed forming the coalition, if you say that that is what that communiqué expresses, I have no further questions on this, and I will pass on to another point. I have made my suggestion, and I maintain the communiqué bears it out.[40]

From Hitler's point of view it would seem that the meeting was at least supposed to have been very secret. As Dietrich relates, the journey to Cologne had been elaborately arranged from the angle of security:

Very early in the morning we all get out at Bonn. Schreck is there at the station with the Führer's car to drive us to Godesberg at dawn. Short interval for breakfast. A closed car drives up. The Führer gets in. He drives off. Destination unknown to us.

But the Führer had given us instructions in advance to continue the journey in the car, without him, in the direction of Cologne. Three kilometres beyond Cologne, on the road to Düsseldorf, we were to stop and wait.

Towards midday we reach the agreed meeting-place. The weather was cold and damp. We wait. We walk up and down on the wet road. We pass the time talking; speculations of every kind as to where the Führer can be. No one knows of a stopping place, no one has a hint of the meaning of this separation.

Two hours later the closed car drives up from Bonn. It stops. The Führer gets out and comes into his car. The closed car turns and vanishes in the direction of Cologne.

On the way to Düsseldorf the Führer dropped hints that he had had an interview with a political notability. I somehow gathered that he was extraordinarily satisfied with the outcome of his secret excursion.[41]

The truth would seem to be that from Papen's point of view he was shrewdly exploring possibilities without making any dangerous commitments as far as he himself was concerned. If Schleicher were to fall, as seemed now more than likely, there would be little doubt in Papen's mind that he (Papen) would be the most appropriate person to come to terms with Hitler. The immediate upshot of the meeting, however, was that Hitler's burden of debt was liquidated through Schroeder's agency, and the door opened towards resolving the stalemate with Hindenburg. Papen returned to Berlin a few days later, and was to become a frequent visitor to both the President and the Chancellor. Schleicher, meanwhile, had been casting around for someone else to take over as Chancellor, and had even approached Schacht and Günther Gereke.

Schacht, as we have seen, was another of Hitler's supporters in banking and industrial circles, though he spent many hours trying to qualify this position during the course of his examination as a defendant in the Nuremberg Trial. Nevertheless, during 1932 he had made up his mind that Hitler must at some stage become Reich Chancellor, and it would seem he was at least forthcoming enough to remind Hitler of his support and assist him in his relations with men in industry who might raise money for the Party.[42] Even at the Trial he was prepared to assert, 'Of course, I did say that Hitler would be Chancellor, and must become Chancellor, and I expressed these convictions in private circles.'[43] Papen indeed asserted that Schacht had come to him in the summer, after the July elections, while he was still Chancellor and had said, 'Give him your position. Give it to Hitler. He is the only man who can save Germany.' Schacht had also written to Hitler himself on 29th August advising him to avoid compromising his policy with any rash statements on economic affairs (where he felt Hitler was weak in judgment), adding, 'You can always count on me as your reliable assistant.' There is no doubt of his sympathy:

> The only purpose of my letter is to assure you of my unchanging sympathy in these times of great trials. I realize that you are not in need of consolation. The rise to a total of 14 million votes cast for you, the perfidious counterblow by the other—theoretically stronger—side, and the loss of the votes of political profiteers, all these are things which could not seriously surprise you. But what you could perhaps do with in these days, is a word of most sincere sympathy. Your movement is carried internally by so strong a truth and necessity that victory in one form or another cannot elude you for long. During the time of the rise of your movement you did not let yourself be led astray by false gods. I am firmly convinced, that now, when you are forced into a position of defence for a short time, you will likewise resist the temptation of an alliance with false idols. If you remain the man that you are, then success cannot elude you.[44]

On 12th November, after the second Reichstag election, Schacht had written to Hitler again, saying, 'I have no doubt that the present

development of things can only lead to your becoming Chancellor.'
This letter had read in full:

Dear Herr Hitler:
Permit me to congratulate you on the firm stand you took immediately after the election. I have no doubt that the present development of things can only lead to your becoming Chancellor. It seems
as if our attempt to collect a number of signatures from business
circles for this purpose was not altogether in vain, although I
believe that heavy industry will hardly participate, for it rightfully
bears its name 'heavy industry' on account of its indecisiveness.

I hope that in the next few days and weeks the slight difficulties
which necessarily appear in the course of the propaganda campaign
will not be so great as to provide the opponents with a reason for
justified indignation: the stronger your internal position is the
more dignified can be your fight. The more the cause develops in
your favour, the more you can renounce personal attacks.

I am quite confident that the present system is certainly doomed
to disintegration.
With German Greetings,
  Yours very truly,
  (sgd) Hjalmar Schacht [45]

Schacht, therefore, equally with Papen and many others, can be considered at this stage as encouraging, indeed actively assisting, Hitler to
hold out for supreme power. No doubt both considered, through
insufficient knowledge or imagination, that once Hitler had got what he
wanted, namely the Chancellorship, he would sober down as a result of
undertaking the responsibilities of office (like so many politicians who
make irresponsible claims when in opposition). They thought they
might bring him up to become, if not exactly a normal member of the
Herrenklub, at least someone whom the Herrenklub could keep under
control. In this, as everyone knows, they were quite wrong, but it is of
course always necessary to see the events of the past as far as ever possible
in the way those conducting them were able to see them at the time,
with no other knowledge than that actually available to them, to which
must be added such capacity for psychological judgment and fore-
sight as they possessed. Whatever their misgivings about Hitler (and
obviously there was no secret about these), they completely failed to
realize the tornado they were about to let loose upon themselves, upon
Germany, and ultimately upon the world, once Hitler was permitted
to become Chancellor. It is doubtful that it was by now in their power to
prevent it, seeing that Hitler had so high a proportion of the nation on
his side, and so weak and divided an opposition to confront him.

Papen returned to Berlin only on 9th January. He went at once to the Chancellery to patch up his relations with Schleicher, and then on to the President's Palace to explain to Hindenburg the significance of his five-day-old meeting with Hitler. Schleicher was labouring badly under the attacks of the landowning class, and as a result was even considering bringing in Hugenberg as his Minister of Economics. The Nazi leaders were away from Berlin concentrating on achieving their symbolic victory in Lippe-Detmold, campaigning even in the villages, where leaders of Goebbels's calibre did not scorn to speak to audiences of a few dozen.

The Lippe-Detmold election was set for 15th January, and was little more than the equivalent of some small-town local election. The State's population of some 165,000 in town and village found themselves the target of the most prominent speakers the Nazis possessed from the 4th to the 14th January in a campaign conducted personally by Goebbels himself. Goebbels claimed he spoke to a 'gigantic assembly' on 4th January at Salzufflen. Hitler himself went to Lippe—'The Leader has actively taken part in the struggle,' wrote Goebbels, 'consequently things are going right from the first. All prominent party members are agitating. It absolutely must be successful.' Although Goebbels had to work and speak also in Berlin, he was back in Lippe on 9th January, in Berlin again on the morning of the 10th, then back in Lippe to speak in the evening. Headquarters were set up in a beautiful medieval castle, Schloss Vinsebeck, which, however, had no telephone. Goebbels claims that he continued to speak to 'overcrowded assemblies'; Hitler arrived again to speak in Lemgo, telling Goebbels afterwards that he had been to the hospital in Berlin and that his wife, dangerously ill since before Christmas, was now over the crisis. They all stayed overnight at the castle of a supporter, Baron von Oeynhausen. Their discussions were, as we have seen, still haunted by the ghost of Strasser's possible inclusion in Schleicher's government. Money was scarce. Otto Dietrich, the Party's press chief:

> At that time I accompanied Hitler as press reporter to the public meetings and could therefore watch the process by which, from one meeting to the next, he literally scraped up the money to cover his travelling expenses. Just seven weeks before he came to power Hitler was spending the night at the Grevenburg near Detmold when his chief adjutant came to me and in great embarrassment asked whether I could advance him 2,000 marks since Hitler had not got another pfennig and the local Party organization had been unable to pay the rental for the hall where the next day's demonstration was to be held.[46]

Working day and night, with transport difficult because of constant fog, Goebbels continued speaking in centre after centre. Others who came included Göring and Ley. More sinister was the invasion of Storm Troopers to augment local supporters at the Nazi rallies, and to apply strong-arm methods at the election meetings of opponents, where posters were torn down from the walls, and where attempts to speak to the electorate were constantly interrupted by violence and heckling.

Goebbels treated their modest gains at Lippe on 15th January as a great national resurgence of Nazism. The principal results (with comparative figures at the previous election) were:

> National Socialists 38,000 (33,000); 17 per cent improvement and 39·6 per cent of votes cast.
>
> Social Democrats 29,000 (25,000); 15 per cent improvement.
>
> The total vote cast was 90,000.

Goebbels gave this 5,000 rise in the Nazi vote a national significance in his paper, *Der Angriff*, on 20th January: 'The decision of the citizens of Lippe is not a local affair. It corresponds to the sentiment prevailing throughout the country. Again the great masses of the people are on the move—in our direction.' Even Papen took due note of the success, writing at the time in his diary, 'The result showed surprisingly high gains for the Nazis and equally surprising losses for the right-wing parties, whose total of votes fell by a third. As a result, the general tension in the country increased.' According to Goebbels, even Strasser was trying now to meet Hitler with the idea of re-establishing relations. But Hitler refused to see him. Strasser, in his view, was now no longer a danger. Support for him in the Party had evaporated. But Gereke reports that even as late as 16th January Schleicher still had hopes of splitting the Party through Strasser.

However, Hugenberg had re-emerged momentarily, meeting Schleicher on behalf of the Right-wing Nationalists on 13th January, Hindenburg on the 14th, and Hitler on the 17th—'without immediate result' writes Goebbels. Hugenberg was casting about for means of entering the Schleicher Cabinet, or forming some kind of alliance with the Nazis. The Reichstag meanwhile had not met, and the re-assembly was in any case to be postponed until (provisionally) the end of the month.[47] The Schleicher government remained in a state of suspension, its days numbered. Now that it seemed impossible to form any kind of broadly based Cabinet, Schleicher was inclined to recommend that a state of emergency should be declared at the end of the month, and Reichstag elections postponed until the autumn.

The days passed in a state of inactive tension. Hitler felt the need to take some initiative. On 20th January he ordered the SA to conduct a mass parade in front of the Karl Liebknecht House, the Communists' headquarters in Berlin. The parade was followed by a mass-meeting of the Nazis at the Sportpalast addressed by Hitler, who was received, Goebbels says, with 'indescribable enthusiasm'. The authorities, according to Goebbels, did not dare to prohibit the mass parade, though they forbade a counter-demonstration by the Communists on the 22nd. Instead, on that day Hitler addressed a mass rally of the SA in the Bülow Platz, with the Communists roaring at them from the side-streets, and police patrols on the ready with armed vehicles and machine-guns. The hero of the day was Horst Wessel, the SA street-fighter and pimp whom Goebbels had chosen to raise to the level of a martyr when he was killed in a brawl in 1930. He had written the words to the 'anthem' which was to become the Nazis' rallying-hymn, using a Communist marching-song for music. The Sportpalast became that same evening the scene of another SA rally, and a further spell-binding address by Hitler.

With this demonstration of strength staged to over-awe opposition to his progress, Hitler then made approaches to meet Papen on 22nd January. He had used Joachim von Ribbentrop, whom Papen had known as a young lieutenant in Turkey during the First World War, as his intermediary. The delicate negotiations which began now to develop have to be scrutinized from a number of points of view—Papen's (either as Chancellor, or at worst as a possible watchdog member of Hitler's government, should this come about), Hindenburg's (faced, at the age of eighty-five, with a situation which could lead straight to civil war), Schleicher's (discredited because he was unable to form a government which could command confidence in the Reichstag), and Hitler's (making his ultimate bid for power by exploiting every aspect of the situation, and with a dangerously restive army of half a million or so men on the streets expecting results commensurate with their adoration of him). Papen, Hindenburg's trusted favourite, was cast in the role of broker; he felt it necessary to intervene. Hitler had made contact with him prior to the 22nd, when an informal meeting took place with Hindenburg's approval at Ribbentrop's house in Dahlem, a suburb of Berlin, in the evening before Hitler was due to speak at the Sportpalast.

This meeting was also attended, on Papen's and Hindenburg's side, by Oskar von Hindenburg and Meissner, and on Hitler's side by Frick and Göring (summoned as usual at the last minute, when he was busy somewhere else, this time in Dresden). Papen's account in his memoirs of what took place is guarded:

I found both Hitler and Frick at Ribbentrop's house, where we were later joined by Goering, who had just made a speech in Dresden, saying that under no circumstances should Hitler join the present Government. Hitler asked me how the President viewed the situation. I told him that Hindenburg had not changed his mind about offering him the post of Chancellor, but realized that the situation itself had changed. It was now more than ever necessary to integrate the Nazi movement into this or some new Government.

Hitler declined flatly to join the Schleicher Government, and insisted again and again that the only circumstances in which the Nazis would co-operate would be under his Chancellorship. He complained that our communiqué on August 13 had declared that he had demanded exclusive power for the party. That had not been true; nor did he make that demand now. It would be easy to reach agreement on a coalition with members of the bourgeois parties, providing these ministers maintained the institution of a Presidential Cabinet and did not remain responsible to their own parties. During the evening, Hitler repeated all these arguments to Meissner and Oscar Hindenburg, on whom he seemed to make a strong impression.

I wish to make it quite clear that the actual question of forming a cabinet with Hitler as Chancellor was not discussed by Oscar Hindenburg, Meissner or myself.[48]

At Nuremberg, where as defendant he was being accused of easing Hitler into the Chancellorship, he was cross-examined by one of the most effective members of the prosecuting team, Sir David Maxwell-Fyfe (later Lord Kilmuir):

MAXWELL-FYFE: Oskar von Hindenburg had private conversations with Hitler which lasted for about an hour, at that meeting in von Ribbentrop's house; is that so?

PAPEN: That is possible. I do not recall it any more.

MAXWELL-FYFE: And thereafter, it was decided that Hitler would be Chancellor in the new government and that he would bring into the government the defendant Frick as Minister of the Interior and the defendant Göring as Minister without Portfolio?

PAPEN: No; on the 22nd, we did not reach any agreement as to this; rather we limited ourselves to—

MAXWELL-FYFE: I said thereafter that had been agreed between you, had it not?

PAPEN: Yes, but it is very important to establish—forgive me if I add this—that we did not begin these talks until after I had ascertained that Herr von Schleicher could not form a government, after the attempt to split the Nazi Party had failed. That is very important.

MAXWELL-FYFE: Now, are you telling the Tribunal that what you did at this time was to bring Hitler into power simply because he was head of the biggest party in the Reichstag; or because you thought he was the most suitable man to be Chancellor of Germany at that date; which was your motive?

PAPEN: My motive, Mr Prosecutor, was very simple. In the situation existing after 23rd January, there were only two possibilities, either to violate the Constitution, which would result in civil war, or to form a government headed by Hitler. I believe I explained that in great detail to the Tribunal.

MAXWELL-FYFE: You had been Chancellor of Germany yourself; you had had contacts with Hitler. What I really want to know, defendant, is did you think that Hitler, taking into consideration his aims, intentions and personality, was a good man for Germany to have as Chancellor? It is a perfectly simple question. I want a straight answer. Did you think it was a good thing to have Hitler, as you knew him then, as Chancellor of Germany?

PAPEN: To that I can say only that the coalition which I formed on behalf of the Reich President was a forced solution. There was no question as to whether it was good or bad. We had to accept it.[49]

Hitler is said to have set out to make a more favourable impression on Oskar von Hindenburg than he had done in the past.

The following day, 23rd January, Schleicher was to make one more bid to remain in power.[50] He admitted at last that he could no longer use Strasser to split the Nazis, and that there was no possibility of forming a government commanding a majority in the Reichstag without Hitler's support, which was not forthcoming unless he was made Chancellor. Schleicher's new proposal to Hindenburg was that the Reichstag should be dissolved with no new election date fixed, and a state of emergency declared, the government to be carried on meanwhile by Presidential decree.

This would be, in effect, a military dictatorship, and it would in any case be unconstitutional. Hindenburg, bound by his oath and burdened now by his growing dislike of Schleicher, stolidly refused. According to Papen, Hindenburg countered Schleicher's arguments in the following terms:

On December 2 you declared that such a measure would lead to civil war. The Army and the police, in your opinion, were not strong enough to deal with internal unrest on a large scale. Since then the situation has been worsening for seven weeks. The Nazis consider themselves in a stronger position, and the left wing is more radical in its intentions than ever. If civil war was likely then, it is even more so now, and the Army will be still less capable of coping with it. In these circumstances I cannot possibly accede to your request for dissolution of the Reichstag and *carte blanche* to deal with the situation.[51]

The meetints behind the scenes between 23rd and 28th January, when Schleicher was finally forced by the President to resign, included further abortive contacts between the Nazis and Hugenberg (Göring and Frick met Hugenberg on the 26th, according to Heiden, while Goebbels records a meeting between Hugenberg and Hitler on the 27th). The various right-wing parties fluttered about in confusion; they wanted to share in a dictatorial cabinet without either Schleicher or Hitler. Hugenberg said as much to Papen at a meeting on 28th January. Papen moved in and out of the President's Palace, seeking means to bring Hitler, Hindenburg and himself into some form of practical alignment. It was agreed by the Reichstag Steering Committee that the Reichstag must assemble, and the date was set for 31st January. From the public's point of view the rumours veered between Schleicher, Papen and Hitler as Chancellor. Papen was bringing Hindenburg round to appointing Hitler Chancellor, with what he held to be a strong Cabinet of non-Nazis.[52] Hindenburg, finally rid of Schleicher, instructed Papen to meet Hitler. This meeting, which took place on 28th January, is described by Papen:

As I expected, he refused flatly to form a Government based on a parliamentary majority. If the President desired his movement to co-operate in the work of government, then he must be allowed to form a Presidential Cabinet with the same rights as those accorded to Schleicher and myself. On the other hand, he had no intention of making exaggerated ministerial demands, and was perfectly prepared to include certain men from the previous Cabinets who enjoyed the President's confidence.

I told him that the mission I have undertaken on behalf of the President did not permit Hitler discretion in choosing the members of the Cabinet. He replied that the President could fill all the ministerial posts, provided the ministers regarded themselves as independent of the political parties. Hitler desired to be Chancellor and Commissioner for Prussia, and wanted a member of his party to be Minister of the Interior in both the Reich and Prussia.[53]

This meant that members of the Papen and Schleicher Cabinets could remain at their posts—relatively trusted men like Baron von Neurath

(Foreign Affairs), Count Schwerin von Krosigk (Finance), and Dr Franz Guertner (Justice). Hitler had, in effect, left it to Papen and Hindenburg to appoint whom they thought fit, except for the positions he had specified. This served as welcome bait to Hindenburg, who suggested Papen should in the circumstances become Vice-Chancellor in order to work closely with Hitler, and General von Blomberg be made Minister of Defence in charge of the Reichswehr.[54] Hugenberg, who had been angling for office during the past weeks as well as meeting Hitler and his representatives, consented the following day to lend his support, and serve as Minister of Economic Affairs, and Agriculture. This would placate the recalcitrant land-owning class, as well as win the support of the Stahlhelm, who in addition were to have their man, Franz Seldte, made Minister of Labour. The proposed government, therefore, could hardly be more right-wing in political character. Papen fondly regarded the Stahlhelm as a stabilizing factor, made up, as he put it, of ex-Servicemen and contrasting with the Storm Troopers and the street-army of the Communists, the *Rotfront*.

Papen conferred with Göring, the Reichstag President, on 29th January.[55] Papen's account of their meeting shows the completion of the business of Cabinet-making:

> They said they wished to appoint Frick as Reich Minister of the Interior, and Goering himself to the same post in Prussia. . . . Both my visitors insisted that the Prussian Police, which had been in the hands of the Social Democrats for ten years, would have to undergo certain changes in personnel. They declared that this would be necessary if the police were to be relied upon to deal effectively with the Communists, and with my experiences in the previous July in mind, I felt that this was by no means a negligible argument. I told Hitler that the President did not intend to give him powers as Reich Commissioner for Prussia, and that these would remain vested in me as Vice-Chancellor. Hitler accepted this decision with a bad grace, but did not make an issue of it.[56]

Göring rushed back in triumph to tell Hitler that at last all was well. He was indeed to be Chancellor. Goebbels almost falls over himself with excitement.

> Göring suddenly comes and reports everything to be A1. To-morrow, the Leader is to be appointed Chancellor. One of our principal conditions is the dissolution of the Reichstag, as the Leader is unable to go on working with it as at present constituted. The Nationalists resist this with might and main. Their motives are more than obvious. This is surely Göring's happiest hour.

And he is right. He has diplomatically and cleverly prepared the ground for the Leader in nerve-racking negotiations for months, or even years.

. . . . A wordless vow to our Leader! As it has been, so it shall remain! The world will witness in us and through us a splendid example of loyalty to the Leader, and an instance of the most beautiful companionship that *can* bind men together.[57]

Again, according to Papen, Schleicher was to make one more desperate effort to save himself:

Schleicher, in the meantime, found another card to play. He sent one of his private emissaries, von Alvensleben, to Goering, who immediately hurried over to me with the news. Schleicher had sent a message that my real intention was to deceive the Nazis, and that they would do very much better to combine with Schleicher, who only wished to retain the post of Minister of Defence. Alvensleben had indicated that means could be found to neutralize Hindenburg. Schleicher had apparently even gone so far as to suggest that if the 'old gentleman' should prove difficult, he, Schleicher, would mobilize the Potsdam garrison. Goering told me that he and Hitler had returned a flat negative to the plan and had immediately told Meissner and Oscar von Hindenburg.[58]

Hitler's response to this danger of what appeared to be a possible military *coup d'état* was to place the SA in Berlin on the alert.

The next day, 30th January, was the day which was to change world history. Hitler and the members of his future Cabinet met in Papen's private house, which adjoined the President's Palace; Hitler was tense with excitement, having been up most of the night. At half-past ten in the morning they walked across the garden to enter the Palace and be received by Hindenburg. Hitler, however, was already beginning to exploit a tactical procedure which was later to become characteristic—having gained what he really most wanted, to raise difficulties at the last minute and ask for more, counting on the consternation a sudden apparent change in attitude would cause to secure some further, last-minute concession. He decided suddenly that, since the subsidiary office of Commissioner for Prussia had been denied him (Papen was to hold this position), he was going to demand that Hindenburg consent to new Reichstag elections. The argument developed, particularly between Hugenberg and Hitler. Düsterberg describes this last-minute altercation.

The new Cabinet, already in a state of tension, went into the

President's room. Papen greeted . . . Hitler as the new Chancellor. Hitler thanked him and stated, to the evident astonishment of everyone there, particularly Hugenberg, that now the German people would have to ratify the new cabinet's composition through a general election. It was clear that Hitler recognized the distinct advantages he and his party would derive from another election. Hugenberg, on the other hand, argued firmly to the contrary, pointing out that the November election results had shown relative party strengths and that their new government was the obligatory democratic consequence of these results. Therefore, he said, new elections were not needed at this time. An increasingly violent debate . . . ensued. Hugenberg stuck firmly to his no. He stood at the pinnacle of his career, and now his dreams of this new cabinet were being ruined. Realizing what was at stake, Hitler, who had been visibly confounded by Hugenberg's opposition, stepped up to him and said something to this effect: 'Herr Geheimrat, I give you my solemn word of honour that, no matter how the elections may come out, I shall never separate myself from any of those here present.'

But Hugenberg still stuck by his no. . . . Papen, however, extremely desirous of the goal he thought so near, exclaimed: 'But Herr Geheimrat! Do you wish to endanger the alliance that took so much work to form? Certainly you cannot question a German gentleman's solemn word of honour. . . .' Suddenly Meissner rushed into the room with his watch in his hand. 'Gentlemen, you were scheduled to take your oaths of office with the President at eleven o'clock. It is now eleven-fifteen. You certainly cannot keep the President waiting any longer.' At this . . . Hugenberg yielded, and Hitler had won.[59]

Papen made the formal introductions to the President, and Hindenburg made a short set speech enjoining them all to co-operate together to serve the nation. Then Hitler and his colleagues were sworn in. Göring records the triumph he felt as a member of the new government:

From 20th January on I was a political delegate, in constant touch with Herr von Papen, with Secretary of State Meissner, with Hugenberg, and the Stalhelm leader, and was discussing with them future developments. . . . At last an agreement was reached. . . . I had, as Hitler's representative, often in the past year gone backwards and forwards between the Kaiserhof and the Wilhelmstrasse, and I shall never forget the moment I hurried out to my car and could be the first to tell the expectant crowds: 'Hitler has become Chancellor.'[60]

Goebbels recalls the emotion of the moment for the rest of Hitler's closest colleagues:

> At noon we are all at the Kaiserhof, waiting. The Leader is with the President of the Reich. The inward excitement almost takes our breath away. In the street the crowd stands silently waiting between the Kaiserhof and the Chancellery. What is happening there? We are torn between doubt, hope, joy and despair. We have been deceived too often to be able whole-heartedly to believe in the great miracle.
>
> Chief-of-Staff Roehm stands at the window the whole time, watching the door of the Chancellery from which the Leader must emerge. We shall be able to judge by his face if the interview was happy.
>
> Torturing hours of waiting! At last a car draws up in front of the entrance. The crowd cheers. They seem to feel that a great change is taking place or had already begun.
>
> The Leader is coming.
>
> A few moments later he is with us. He says nothing, and we all remain silent also. His eyes are full of tears. It has come! The Leader is appointed Chancellor. He has already been sworn in by the President of the Reich. The final decision has been made. Germany is at a turning-point in her history.
>
> All of us are dumb with emotion. Everyone clasps the Leader's hand; it would seem as if our old pact of loyalty were renewed at this moment.[61]

II. From Hitler's appointment as Chancellor to the Enabling Bill of March 1933 which made him Dictator of Germany

i

Word of mouth was sufficient to spread the news. Like some giant lodestone, the Wilhelmstrasse drew the crowds as mid-winter darkness fell during that Monday afternoon in January. Torches were lit, and at seven o'clock the Nazi processions began to mass, celebrating the victory of the Führer. The columns of torch-bearers filed past the windows of the Chancellery, where Hitler and Göring stood on a balcony to receive the salutations of their followers. Hindenburg also stood near by sheltering behind a closed window, and peering down at the marching masses of the new Germany—the Storm Troopers and their brown shirts, the Hitler Youth, the Stahlhelm in grey, the excited ranks of women and children. The endless processions, marching on until one o'clock in the morning of 31st January, were greeting a man whose strength was soon to exceed any dream they could envisage. Papen stood behind Hitler, watching the flood of people, and proud perhaps of the part he had played in the release of this pent-up enthusiasm which he felt had been so dangerously dammed. He described the scene as he experienced it:

> We watched an endless procession of hundreds of thousands of delirious people, from every level of society, parading with lighted torches before Hindenburg and the Chancellor. It was a clear, starlit night, and the long columns of uniformed Brownshirts, S.S. and Stahlhelm, with their brass bands, provided an unforgettable

picture. As they approached the window at which the old Reich President appeared to the crowd there were respectful shouts. But about a hundred yards further on, Hitler stood on the little balcony of the new Reich Chancellery. As soon as they saw him, the marchers burst into frantic applause. The contrast was most marked and seemed to emphasize the transition from a moribund régime to the new revolutionary forces. I had preferred not to push myself forward and was sitting quietly in the room behind the balcony, leaving Hitler and Goering to take the salute. But every now and then Hitler turned round and beckoned me to join him. The fantastic ovation had put even these hardened party chiefs into a state of ecstasy. It was an extraordinary experience, and the endless repetition of the triumphal cry '*Heil, Heil, Sieg Heil!*' rang in my ears like a tocsin. When Hitler turned round to speak to me, his voice seemed choked with sobs. 'What an immense task we have set ourselves, Herr von Papen—we must never part until our work is accomplished.'[1]

The crowds stood below, singing the Horst Wessel Lied, as a choral finale to the night's celebration. 'At length the square is empty,' wrote Goebbels. 'We close the windows and are surrounded by absolute silence. The Leader lays his hands on my shoulders.'

Hitler's first Cabinet had already sat.[2] They had met at five o'clock in the evening, before the torch-lit processions had begun; the minutes of this meeting survive.[3] Hitler masked his move towards authoritarianism by insisting that support of the Centre Party should be sought before the Reichstag was formally dissolved; in his heart, Hitler knew perfectly well the Centre would not co-operate. Hugenberg was dubious. But the promise to Hindenburg that the new Cabinet would seek majority support in the Reichstag must be upheld, and Hugenberg had to rest content with Hitler's reiterated undertaking that the Cabinet would stay the same after the elections, whatever their outcome. Once again, Hugenberg was pressed by Hitler into agreeing with great reluctance that the dissolution of the Reichstag should follow if the Centre Party refused to collaborate. Hitler saw Kaas, leader of the Zentrum, the next day and, in effect, did not even trouble to consider the points he raised for initial discussion. At the next meeting of the Cabinet he merely reported that there was no possibility at all of coming to terms. Papen saw that Hindenburg signed the necessary decree of dissolution the following day, and on 1st February the Reichstag, as elected less than three months previously, no longer existed. In the decree, the President stressed that he wanted to discover the nation's attitude to the new Government. The election was fixed for 5th March. The

Centre Party protested in vain, and too late, for they had never had the opportunity to discuss co-operation with Hitler.

Goebbels knew the battle was by no means won, though the cards were stacked more in their favour than ever before. 'Radio and press are at our disposal. We shall achieve a masterpiece of propaganda,' he wrote in his diary. 'Even money is not lacking this time.' However, he added, 'The situation throughout the country is not so clearly defined as to allow me to call our position absolutely secure.' The main target was obvious—'This time we are going definitely to attack Marxism.' The question was tactics: 'For the present we shall abstain from direct action. First the Bolshevist attempt at a revolution must burst into flame. At the given moment we shall strike.' Could it be that Goebbels already had in mind the precipitating event to be staged in three weeks' time on 27th February?

In addition to the dissolution of the Reichstag, Hindenburg decreed that the Diet of Prussia should be dissolved. Papen, as Reich Commissioner for Prussia, carried this out once again on 6th January, in spite of the protests of Otto Braun and his Cabinet. Prussia was now to be governed again by decree, and this was an opportunity to be seized by Göring as Papen's deputy. The Diets of many other states were correspondingly dissolved—'We are making a clean sweep of it,' wrote Goebbels ferociously.

The position was one in which a number of actions were being carried out in parallel. Papen represented himself as trying to curb Hitler's extremism, influencing his policy statements for the new government, and bringing the moderating influence of the centre parties to bear upon him. Hitler himself broadcast to the nation in terms which suggested a new age was to begin, with a great challenge to all classes:

> Fourteen years have passed since the German people lost the war, in which they had been attacked and for which, therefore, they had no responsibility. . . . Fourteen years of Marxism has ruined Germany. . . . Our grey haired leader in the World War has called upon the men of the national parties to link up with a view to saving the Fatherland, and they have responded to his appeal. Their task is a terrible one, but they have confidence in themselves and in the German nation. I feel sure that the peasants, workers and middle-class citizens will join with us in the task of building up a Third Reich. . . . In foreign politics the National Government will regard as its supreme mission the protection of our vital rights and the reconquest of our freedom.[4]

Hitler played for safety with bare-faced cynicism in the government proclamation of 1st February, which included the words:

> The national government will consider it as its first and foremost task to retore the spiritual and political unity of our people. It will consider Christianity as the basis of its general moral outlook and will firmly protect the family as the determining unit of the nation and the State.[5]

Such phrasing (the words were Papen's) was meant to keep not only the German middle-class but Hitler's own conservative colleagues in the Cabinet sweet during the dog-days leading up to the election. Papen, the leading light in the Cabinet to whom the other non-Nazis looked for safety, was thoroughly taken in by Hitler's unexpected reasonableness. As Papen wrote in his memoirs:

> I experienced much less difficulty than I had expected in formulating a coalition programme. Hitler thought the moral regeneration of the nation to be our principal task. He suggested that economic reconstruction should be accomplished in two four-year plans, and mentioned, for the first time, the necessity of passing an Enabling Law for this purpose. I thought a four-year plan sounded too much like Soviet methods, but agreed that a set programme was necessary. For my part, I laid down those lines of conservative thought which I considered should serve as a framework for our policies, and suggested one or two phrases: 'The Government recognizes the Christian basis of moral existence and regards the family as the basic unit in the nation, requiring the particular protection of the State.' We agreed to strengthen the federal structure of the country by promoting healthy State and Municipal Government, while maintaining sound central direction. In the field of foreign affairs, the Government intended to strive for equal rights in the community of nations, 'fully aware of the responsibilities of a great and free nation in the maintenance and consolidation of peace, more necessary to the world than ever before'. Hitler gave his full approval to these declarations, to which we added the suggestion that a general reduction in armaments would do away with the necessity for any increase in our own.[6]

Schwerin-Krosigk has testified how reasonable Hitler appeared at this time, humouring his colleagues and drawing on their advice as 'experienced' politicians.

Having made their general proclamation, each section in the Cabinet went its own way in the election campaign. At the Nuremberg trial, Papen vindicated his own good faith:

I did everything within my power, together with my political friends, to carry through the ideas which I myself had contributed to this political programme. At that time, the essential point seemed to me the creation of a counter-balance to National Socialism, and, therefore, I asked the leaders of the Rightist parties to give up the old party programmes and to unite in a large, common political organization with the aim of fighting for the principles which we had enunciated. However, the party leaders did not act on this suggestion. Party differences were too marked and no changes took place. The only thing I accomplished was the establishment of a voting bloc of all these parties, and on behalf of this voting bloc I made many speeches in which I presented this programme, this coalition programme, to the country.[7]

Hitler, however, went rip-roaring round the country, in effect repudiating the words just issued in his name:

If, today, we are asked for the programme of this movement, then we can summarize this in a few quite general sentences: programmes are of no avail, it is the human purpose which is decisive ... therefore the first point in our programme is: Away with all illusions![8]

That is what he said at Munich on 24th February.

Hitler's meeting with the industrialists summoned by Göring on 20th February was the subject of an affidavit which Georg von Schnitzler of I.G. Farben made during the period of the Nuremberg trial:

I, Georg von Schnitzler, a member of the Vorstand [Board] of I.G. Farben, make the following deposition under oath:

At the end of February 1933, 4 members of the Vorstand of I.G. Farben including Dr. Bosch, the head of the Vorstand, and myself, were asked by the office of the president of the Reichstag to attend a meeting in his house, the purpose of which was not given. I do not remember the two other colleagues of mine who were also invited. I believe the invitation reached me during one of my business trips to Berlin. I went to the meeting which was attended by about 20 persons who I believe were mostly leading industrialists from the Ruhr.

Among those present I remember:

Dr. Schacht, who at that time was not yet head of the Reichsbank again and not yet Minister of Economics.

Krupp von Bohlen, who in the beginning of 1933 presided over the

Reichsverband der Deutschen Industrie which later on was changed into the semi-official organization 'Reichsgruppe Industrie'.

Dr. Albert Vogler, the leading man of the Vereinigte Stahlwerke.

Von Lowenfeld, from an industrial works in Essen.

Dr. Stein, head of the Gewerkschaft August Victoria, a mine which belongs to the I.G. Dr. Stein was an active member of the Deutsche Volkspartei.

I remember that Dr. Schacht acted as a kind of host.

While I had expected the appearance of Göring, Hitler entered the room, shook hands with everybody and took a seat at the top of the table. In a long speech he talked mainly about the danger of Communism over which he pretended that he had just won a decisive victory. He then talked about the 'Bündnis' (alliance) into which his party and the Deutsch-Nationale Volkspartei had entered. This latter party in the meantime had been reorganized by Herr von Papen. At the end he came to the point which seemed to me the purpose of the meeting. Hitler stressed the importance that the two aforementioned parties should gain the majority in the coming Reichstag election. Krupp von Bohlen thanked Hitler for his speech. After Hitler had left the room, Dr. Schacht proposed to the meeting the raising of an election fund of—as far as I remember—RM 3,000,000. The fund should be distributed between the two 'Allies' according to their relative strength at the time being. Dr. Stein suggested that the Deutsche Volkspartei should be included which suggestion ... was accepted. The amounts which the individual firms had to contribute were not discussed.[9]

Notes on the statements made by Hitler and Göring were found in Krupp's file of private correspondence for 1933, and among the points Hitler is said in this document to have made are the following:

Private enterprise cannot be maintained in the age of Democracy; it is conceivable only if the people have a sound idea of authority and personality. Everything positive, good and valuable, which has been achieved in the world in the field of economics and culture, is solely attributable to personality. When, however, the defence of the existing order [*des Geschaffenen*], its political administration, is left to a majority it will irretrievably go under. All the worldly goods which we possess, we owe to the struggle of the chosen [*Auserlesenen*] ...

... As I lay in the hospital in 1918 I experienced the revolution in Bavaria. From the beginning I saw it as a crisis in the development of the German people, as a period of transition. Life always tears up humanity. It is therefore the noblest task of a Leader to find ideals that are stronger than the factors that pull the people apart. I recognized even while in the hospital that one had to search for new ideas conducive to reconstruction. I found them in Nationalism, in the value of personality, in the denial of reconciliation between nations, in the strength and power of individual personality. . . .

. . . We have withstood all attempts to move us off the right way. We have turned down the benevolence of the Catholic Centre Party (Zentrum) to tolerate us. Hugenberg has too small a movement. He has only considerably slowed down our development. We must first gain complete power if we want to crush the other side completely. While still gaining power one should not start the struggle against the opponent. Only when one knows that one has reached the pinnacle of power, that there is no further possible upward development, should one strike. . . .

. . . We must penetrate with our SA men into the darkest quarters of the cities and operate there from mouth to mouth and fight for every single soul. Göring considered to some extent the great dangers connected with this election battle. He then led over very cleverly to the necessity that other circles not taking part in this political battle should at least make the financial sacrifices so necessary at this time. These were so much more necessary because not even one penny of the tax-payers' money would be asked for. Government funds would not be used. The sacrifices asked for purely would be so much easier for industry to bear if it realised that the election of March 5th will surely be the last one for the next ten years, probably even for the next hundred years.[10]

Papen was later to admit that he made a terrible, basic error in his calculations about Hitler. 'My own fundamental error was to underrate the dynamic power which had awakened the national and social instincts of the masses.'[11] He was, although still only fifty-four, wholly conditioned by the past, by traditions going back to the Kaiser-Reich, and the values of the old-time professional soldier, the professional diplomat, the career politician. The duplicity he and his peers had used was a duplicity functioning within a conservative and Christian moral framework, tactics of which Hitler had had no direct experience, and for which he entertained only contempt. Papen had gambled on his becoming overawed by the office of Chancellor and the responsibilitias it represented, coupled by the restraints of having eight Conservatives in his Cabinet compared with only two Nazi colleagues, Göring and

Frick.[12] But if Hitler was overawed by anything, it was the plethora of opportunities open to his genius if he could only consolidate his power; indeed he regarded his colleagues in the Cabinet, other than Göring, that is, as little more than paper men.

Papen's apologia continues:

> In practical terms, the mistake was to consider the apparatus of the State sufficiently intact and independent to assert itself, under Conservative leadership, against the propaganda methods and machinery of the Nazi movement. What had happened was that the long years of party warfare had undermined the apparatus, though none of us realized how far the process had gone.

There were, perhaps, odd moments when Hitler did seem overwhelmed by the protocol of Chancellorship:

> During the first weeks of his Chancellorship he seemed distinctly ill at ease, particularly when he had to appear in a top hat and formal dress. His party colleagues soon persuaded him to abandon these bourgeois trappings in favour of the party uniform. With me he was invariably polite, even modest—at any rate as long as the effect of his first electoral victory lasted. It took me a long time to see through him. At first I had the impression that even though he was not easy to handle, it would still be possible to attract him to my own professed political ideas. In this I was to be grievously disappointed.[13]

Papen's position was further weakened by the incorrigible divisions among the parties which might have combined to oppose Hitler, as democracy went by default. The Communists imagined they were 'infiltrating' the Storm Troopers, the leaders still deluded by the theory that a brief reign of Hitler would be the prelude to their own seizure of power.[14] The Centre Party fluctuated with no firm line of policy, and the Social Democrats (allied to the Trade Unions) were weak from lack of leadership. The middle classes on the whole kept to the Right, many of them turning to Hitler through fear of Communism or any policy which seemed to favour the Left.

Hitler left it to Göring to further the Nazis' cause on the plane of sheer *coup d'état*. While Hitler and Goebbels were handling the election campaign, constantly moving about the country to address rallies and spur the local Party organizers, Göring, as Deputy Commissioner and Minister of the Interior of Prussia, took possession of the security forces of Germany's premier state, with its headquarters in Berlin. Gritzbach, Göring's official biographer, claims that he virtually lived in the Prussian government building during February and March, eating and at times even sleeping there. His governing philosophy was to be stated clearly enough at the Nuremberg trial in 1946—'The conception "illegal" should perhaps be clarified,' he declared. 'If I aim at a revolution then it is an illegal action for the State then in existence. If I am successful, then it becomes a fact, and thereby legal.' On the day he moved into the Prussian Ministry of the Interior, he assembled his staff of Civil Servants and told them they were now 'representatives of the new patriotic spirit that has arisen'. He was going, he said, to purge the Service of any taint of Communism; anyone who thought he was going to find the new Minister difficult to work with had better seize his opportunity forthwith to resign. Then, without reference to Papen, his superior as Commissioner for Prussia, he began his purge of the key posts in the Service and the police. He had had his blacklist prepared against this golden day. Even Goebbels, prone to be jealous of any man too close to his beloved Leader, was filled with admiration: 'Göring is cleaning out the Augean stables,' he wrote on 15th February. 'One Lord Lieutenant after another is removed.' The Right-wing Admiral von Levetzow became Police-President of Berlin; similarly, though outside Göring's jurisdiction, Viktor Lutze became Police-President of Hanover, and Wilhelm Scheppmann of the SA Police-President in Dortmund. The Reich Ministry of the Interior, it should be remembered, was under the control of the only other Nazi in the Cabinet, Frick.

In the short book Göring wrote the following year for special publication in Britain, *Germany Reborn* (1934), he declared quite frankly:

> To begin with it seemed to me of the first importance to get the weapon of the police firmly into my own hands. Here it was that I made the first sweeping changes. Out of 32 police chiefs I removed 22. Hundreds of inspectors and thousands of police sergeants followed in the course of the next month. New men were brought in, and in every case these men came from the great reservoir of the Storm Troopers and Guards.[15]

The whole administrative purge was carried out in a matter of weeks. Indeed, it was completed before the election itself, while most people who might have been critical were distracted by the fiercely fought campaign. Having got rid of control by the Prussian Diet, and studiously neglecting to keep Papen informed, Göring proceeded to rule Prussia by decree. 'The weakness of our position was that we were not able to criticize our new coalition partner openly,' wrote Papen, with extraordinary understatement. And again, 'I see that there were many times when I should have invoked the President's authority.' Papen, it must be remembered, was virtually alone; he had no Party to support him, and only the President to turn to. Blomberg, who was in charge of the only independent force in the State, the Reichswehr, became Hitler's man. Papen claims that he did indeed try to control Göring, and even went so far as to ask him to resign. Göring merely rounded on him and said, 'You will only get me out of this room flat on my back!'

On 17th February Göring's celebrated Manifesto was published:

> I do not think it necessary to point out that the police must in all circumstances avoid even the appearance of a hostile attitude towards, or even the impression of any persecution of, the national associations and parties. I expect rather from all the police authorities that they will create and maintain the best understanding with the above-mentioned organizations, in the ranks of which the most important forces of political reconstruction are to be found. Moreover, every kind of activity for national purposes and national propaganda is to be thoroughly supported. On the other hand, the activities of organizations hostile to the State are to be checked by the strongest methods. With Communist terrorism and raids there must be no trifling, and, when necessary, revolvers must be used without regard to consequences. Police officers who fire their revolvers in the execution of their duty will be protected by me without regard to the consequences of using their weapons. But officials who fail, out of mistaken regard for consequences, must expect disciplinary action to be taken against them.[16]

Speaking in the election campaign at Dortmund, Göring made a further notorious statement:

> In the future there will be only one man who will wield power and bear responsibility in Prussia—that is myself. Whoever does his duty in the service of the State, who obeys my orders and ruthlessly makes use of his revolver when attacked, is assured of my protection. Whoever, on the other hand, plays the coward, will have to reckon on being thrown out by me at the earliest possible moment. A bullet fired from the barrel of a police pistol is my bullet. If you say that is murder then I am a murderer . . . I know two sorts of law because I know two sorts of men: those who are with us and those who are against us.

On 1st March Sir Horace Rumbold, Britain's Ambassador to Berlin, reported to the Foreign Office that the daily press contained three lists: of government and police officials who have either been suspended or sent away altogether; of journals suppressed or suspended; of persons who have lost their lives or been injured in political disturbances. Sir Horace also quoted Neurath's opinion of Göring, his new colleague in the Cabinet, as a 'dreadful man', whom Papen was unable to control. Göring, said Neurath, was regarded as the real Fascist in the Hitler Party.[17]

On 22nd February Göring made the boldest move of the period; he infiltrated the Prussian police with a large auxiliary force recreated from the SA, the SS, and the Stahlhelm. The decree made what purported to be an explanation.

> The demands made on the existing police force, which cannot be adequately increased at the present juncture, are often beyond its power; by the present necessity of utilizing them outside their places of service, police officers are often removed from their proper field of activity at inopportune times. In consequence, the voluntary support of suitable helpers to be used as auxiliary police officers in case of emergency can no longer be dispensed with.[18]

Some 50,000 men, still dressed in Party uniform but with a white arm-band to show the new extension to their authority, raising them from street-roughs to police auxiliaries, were added in this way to Göring's police control. They were given free transport, and a daily allowance of three marks. This substantial force could go into action against the Left and all who dared openly to oppose the Nazis.

The election campaign itself became the most violent in Germany's history; at least fifty-one were killed (a conservative, official figure), and several hundred injured. Not all of these were Communists; some leading figures, including the former Minister in the Brüning Government, Adam Stegerweld, Leader of the Catholic trade unionists, were badly beaten up. The SA broke up rival election meetings, their colleagues in the auxiliary police making no pretence of interference. In any case, by an order of 4th February, permission had to be obtained to hold any political meeting, which enabled Göring to put pressure on the opposition parties and to ban Communist rallies. Oppression of the Communists led to many arrests and detentions. On 17th February Göring issued an order forbidding the police to interfere with SA and Stahlhelm activities. Goebbels was right to call this a merciless election.

But more sinister than these open, strong-arm methods of conquering the State were Göring's plans for establishing a secret political police. To further this, he promoted a handsome young official in the Political department of the Prussian Police, Rudolf Diels, whom he had come to know the previous year, and who had supplied him, as Reichstag President, with information from police dossiers on individuals whose Leftist background interested him. Diels was further involved through being the husband of Göring's cousin, Ilse. Göring promoted this smooth, conscienceless young man head of his Political Department.

Göring considered the establishment of a secret police service to be essential to the capture of the State. In *Germany Reborn* he wrote:

> I have created, on my own initiative, the State Secret Police Department. This is the instrument which is so much feared by the enemies of the State and which is chiefly responsible for the fact that in Germany and Prussia there is no question of a Marxist or Communist danger. . . . We had to proceed against these enemies of the State with complete ruthlessness. . . . And so the concentration camps were set up, to which we had sent first of all thousands of officials of the Communist and Socialist democratic Parties. It was only natural that here and there beatings took place. . . . But if we consider the greatness of the occasion . . .[19]

This was the origin of the Gestapo, which was not to be founded officially until April 1933. By that time Hitler had Germany in his grasp.

Göring needed evidence for publication before the election to demonstrate that the Communists were planning some strong counter-move to the lightning tactics of the Nazis. He wanted to show that they were planning a *coup d'état*. On 24th February, three and a half weeks after Hitler's appointment as Chancellor, Göring ordered a raid by the Political Police on the Karl Liebknecht House, Communist head-quarters in Berlin. The leadership were absent; their centre was no place in which to be found at this time. But routine Marxist literature abounded in the cellars, which Göring immediately referred to as the Communist 'catacombs'. Here, he was to claim when the appropriate moment arrived, were documents proving that the Communists were planning a *coup d'état* in Germany. Actually the Communist leadership had resigned itself to the Nazis taking over the Government; they hoped this would result in a mass movement of the workers to their ranks from such parties as the Social Democrats. Göring kept the 'secret' of the evidence for this *coup d'état* strictly to himself. There is nothing in Goebbels's diary about it on 24th February or on the days immediately following. The only reference was that which occurred three weeks earlier—'the Bolshevist attempt at a revolution . . .'. But this threatened *coup d'état* was to be 'planted' on the Communists in good time for the election, accompanied by a resounding proof that mischief was afoot.

It happened on the night of 27th February. The protagonists were all in Berlin, having a quiet evening in spite of the impending elections, now a bare week off. Hitler was paying a social call on Goebbels and his wife at their flat; only music and gossip were in progress. Göring was working at the office in the Prussian Ministry of the Interior on the Unter den Linden. Papen and others were dining at the Herrenklub with Hindenburg. Torgler, the leader of the Communists in the Reichstag, was at one of the Aschinger Restaurants, near the Reichstag, having left his office there relatively late, around 20.30.

The Reichstag building was virtually empty. It had been, after all, in recess since December. Many Communist members were lying low or even under arrest, following Göring's raid on their Party headquarters four days previously. About the time Torgler had left, one of the Reichstag's caretaking staff, a man called Scholz, passed by the large session chamber while on his rounds. It was, he testified subsequently, about 20.30, and nothing seemed amiss. The southern entrance to the building had been locked by the night porter at 20.07. Again, at about 20.50, a postman called Willi Otto passed along the corridor between the door to the Reichstag restaurant and the entrance to the session chamber, and heard nothing untoward.

Outside the building the night was calm and clear, and the ground snow-covered. At about 21.05 a student named Hans Flöter was passing by when he heard breaking glass and his eye caught the astonishing sight of a man who appeared to be carrying a burning brand or torch standing momentarily on the first-floor balcony outside one of the windows of the Reichstag. Unsure what to do, the student went in search of a policeman, and reported what he thought he had seen. Another passerby, Werner Thaler, who was a type-setter by trade, also heard breaking glass and saw something strange—a man climbing through the window of the restaurant. As he was considering what to do, he was joined by a police-sergeant named Karl Buwert, who had hurried up to investigate, having been told something suspicious was happening in the Reichstag by yet another passerby who was not subsequently identified. Buwert and Thaler both saw lights moving inside the ground-floor windows. Buwert drew his revolver and fired. The lights disappeared.

At about this time, 21.14, a fire alarm for the Reichstag was received at a fire station near by. At 21.17 a Police-Lieutenant, Emil Lateit, with a contingent of officers arrived from the nearby Brandenburger Tor police station; they entered the Reichstag. All these events, relating to observers outside the Reichstag, had happened within less than fifteen minutes. The first fire-engine arrived at 21.18. Lateit, by now inside the session chamber itself, found a fire alight in the area round the Reichstag President's chair. The House Inspector joined him as fires were starting up among the members' seats. By 21.24 the firemen were in the building, supervised by Fire-Captain Klotz, and a thick haze of smoke was developing in the session chamber, accompanied by growing heat. Then, at 21.27, there was a huge explosion under the glass dome of the session chamber, and the flames leaped up from floor level. The great chamber was fully alight.

At the same time a man was discovered in the Bismarck Hall, at the rear of the building. He was half-naked, streaming with sweat, and covered with grime. He was arrested immediately, and was later identified as a twenty-four-year-old Dutchman, Marinus van der Lubbe. He carried a pocket knife, wallet and passport.

'Why did you do it?' he was asked.

'As a protest,' he replied. He claimed he had entered the building only at nine o'clock.

This was the position at around 21.30, less than half an hour since the student, Flöter, had made his first observation of the man with the burning brand (who was evidently van der Lubbe), and only some forty minutes since the postman, Otto, had passed the session chamber and heard no sound, and barely an hour since Scholz, the caretaker, had passed by the chamber itself. Now the whole building, some 11,000 cubic metres, was an inferno of leaping flame, reaching through the broken dome some 75 metres from the ground and out through twisted metal and melted glass into the night sky. It was a spectacle to draw crowds from the area nearby.

The first of the Nazi leaders to arrive on the scene was Göring, wearing his long trench coat and rushing by car to the blazing building from the Unter den Linden, a bare half-kilometre away. It was now 21.35, and large crowds were gathering, drawn by the flames glowing in the sky above the ruined cupola. At the same time as Göring arrived, Douglas Reed, the Berlin correspondent of *The Times* of London, drove up. He saw Göring's massive figure running into the building through the deputies' entrance. Reed followed; one or two other pressmen were already there. The session chamber was a mass of flames. Göring ordered everyone out, and immediately took charge. He claimed that someone in the crowd outside had shouted 'arson' and that, as he chose to put it, a veil had immediately dropped from his eyes. It was the Communists! It was the signal for a *coup d'état*! 'It never even occurred to me that the Reichstag might have been set alight; I thought the fire had been caused by carelessness. . . . At this moment I knew that the Communist Party was the culprit.' When Papen arrived later, having just driven the President back from the Herrenklub to his palace, Göring was furiously directing the fire fighting. He shouted to the Vice-Chancellor as he drove up, 'This is a Communist crime against the new Government.'[20]

Goebbels and Hitler learned of the fire by telephone. Hitler's friend, Ernst 'Putzi' Hanfstaengl of Munich, was living at the time at Göring's

Presidential palace, and saw the fire raging from the window of his rooms, which were close by the burning building:

> After an hour or so of alternate draughts, with the bed-clothes up to my nose, I could feel the shivering lessening and a welcome warmth coursing through my limbs. I was nicely bathed in perspiration when the telephone in the adjacent sitting-room began to ring. It went on and on, no one came to answer it, so in the end I heaved myself out of bed, mopping my face with a towel, and went next door. It was Brückner, or one of the adjutants, I do not remember: 'The Führer insists that you come this evening to Goebbels. He wants you to play the piano for him.' I explained rather tersely my position, said he had undone all the good work I had started, that I could not possibly come out with a feverish cold on me and that I was going back to my bed. I had just re-arranged everything and was starting to warm up when the telephone shrilled again. This is too much, I thought, it can ring till it stops. It failed to do so, so I dragged myself next door again. This time it was Magda herself calling. I was ruining her whole party. I only had to wrap up and come along and sweat later, and so forth. I was suitably firm, took care to leave the earpiece off its hook, and started my self-imposed régime all over again.
>
> I tried to doze, and slowly realized that there was too much light to do so in comfort. I had left the door to the other room open. You idiot, I groaned to myself, you have left the reading-lamp on at the desk. I tried counting sheep but it was no good. Moreover there was a curious quality about the light. It seemed to flicker and was penetrating into my bedroom from some other source than the open door. Suddenly Frau Wanda, the housekeeper burst in: 'Herr Doktor! Herr Doktor!' she screamed in her falsetto, 'the Reichstag is on fire!' This time I was up in a bound, ran to the window, which faced across the square, and there, in very truth, was the whole building enveloped in flames.
>
> This time I did the telephoning and got Goebbels himself on the line: 'I must talk to Herr Hitler,' I said. What was it all about, the little gnome wanted to know, was it nothing I could tell him to pass on? In the end I lost patience: 'Tell him the Reichstag is on fire.' 'Hanfstaengl, is this one of your jokes?' Goebbels answered rather curtly. 'If you think that, come down here and see for yourselves,' and I hung up.[21]

Goebbels takes up the story in his Diary:

> Work at home in the evening. The Leader comes to dine at nine o'clock. We have some music and talk. Suddenly a phone call

from Dr. Hanfstaengl: 'The Reichstag is on fire!' I take this for a bit of wild fantasy and refuse to report it to the Leader. I ask for news wherever possible and at last obtain the dreadful confirmation it is true! The great dome is all ablaze. Incendiarism! I immediately inform the Leader, and we hasten at top speed down the empty streets to the Reichstag. The whole building is aflame. Clambering over thick fire-hoses we reach the great lobby by gateway number two. Göring meets us on the way, and soon von Papen also arrives. That this is the work of incendiaries has been ascertained to be the fact at various spots. There is no doubt but that communism has made a last attempt to cause disorder by means of fire and terror, in order to grasp the power during the general panic.

The decisive moment arrives. Göring is amazingly active. Not for a moment does the Leader lose his composure; wonderful to watch him giving his orders here, the same man who sat at table with us, chatting cheerfully, half an hour ago.

The Assembly Hall presents a desolate spectacle of devastation. The flames have reached the ceiling, which threatens to crash every moment.

Now we have to act.

Göring at once suppresses the entire Communist and Social Democrat Press. Officials of the Communist Party are arrested during the night. The S.A. is warned to stand by for every contingency.

Dash to the district, to inform everybody, and to prepare for all eventualities. The Leader confers with a hurriedly summoned Cabinet council. We meet again shortly after at the Kaiserhof and discuss the situation. One culprit has already been caught, a young Dutch Communist called van der Lubbe.

Drive with the Leader to the editorial office of the *Völkischer Beobachter*. We both set to work there at once, writing leading articles and proclamations. I retire to the district hall, to be able to dictate without being interrupted. In the middle of the night, Counciller of State Diels, of the Prussian Ministry of Interior, comes to give me a detailed report as to all the steps that have hitherto been taken. The arrests have been effected without difficulty. The entire Communist and Democratic Press is already suppressed. If resistance is offered, it will be 'line clear' for the S.A.

It is already morning when I meet the Leader again at the Kaiserhof. The Press is in order. The direction of our action has been set by events themselves. Now we can set to work with a vengeance. The Communists will have been very much mistaken. They have proposed our downfall, but have dealt themselves the mortal blow.[22]

Göring himself was less than frank about the action he took when defending his position at the Nuremberg Trial while being interrogated by the American prosecutor, Mr Justice Jackson:

GÖRING: . . . Relatively few arrests were made in connection with the Reichstag fire. The arrests which you attribute to the Reichstag fire were the arrests of Communist functionaries. These arrests, as I have repeatedly stated and wish to emphasize once more, had nothing to do with this fire. The fire merely precipitated their arrest and upset our carefully planned action, thus allowing several of the functionaries to escape.

JACKSON: In other words, you had lists of Communists already prepared at the time of the Reichstag fire, of persons who should be arrested, did you not?

GÖRING: We had always drawn up beforehand fairly complete lists of Communist functionaries who were to be arrested. That had nothing to do with the fire in the German Reichstag.

JACKSON: They were immediately put into execution—the arrests, I mean—after the Reichstag fire?

GÖRING: Contrary to my intention of postponing this action for a few days and letting it take place according to plan, thereby perfecting the arrangements, the Führer ordered that same night that the arrests should follow immediately. This had the disadvantage, as I said, of precipitating matters.

JACKSON: You and the Führer met at the fire, did you not?

GÖRING: That is right.

JACKSON: And then and there you decided to arrest all the Communists that you had listed?

GÖRING: I repeat again that the decision for their arrests had been reached some days before this; it simply meant that on this night they were immediately arrested. I would rather have waited a few days, according to plan; then some of the more important men would not have escaped.

JACKSON: And the next morning the decree was presented to President von Hindenburg suspending the provisions of the Constitution which we have discussed here, was it not?

GÖRING: I believe so, yes.[23]

The decree mentioned here was issued on 28th February, the day after the fire, and signed by the President. It was of significance for the liberties of the German people. It was described as 'for the protection of the People and the State', and 'as a defensive measure against Communist acts of violence'. It gave sweeping powers to Hitler and Göring over the individual liberty of German citizens; it authorized them to restrict the freedom of the individual, censor or ban the press and other forms of communication, and over-rule the inviolability of property. The death penalty was extended to include those found guilty of treason, sabotage, and arson, and those convicted of conspiracy to assassinate members of the government. The Communist Party was cunningly left intact until after the elections—in order to ensure splitting the working class vote between the Communists and the Social Democrats.

With the Reichstag fire, which Hitler described as a beacon (*Fanal*) sent from heaven, now behind them, the Nazis could launch into the full savagery of their anti-Communist pre-election campaign. Göring, speaking at Frankfurt on 3rd March, just prior to the election, declared categorically:

> Fellow Germans, my measures will not be crippled by any judicial thinking. My measures will not be crippled by any bureaucracy. Here I don't have to worry about Justice, my mission is only to destroy and exterminate, nothing more. This struggle will be a struggle against chaos, and such a struggle I shall not conduct with the power of the police. A bourgeois State might have done that. Certainly, I shall use the power of the State and the police to the utmost, my dear Communists, so don't draw any false conclusions; but the struggle to the death, in which my fist will grasp your necks, I shall lead with those down there—the Brown Shirts.[24]

Everything, in fact, as Göring said at Nuremberg, had been made ready to assault the Communists, the most immediately vulnerable of Hitler's opponents in the election, and in the Reichstag. All that was needed was the open sign, obvious to all, which would enable the Nazis to attack them in the name of state security. The Reichstag fire came pat on cue—a completely useless gesture from the point of view of the Communists, but a blessing to the Nazis, who were universally suspected of having set the building alight themselves.[25] Almost half a century has been occupied since in endless discussion, often at book length, as to whether the Nazis, or the mentally disturbed Dutchman with his waving torch, had set the place alight at some moment after nine o'clock that winter evening. So little time was lost that the whole night of 27th–28th February was spent putting the right political gloss on the fire through the Nazi organs of speech and journalism. Arrests were accelerated while the Reichstag embers were still warm.[26]

Torgler, chairman of the Communist deputies in the Reichstag and the principal Communist suspect, went straight to the police on the day after the fire, declaring Göring's accusations to be as ridiculous as they were impossible. He declared he had no acquaintance with, or knowledge of, van der Lubbe. Nevertheless, he was arrested, as were certain other Communists who were later to be charged with the arson alongside van der Lubbe—Georgi Dimitroff, Blagoi Popov and Wassil Tanev, all three Bulgarians.[27]

Göring knew that the onus of proof lay with him, but he adopted his usual buccaneering attitude in failing to provide it in the rush of events which followed. The raid on the Karl Liebknecht House provided him with the opportunity to produce any evidence he might care to produce, or say he would produce. With Hitler away in Breslau on 1st March, no Cabinet was called to discuss the emergency (if indeed Hitler wanted to discuss it) until 2nd March. The official minutes of this meeting fortunately survive:

> Reich Minister Göring stated with regard to the measures directed against the Communists that last night important material on the Communist plans had been found. The time for setting off the operation had first been fixed for the evening and the night of Election Day, but had then been postponed to the middle of March. A Pharus* map of Berlin had been found in duplicate, on which all important electrical control stations, subways, transformer stations were indicated. One copy had been in the hands of headquarters; the other had been cut up and distributed to the individual groups. The map was being photographed. In consequence of this the power lines were being guarded with especial care.
>
> From the material the close connection that existed with Moscow was also evident. The German Communists had been given a time limit within which to do something. Otherwise they would be deprived of their subsidies. The directive concerning the operation and the photograph of the map would be sent to the Ministers personally. He did not consider it feasible to publish it because it might provoke acts of sabotage.
>
> The police would have to turn over the examining of the culprit to the Reich Supreme Court [*Reichsgericht*] at once. The examining judge was the *Landgerichtsdirektor*, Dr Braune, who had formerly conducted the examinations of members of the NSDAP. He had always proceeded most severely against the party.
>
> Even if it had to be assumed that he would work objectively, he was hardly a suitable person to handle this important matter.

*A popular type of street map.

It is possible that he might confine the examination merely to the one that committed the outrage although, in the opinion of the experts concerned, at least 6 to 7 persons must have been involved. He might possibly also release Deputy Torgler prematurely from prison. Inept handling might have intolerable results. Whether another more suitable person might not be entrusted with the investigation of the arson in the Reichstag, which had to be regarded not as such, but as high treason, must be considered.

The funds at his disposal for fighting criminal elements amounted to only 30,000 Reichsmarks and would not be replenished until April 1. This amount was not nearly enough to take care of the very considerable outlays for rewards to informers and similar expenditures.

Also to be considered was whether something could not be done about the foreign press, which in part reported that he himself had set fire to the Reichstag, and was also making similar statements about the Reich Chancellor too. In addition Stampfer had stated that he did not mean to say that the Reichstag had been set afire by Göring the Reich Minister but by Göring the National Socialist.

The Reich Chancellor likewise considered the agitation of the world press against the German Government very dangerous. All grounds for the clamor would have been removed if the culprit had been hanged right away.[28]

Papen gives his own description of what happened at this Cabinet meeting:

> Göring presented some of the documents which had allegedly been found during a raid on the Communist headquarters in the Karl Liebknecht House. I remember they included plans for the liquidation of a number of political leaders, among them most of the Cabinet ministers and myself. I must confess that it did not occur to me that the Nazis, now a responsible government party, would find it necessary to forge such documents in order to bolster up their case. We were all convinced that the Communists had planned an armed uprising and represented a menace to the security of the state.

Needless to say, the documents were never produced. The elections followed hard upon the Cabinet meeting, and the energies of both Hitler and Göring were turned elsewhere. It was not even worth the trouble to forge the necessary material.

Nevertheless, later in the year van der Lubbe was brought to trial, along with Torgler and the Bulgarians. The trial was held between 21st September and 23rd December in the Supreme Court in Leipzig, and it was conducted scrupulously by a process of law still uncontaminated by Nazi infiltration. Hitler did not choose to interfere with the German Law Courts during Hindenburg's lifetime. The trial was public, and attended by the world press. Van der Lubbe refused to speak in the courtroom, having previously testified that it was he, and he alone, who achieved the feat of firing the Reichstag; it was evident he did not want anyone to rob him of the glory attaching to his proudest act of incendiarism. The other defendants stoutly protested their innocence, and Dimitroff, who conducted his own defence vociferously, had constantly to be called to order in the court. He made Göring lose his temper when he appeared as a witness on 4th November, accusing the alleged Communist traitors and incendiaries of wearing Nazi uniforms—'I knew as by intuition that the Communists fired the Reichstag', he declared. The interchanges between Göring and Dimitroff descended to the level of a slanging match, and the President had to order the police to remove the prisoner. It is notable that the documentation Göring had promised to produce in February still made no appearance. Van der Lubbe sat silent and remote throughout the trial. He was finally convicted in December and executed by the axe on 10th January 1934. But not a single shred of evidence could be produced during the fifty-seven days of the trial against Torgler and the Bulgarians, or indeed against the Communists as such, though the judgment of the Court included a statement which implied that radical elements must have been responsible for the fire. In spite of their acquittal, Torgler and the Bulgarians were kept in custody.[29]

This, however, was in the future. Heiden describes the atmosphere in which the election campaign was conducted during the last days of February and early March:

> Before the ashes of the Reichstag building were cold the air waves were alive with National Socialist voices blaring forth details about the murderous, incendiary plans of the Communists, that had been frustrated just in time; SA men rushed about in trucks, drunk with victory and roaring threats at people; in the cellars of the SA barracks woollen blankets stifled the cries of the victims. . . . Outside the polls, giant posters screamed: 'Your vote for Adolf Hitler!' or 'Stamp out Communism! Crush Social Democracy!' Other placards, here and there, advocated a so-called 'Black, White and Red Fighting Front'. This, for practical purposes, was the old German Nationalist Party, led by Hugenberg, Papen,

and Franz Seldte of the Stahlhelm. Of other parties the voter saw and heard next to nothing; the Social Democrats made no speeches and issued no literature. In many smaller localities the polls were manned only by National Socialists; occasionally the secret ballot was discarded and voting took place publicly; and after the secrecy of the mails and of telephone conversations had been suspended, many people ceased to believe in the secret ballot even where it was still observed.[30]

Goebbels's cynical description of Hitler's final speech, which was broadcast from Königsberg to the nation at large, shows the difference when the Nazis' leading propagandist describes what happens:

> The Leader speaks with utmost fervour and devotion. When at the end he mentions that the President of the Reich and he had clasped hands—the one having released Prussia from the enemy as a Field-Marshal, and the other having done his duty in the West as simple soldier—solemn silence reigns and deep emotion holds the whole assembly. The Netherland Hymn of Thanksgiving, the last verse of which is drowned in the clamour of the bells from the Königsberg Cathedral, forms a mighty chorus to crown his speech. This hymn goes throbbing on the ethereal waves of the radio over the whole of Germany. Forty million people are now standing in the squares and in the streets, or are sitting in the Bierhallen and their homes by the radio, and become conscious that the new era has dawned. At this moment hundreds of thousands will decide to follow Hitler, and fight in his spirit for the revival of the nation.[31]

Fogbound overnight at Königsberg, Goebbels and Hitler cast their votes on the following day, 5th March, at a small local polling booth, to the astonishment of the Returning Officer.

This, Germany's last election which can still be termed, with some reservations, relatively free and secret, gave Hitler some 6 million additional votes, representing in all the support of some 44 per cent of the electorate. The principal results are engraved in Germany's history.

	Seats	Votes
National Socialists	288	17,277,180
Social Democrats	120	7,181,629
Communists	81	4,848,058
Centre Party	74	4,425,000
Nationalists	52	3,136,760
Bavarian People's Party	18	1,072,893

The Prussian Diet election also took place on the same day, with similar results. Goebbels made this relative success into a triumph: '. . . the victory is ours. It is far greater than any of us had dared to hope. But what do figures signify any longer? We are masters of the Reich and of Prussia. . . . We are all intoxicated with success.'

The first major act of the Nazis, in the progress towards absolute power, was to repeat in Bavaria the technical *coup d'état* they had already achieved in Prussia. Bavaria, Germany's second state in size and political significance (though in population only 7 million to Prussia's 35 million), always regarded itself as alien to the north. Hitler himself had once exploited this situation, though to his cost, in the Munich *Putsch* undertaken ten years before. Now that he himself was in charge of the federal government, he realized the importance of losing no time in bringing Bavaria to heel. A new political word appeared: *Gleichschaltung* (meaning to achieve a 'unifying process' of the country under Nazi control) was to imply first of all loss of the individual controls enjoyed by the various State administrations, and their absorption into a single uniform state system.

Bavaria, as usual, had already shown signs of recalcitrance, of its traditional separatism. The Catholic Prime Minister in Bavaria, Heinrich Held, did not command a majority in the Diet; on the other hand, his opponents, including the National Socialists, could not form a combined front to oust him. The Held régime, it was known, favoured placing Prince Rupprecht, son of the last reigning monarch in Bavaria, at the head of the State as a kind of regent. This was to be a separatist act, a declaration of independence. However, the Prussian story was to be repeated; on 8th March the Bavarian National Socialists demanded that Franz Ritter von Epp,[32] a Catholic general, a sound Nazi, and former Freikorps commander of the early 1920s, be appointed State Commissar, the position earmarked for the Prince. When this was rejected by the Bavarian government, Epp, on orders from Berlin, brought out the Storm Troopers, who marched through the streets of Munich and occupied the government offices. Held immediately protested to the local Army commander, General von Leeb, demanding help; Leeb, appealing for advice to the Ministry of Defence, was told not to interfere. In the background, supporting Epp, was the police president of Bavaria, Heinrich Himmler. Held was forced to give way, and Prince Rupprecht disappeared to Greece. Epp, taking control of Bavaria, appointed National Socialist Ministers, and the *coup d'état* was complete. Similarly on 10th March Nazi Reich Governors (Reichsstatthalter) took over in Saxony, Württemberg, Baden, and Thuringia; their powers enabled them to dismiss state officials unsympathetic to the Nazis, and have full control of the Police.[33] Those states not included at this stage were to find their Diets dissolved by decree at the end of the month.

ii

Hitler was working now at high speed. He knew that he had to take the State and its institutions by storm, leaving his slower-moving opponents breathless and faced by now one, now another *fait accompli* which they had no power actively to resist. The fear of physical reprisal if personal protests were offered in the face of the triumphant Nazis, made the Germans, and their silenced officials and politicians, appear supine during these terrible days. The Reichstag was not due to meet until 21st March. Meanwhile complaints had begun to pour in addressed to Hindenburg, to Hitler, to Göring appealing for action against the Storm Troopers whose violence was horrifying peaceful citizens.[34] For example, on 26th February Dr Richard Moeller, a former Federal Prime Minister, had written to Hindenburg asking him to exert his authority so that 'peaceful citizens who do not approve of the party politics of the present Government are not deprived of the protection the State owes them by being degraded to second-class citizens'. Hindenburg merely passed the complaint on to Hitler, as Reich Chancellor. On 13th March the Labour Party of Birmingham, England, sent a resolution to Hitler expressing strong indignation at the terrorist methods used by him and his party members prior to and during the recent elections. Complaints arrived from the Polish Embassy concerning the brutal treatment of Jews in Germany who were Polish subjects and whose shops had been robbed by uniformed SA men. No notice was taken of these complaints.

Protests came from other quarters. On 7th March a statement signed by Cardinal Schulte, Archbishop of Cologne, and five Catholic bishops called attention to the serious danger which threatened the morals of Catholics through National Socialism. As early as September 1931 the Church, through the agency of the Vicar General of the Diocese of Mainz, had condemned the heretical views of National Socialism; members of the Party were forbidden in this statement Catholic burial unless they had signified their repentance. Catholics were being forced increasingly into a dilemma—could they accept the political doctrines of the Nazis while at the same time rejecting its anti-religious ethic?

Both Hitler and Goebbels were still nominal Catholics. Goebbels had become a non-believer, but Hitler, according to Otto Dietrich, his Party press chief, combined belief in Darwin's theories of natural selection and survival of the fittest with 'a highly general, monotheistic faith. He believed in guidance from above and in the existence of a

Supreme Being whose wisdom and will had created laws for the preservation and evolution of the human race. He believed that the highest aim of mankind was to survive for the achievement of progress and perfection. From this belief there followed directly for him a sense of his own mission to be the Leader of the German people. He was acting, he believed, on the command of this Supreme Being. . . . In his speeches he often mentioned the Almighty and Providence. . . . But he personally was sharply hostile to Christianity and the churches, although the Party programme came out for a " positive " Christianity.' However, he was never formally to withdraw from membership of the Catholic Church, while at the same time he endeavoured to establish a State-controlled Protestant Church. He appeared himself now and then at Church ceremonials.

In private he ridiculed Christianity and what he held to be the effete nature of much Christian practice. Shortly after the election he said to Rauschning during a private conversation among friends:

> For our people it is decisive whether they acknowledge the Jewish Christ-creed with its effeminate pity-ethic, or a strong, heroic belief in God in Nature, God in our own people, in our destiny, in our blood. . . . One is either a German or a Christian. You cannot be both. . . . I'm a Catholic. Certainly that was fated from the beginning, for only a Catholic knows the weaknesses of the Church. I know how to deal with these gentry. Bismarck was a fool. In other words, he was a Protestant. Protestants don't know what a church is.[35]

However, it was not politic at this stage in the development of Nazi power for the Leader openly to tangle with the Churches. Rather, it was necessary to bring the right pressure to bear on them to accept Nazism as the force which opposed the Church's greatest enemy, the Communists. When Göring openly attacked the Catholics as politicians in a speech at Essen on 11th March, the Church temporized. By the end of the month the Archbishop of Cologne revised his opposition, permitting Nazis in uniform to take the sacraments, and raising his ban on religious burial for Party members. Later in the year the German Catholics were to find it politic to come to terms with the Nazis, though many Catholics, both prominent and not so prominent, were to resist.[36]

Another significant protest came from Theodor Leipart, the Trade Union leader. On Hitler's accession to power he had issued a temporary directive to the Unions: 'Though we are against the new Government, the present hour commands "Organization", not "Demonstration".' After the Reichstag fire, when it seemed that the suppression of the Unions, and even of the Social Democratic Party, was likely, Leipart advised the Party Leader, Otto Wels, who was pondering some form of active resistance to Hitler, in the same temporizing vein as on the occasion of Papen's Prussian coup in the previous July; he claimed he could not 'press a button to start a civil war, all the more because the result was obvious'. However, even Leipart in the period of his weakness felt impelled to address an appeal direct to the President, especially as the SA began systematic raids on Trade Union offices in March. On 10th March he wrote on behalf of the Federal Executive of the Trade Unions:

> Dear Herr Reich President,
> In the sign of the day of mourning which next Sunday is to unite the German nation, regardless of political creed, in remembrance of those who fell in the war, the Federal Executive of the German General Federation of Trade Unions, again approaches you as the German leader who in his person combines the tradition of the old and the dignity of the new Germany.
>
> In our Fatherland, torn by antagonisms, you, Mr Reich President, represent the unity of our people beyond the frontiers of party. In the confidence that you are still the guardian and guarantor of the popular rights laid down in the Constitution, in the conviction that you are still prepared and resolved to oppose any party-political arbitrariness, we approach you on behalf of many millions of organized German workers and their families with the request to cry a halt to the legal insecurity which in many German towns threatens the life and property of the German workers.[37]

Hindenburg, however, was by now beyond appealing to, if not praying for.

Hitler meanwhile worked from day to day to consolidate his seizure of the State. On 12th March Hindenburg was brought out to take the salute from a combined march-past made up of the Reichswehr, the SA and the Stahlhelm. A new official flag was proclaimed by Presidential decree on 13th March—the former black-and-white-and-red Imperial flag had now to be flown along with the Nazi Swastika flag; this decree concerning the twin flags was the following day made applicable also to the Army.[38] The day before, Hitler had flown to Munich, saying as he stepped down from the plane: 'Years ago I took up the struggle here, the first phase of which may be considered now as ended. A co-ordination [*Gleichschaltung*[39]] of political life, such as we have never before experienced, has been completed.' He was in the sixth week only of the Chancellorship.

But Hitler remained careful about the image he presented to the public eye, at least abroad. When Sefton Delmer, the English correspondent, asked him in March 1933, with aftermath of the Reichstag fire in mind, whether the suspension of liberty was to remain permanent, Hitler replied, 'No, when the Communist menace is stamped out, the normal order of things shall return. Our laws were too liberal for me to be able to deal properly and swiftly with this Bolshevik underworld. But I myself am only too anxious for the normal state of affairs to be restored as soon as possible. First, however, we must crush Communism out of existence.'[40]

On 14th March Goebbels, aged only thirty-five, took up his appointment as Minister for Propaganda and Public Enlightenment; a decree to this effect had been signed by the President the previous day. 'What a happiness for all of us to have this venerable and remarkable man yet over us,' wrote Goebbels, his emotions on show. Since early February he had been planning the new Ministry he had been promised after the election; it was, he says, to be built up on exactly the same lines as the Propaganda Department of the Party, and 'is to be absolutely modern, unique, and novel'. By 8th March the initial plan had been completed, the Ministry was to have five large departments controlling Press, Film, Radio, Theatre and Propaganda. He was assigned an old building on the Wilhelmplatz; this he planned to strip of its old-fashioned plush and stucco, as he put it 'to let the sunshine in at the windows'; work began on 13th March, carried out by SA men, to the horror of the old-fashioned civil servants. As soon as he was satisfied the renovations were going well, Goebbels turned his attention to planning the special ceremonial designed to make a spectacle out of the opening day of the new Reichstag. A preliminary ceremony of inauguration was planned to take place at the Garrison Chapel in Potsdam, and broadcast to the nation. Hindenburg was once more to be led on parade to lend the Nazis tradition and respectability.

Hitler introduced a further supporter to a key position—Schacht was appointed Governor of the Reichsbank (an office he had held three years previously) in succession to Dr Hans Luther, who was told to resign and was subsequently packed off to Washington as German Ambassador. The appointment of Schacht foreshadowed the future streamlined economy which Hitler envisaged for Germany and placed under Schacht's control.

On 15th March Hitler held a Cabinet meeting to prepare his 'colleagues' to accept the Enabling Act which was to be the cornerstone of his power. It was to be entitled the 'Law for Removing the Distress of People and Reich' (*Gesetz zur Behebung der Not von Volk und Reich*). It represented a change in the Constitution, and so required a two-thirds majority in the Reichstag. Hitler's task was to cajole his Nationalist colleagues into supporting him when the Bill was presented at the opening session of the Reichstag; as a bait, the Bill permitted the President's authority to remain intact. At the same time negotiations were taking place with the Centre party to win their support. The Communists no longer counted; those deputies who were not already under arrest (like their leaders Thaelmann and Torgler) would soon find themselves detained if they dared to set foot inside the assembly, which was to be convened, after the Potsdam ceremonial, in temporary premises set up in the Kroll Opera House.

The Cabinet Minutes of 15th and 20th March survive, and show Hitler's tactics in dealing with his Ministers, and the utter lack of any opposition to his proposals for such sweeping changes as the proposed Enabling Bill represented:

15th March:

> The Reich Chancellor opened the session and stated that the political situation was completely clarified now that the elections of the municipal councils had taken place.
>
> The clarification of the relations between the Reich and the south German states was of decisive importance, especially that of the relationship between the Reich and Bavaria. The Reich idea (*Reichsgedanke*) had shown itself surprisingly strong everywhere. The revolution in Bavaria was perhaps the most thorough one. In his opinion, further internal political developments would progress without disturbance. In Württemberg a government had already been formed. In Bavaria it was still necessary to clarify certain separatist activities. For this reason it would, in his opinion, be practical to wait a while with the formation of a government in Bavaria. The national revolution had taken place without great upheavals. He stated that henceforth, it would be necessary to detour all activities of the people towards the purely political, because economic decisions had to be awaited.
>
> In his opinion there would be no difficulties in getting the Enabling Act (*Ermächtigungsgesetz*) through the Reichstag with a two-thirds majority.
>
> The foreign political situation had in no way become worse. He was firmly convinced that foreign countries would take a totally different attitude towards the present Reich government than to the former ones, that is, they would treat it with greater respect.
>
> The situation in Austria could not yet be surveyed clearly. As long as the political centre of gravity was in Vienna, France would always be able to assert a strong influence.
>
> The Reich Minister of the Interior gave the information that he

had attended the session of the Reichstag Committee of Oldest Members (*Aeltestenrat*). The five Reichstag parties still existing were all represented, namely the National Socialists by Reich Minister Göring and himself, the Social Democrats by Loebe and Hertz, the Centre Party by Leicht and Rauch. The German National Party was also represented. Immediate agreement was reached that a seniority president was not necessary and that Reichstag President Göring should preside over the sessions of the new Reichstag.

He, the Reich Minister of the Interior, had pointed out that the Reichstag ought to pass within three days an Enabling Act with the majority necessary to change the constitution. The Centre Party (Zentrum) had not expressed any objection. Representative Esser had, however, asked to be received by the Reich Chancellor.

There still remained the question of what should happen to the drafts of bills not presented, which ought to be supported by the present administration, and formerly had already been presented to the Reichstag. In his opinion it was best, in consideration of the Enabling Act, not to present the list to the Reich Council and the Reichstag, but to pass the list later on the basis of the Enabling Act.

The Enabling Act would have to be so broadly framed that every provision of the German constitution could be side-tracked. It would have to have a time limit of four years for the time being. He, the Reich Minister of the Interior, had in mind something like the following text for the law:

'The Reich administration shall be enabled to take such measures as it deems necessary in view of the needs of the people and State. In doing so the provisions of the Reich constitution can be waived.'

It was still to be determined if an addition to the content would be practical, according to which the validity of the Enabling Act (*Ermächtigungsgesetz*) would depend on the present composition of the Reich government.

As regards the two-third majorities demanded by the Reich constitution, altogether 432 representatives would have to be present to pass the Enabling Act, with the Communists included and the number of elected Reichstag representatives assumed to be 647. If the Communist representatives are deducted the total number of representatives would have to be present in order to pass the Enabling Act. He believed it better not to eliminate the Communist mandates. On the other hand, prohibition of the Communist Party would be practical. The prohibition would result in dissolution of the organizations. Eventually all the persons who would still insist on professing Communism would have to be sent to labour camps.

Reich Minister Göring expressed his conviction that the Enabling Act would be passed with the necessary two-thirds majority. Possibly a majority could be obtained by banishing several Social Democrats from the hall. Possibly, the Social Democrats would even refrain from voting on the Enabling Act. At the election of the President of the Reichstag the Social Democrats would certainly hand in blank slips.

20th March:

The Reich Chancellor reported on the interview which he had just had with representatives of the Centre Party. He explained that in this interview he had established the necessity for the Enabling Act and that the representatives of the Centre Party had recognised this necessity. The representatives of the Centre Party had only asked that a small committee be formed which was to be continuously informed about the measures which the Reich Government would take on the basis of the Enabling Act. In his opinion this request should be granted; then there would be no doubt that the Centre Party would agree to the Enabling Act. The acceptance of the Enabling Act by the Centre Party would mean a strengthening of prestige abroad.

On Wednesday the discussion of individual concrete questions with representatives of the Centre Party was to be continued.

The Reich Minister for Foreign Affairs suggested that written notes be made of the settlements arrived at with the representatives of the Centre Party.

The Reich Minister of the Interior then presented the contents of the accompanying bill to relieve the distress of the people and of the Reich. He said that in his opinion it would be most practical to introduce the bill as an initial motion in the Reichstag. It would be best if the Party Leaders should sign it.

A change in the parliamentary procedure of the Reichstag was also considered necessary. A specific ruling would have to be made that even those Reichstag members who were absent without being excused would be counted as present. Presumably it would be possible to pass the Enabling Act in all of the three readings on Thursday.

The deputy of the Reich Chancellor and Reich Commissioner for Prussia stated that a new basic state law would have to be formulated, which would above all be free of exaggerated parliamentarianism. Perhaps the Reich Chancellor in his government statement (*Regierungserklärung*) would be able to make some statements to this effect.

The Reich Chancellor said that he had already made clear to the representatives of the Centre Party that the Reichstag could become a national assembly when the advance work for the outline of a new Reich constitution should be ready.

The Reich Minister of Economics and Reich Minister for Nutrition and Agriculture stated that the proposed Enabling Act could perhaps have a passage inserted, specifically declaring the Reichstag to be a national assembly.

Reich Minister Göring declared that he had made an intensive study of this question. He considered it more practical, however, that such a form should not be chosen.

The Reich Cabinet approved the drafting of a law to relieve the distress of the people and the nation.[41]

In private, Hitler mocked his Cabinet colleagues. 'They regard me as an uneducated barbarian,' he said in Rauschning's hearing. 'Yes, we are barbarians! We want to be barbarians! It is an honourable title. We shall rejuvenate the world. This world is near its end. It is our mission to cause unrest.'[42]

The civil ceremony commemorating the opening of the new Reichstag on Tuesday 21st March took place in the Protestant Garrison Chapel of the new Reichstag; the Catholics held their own religious ceremony in the Potsdam Pfarrkirche, and the Protestants in various churches. Hitler did not attend either the Catholic or the Protestant religious celebrations. Instead, he visited the graves of Nazis who had died for the cause.

It was a brilliantly sunny day, warm and spring-like. Hitler was deeply conscious that the civil ceremony in the Garrison Church echoed that attended by Bismarck in 1871, when he had opened the first Reichstag of the new German Empire.[43] By adopting this ceremony in Potsdam, Hitler was proclaiming the inauguration of a new order, the Third Reich.

Although the Communist deputies and Social Democrats were entirely absent (they had not been invited), the other deputies (the Nazis—in brown shirts—the Centre Party, the Nationalists) were marshalled in their seats, while the rest of the cast were also carefully selected for the occasion. The intention was to combine as obviously as possible the old (the Imperial régime) with the new (the Nazis)—field-marshals, generals, admirals (all in pre-war uniform) were present, including Field-Marshal August von Mackensen and General Hans von Seeckt. A chair, conspicuously empty, stood by for the absent Kaiser, while the ex-Crown Prince attended in the uniform of a Lieutenant-General of the Death's Head Hussars. Outside, the Reichswehr were on parade, marching alongside the ranks of the SA and the Stahlhelm.

The civil ceremony began with a procession. The congregation rose from their seats, looking towards the entrance to the Church. Hitler, dressed formally in morning clothes (in which he always looked out of place), led in his ministers; the line was brought up by the huge bulk of Hindenburg, walking with slow, stiff deliberation towards the empty chair of the Kaiser, which he saluted with his Field-Marshal's baton. If the ceremony had been staged to win the support of Hindenburg and the Junker class for the Nazis, it was also meant to act as a sign to the German people and to the world that Hitler wanted his régime to be associated with the ancient imperial tradition of Prussia and the pre-war German Empire. But Hindenburg, in turn, had to appear in the guise of patron of National Socialism.

The speeches were short, but significant, and carefully composed for the occasion. They were broadcast. First Hindenburg read his speech:

> By my decree of February 1, I dissolved the Reichstag so that the German people might themselves define their attitude towards the Government of national concentration appointed by me. In the election of March 5 our people gave their support by a clear majority to the Government in whom I put my confidence, and by doing so have given them the constitutional foundation for their work.
>
> The tasks which you, Chancellor and Ministers, see before you are many and arduous. In both internal and foreign politics, in our own economic situation as in that of the world, there are difficult questions to solve and big decisions to make. I know that you will tackle these tasks with resolution. And I hope that you for your part, members of the new Reichstag, will, on your part with a clear recognition of the needs of the situation, support the Government and do all in your power to help them in their arduous labours. The place where we are met today recalls to our minds the old God-fearing Prussia which by conscientious work, unfailing courage and devotion to the Fatherland became great and on this foundation brought unity to the German family. May the spirit of this historic place also inspire the generation of today, may it free us from self-seeking and party strife, and draw us together, conscious of our national greatness and spiritually revived, for the good of a united, free and proud Germany.

He was followed by Hitler, who spoke at greater length, though more briefly than usual. He repudiated German responsibility for the First World War.

The Revolution of November 1918 brought to a close a struggle into which the German nation had entered with the most sacred conviction of defending its freedom and therewith its right to live. For neither the Kaiser, nor the Government, nor the people wanted this war. Only the disintegration of the nation compelled a weak generation, against its own conscience and against its most sacred inner conviction, to accept the assertion of German war guilt.

This collapse had been followed by decay in all spheres, political, moral, cultural, and economic. Worst of all was the destruction of faith in the nation's own strength, the degradation of traditions of confidence. Crisis after crisis had shaken the people. But the rest of the world had not become happier and wealthier through the political and economic bleeding of an important member of its commonwealth. From the crazy theory of permanent victors and vanquished had sprung the madness of reparations, and in consequence the world economic catastrophe.

Meanwhile the new rally of Germans who, trusting in their own people, sought to shape them into a new community, had begun. On January 30, 1933, the leadership of the Reich was entrusted by the Field-Marshal to this young Germany, and on March 5 it was acclaimed by the majority of the people.

In an unparalleled uprising it has restored the national honour in a few weeks and, thanks to your understanding, Herr Reich President, has consummated the marriage between the symbols of the old greatness and the young strength.

The new Chancellor proclaimed it his task to renew the spirit of the German people: those who proved themselves enemies must be made harmless. A new German nation was to be forged; a nation which was to offer peace to Europe:

In the spirit of the Imperial proclamation of 1871 our people has done its share to strengthen and increase the benefits of peace, civilization and culture. While conscious of its power, it never forgot its responsibility towards the mutual co-operation of European nations.

Hitler closed his speech with a panegyric of Hindenburg, which ended with the words:

Field-Marshal von Hindenburg, you have seen the rise of Germany; you have lived to see the work of the great Chancellor Bismarck; you have led us in the great war, and today Providence has made you the protector of the re-birth of our people.[44]

Hitler strode forward and clasped the President by the hand for all to see. The cameras flashed and clicked. Goebbels saw to it there were tears in the President's eyes, and that they were visible. Then Hindenburg and his son Oskar walked to the crypt where the body of Frederick the Great lay buried. He placed a wreath on his sarcophagus. Guns were fired, and the ceremony was over.

After witnessing a march-past, the President returned to Berlin, along with the deputies who later in the day met formally to elect the Reichstag President. The office, it goes without saying, went to Göring. But it was what Heiden describes as a 'rump parliament'; the Communists dared not put in an appearance and, according to Heiden, more than twenty of the Social Democrats failed to appear, most of them either under arrest or in hiding. The deputies present, led by the Nazis, readily agreed to hear Hitler's initial speech two days later, on 23rd March. The evening concluded with a performance of the *Meistersinger* at what used to be the Imperial Opera House.

March 21st saw the publication of decrees further undermining civil liberty. Special courts were established to deal with political offences against the new régime, while at the same time a Presidential amnesty was declared for criminal acts committed by Nazis in the course of their struggle for the 'national resurgence'.

The Enabling Bill itself was presented and debated on 23rd March, the Reichstag meeting as before in the Kroll Opera House. The Bill read as follows:

> I. Reich laws may be passed by the Reich Government by means other than the process laid down in the Reich Constitution.
>
> II. Reich laws decided upon by the Reich Government may deviate from the Reich Constitution, unless they relate to the institution of the Reichstag and the Reich Council. The rights of the Reich President remain unaffected.
>
> III. Reich laws decided upon by the Reich Government will be drafted by the Reich Chancellor and published in the official Gazette.
>
> IV. The Reich's agreements with foreign States relating to subjects of Reich legislation do not require the consent of the bodies participating in legislation.
>
> V. The present Law comes into force on the date of its promulgation. It becomes invalid on April 1, 1937. It also becomes invalid if the present Reich Government is replaced by another.[45]

The representatives of the German Centre Party, the Bavarian People's Party, the State Party (Democrats), the Christian Socialist Volksdienst, all spoke in support of the proposed law giving Hitler dictatorship. The Social Democrat leader, Otto Wels, however, spoke against the Bill, a brave gesture. While supporting Hitler's foreign policy, he opposed the Enabling Bill:

> No blessing will come out of a peace of violence, particularly at home. It is not possible to found a real national community upon it. The first condition is equal rights. The Government may protect itself against flagrant excesses of controversy, it may prevent with severity appeals to violence and violence itself. This may be done if it is done uniformly and impartially in all directions, and if defeated opponents are not treated as if they were outlaws. Freedom and life can be taken from us, but not honour.[46]

Hitler replied with a brutal attack on the Social Democrats, his sole opponents left in the House. When the deputies tried to protest, Göring used his authority to shout them down with the words 'Quiet! The Chancellor's settling accounts.' When the Bill was finally put to the vote, it was passed by 441 votes of the Nazis and their supporters against 94 Socialist opponents.

The Enabling Bill need not have been passed on 23rd March. Since it represented a change in the Constitution, it needed (as we have seen) a two-thirds majority vote to become law. But not only this, it also needed a two-thirds attendance of the House to make the two-thirds majority vote valid. If deputies, additional to the Communists, had stayed away in large enough numbers, they could have prevented the Enabling Bill being put to the House for vote. If the whole Social Democrat roster together with not less than fifteen Centre Party members had absented themselves on 23rd March, the Enabling Bill would at least have been delayed. However, in the circumstances, it was braver to attend and vote against the Bill than to be absent and let it go by default for some brief period.[47]

A further subsidiary law was passed at the same time, giving legal weight to the Reich Commissioners (*Statthalter*) to act as local dictators on behalf of their Führer:

> I. The Reich President will appoint Statthalter proposed by the Chancellor to all the Federal States, with the exception of Prussia. The duties of these officials will consist in supervising the execution of political directives given by the Chancellor.
>
> II. Appointed for the duration of the Reichstag, the Statthalter are invested with power to dissolve the Diet (Landtag), to appoint and recall the head of the Government, to nominate and depose officials and judges.[48]

Thus, in these few words, the German Federal States lost their autonomy.

In the street outside the Kroll Opera House, Storm Troopers were gathered to cow the Social Democrats with constant shouts of 'We want the Bill', 'We want the Bill', '*Or* fire and murder'. Inside, as Göring read out the figures almost five to one in favour of the Bill, the Nazis rose to their feet and saluted their leader by chanting the Horst Wessel anthem.

The hundred days crowded with anxiety, pressure, violence, hard labour, despair as well as the seeds of defeat for Hitler were over. Hitler was in power. Rule by decree was paramount. The twelve years' dictatorship in Germany which was to disrupt the world had begun.

Part 3

Aftermath:
The Night of the Long Knives: 30th June, 1934

These many men shall die, their names are pricked ...
He shall not live; look, with a spot I damn him.
Shakespeare, *Julius Caesar*, IV, i, 1,6.

Fifteen months separated Hitler's achievement of dictatorship in Germany and his final act of revenge on the leading characters in the drama who had opposed his assumption of power. There were many reasons for this. First there was the vast administrative task of national 'co-ordination' (*Gleichschaltung*), of bringing German political, social, administrative and cultural life into a single unified whole under the direct control of the Party. Though the Party was to remain intact, with its own central and regional administration, operated by the Gauleiters in the various regions (*Gaue*) into which Germany had already been divided for Party political purposes, the function of the Party and of the State drew closer together until (in practice at least), they were virtually integrated, in the symbolic person of Adolf Hitler. *L'État, c'est moi*, was Hitler's deepest conviction, and the Party was the immediate instrument of his will, an extension of his personal authority throughout the State.

These fifteen months saw the enactment of a constant stream of laws and decrees all of which were aimed at fulfilling the policy of *Gleichschaltung*. It was a period of ceaseless activity, of constant speechmaking by Hitler and other Nazi leaders. It was to see, during April 1933, the official exclusion of the Jews from state and professional employment, and the suppression of the opposition press; in May, the abolition of the trade union movement, and the confiscation of the property of the Social Democratic and Communist parties preparatory to the dissolution and banning of them and all parties, except, of course, the Nazi party, the following month; in June and July, conformity to Hitler's wishes by a large wing of both the Protestant and Catholic Churches, in the latter case culminating in the Concordat signed with the Vatican; the establishment in September of the Reich Chamber of Culture to control the arts and all forms of communication—the press, radio and cinema. October saw the withdrawal of Germany from the League of Nations and from the Disarmament Conference. On 1st December Germany was officially proclaimed a Nazi state, its constitution to be remodelled in the following February, the month in which Hitler exacted an oath of personal allegiance from all Nazi officials, totalling by now (according to Rauschning) some million men.

During this period, in which Hitler's tyranny began to be revealed with increasing force, the flow of émigrés from Germany developed into a tide which forced the nations to which they fled to recognize that there was a dictatorial power being established in central Europe's most powerful nation. Some 235,000 of Germany's Jews were to depart during the five years 1933–8, some 50,000 by the end of 1933; those leaving paid expropriation taxes to the State estimated for the year 1933–4 alone at 50 million marks.[1] The severe restrictions imposed on the Jewish professional classes caused them to be among the first to leave Germany in any numbers. In addition to the Jews, many Germans, prominent or not so prominent in the political parties which had opposed Hitler, left Germany, taking refuge mainly in Britain, the United States, Austria and Czechoslovakia. Among these were to be Brüning and Kaas of the Centre Party and Otto Wels, leader of the Social Democrats. The Communist leaders were already under arrest, including Thaelmann and Torgler; a number fled to Russia.

The manner in which the trade union movement collapsed—its executive calling on members to take part in Hitler's May Day labour celebrations, which occurred a bare twenty-four hours before the official abolition of the trade union movement—made a melancholy spectacle. Even worse is the manner in which the Churches in great measure appeared to welcome collaboration with Hitler; the bishops of the Catholic Church in Germany issued a pastoral letter in June 1933 which welcomed the fact that 'the men at the head of the State have to our great joy given a formal assurance that they take their stand on Christianity', and added that this required, 'a sincere attitude [response] on the part of all Catholics'. The Concordat sealed this rapprochement between religion and fascism. The Protestants established a Nazi-inspired branch of their Church, headed by Reich Bishop Mueller. On the other hand, many individual Catholics on all levels were courageously to oppose Hitler, as did the Protestant Bekennende Kirche (Confessional Church) of Pastor Niemoeller. Hitler appointed a special member of Cabinet to deal with Church affairs, Hans Kerrl, a Party veteran and Reichstag deputy of no distinction or ability.

Hitler reorganized his Cabinet, retaining only those former Right-wing members who were prepared to support him unquestioningly. Papen remained for a while as Vice-Chancellor, though in April 1933 he was removed from his position as Prime Minister and Reich Commissioner for Prussia in favour of Göring. The Ministers who kept their positions were: Blomberg (Defence), Neurath (Foreign Affairs), Guertner (Justice), and Schwerin-Krosigk (Finance). Others were displaced—Gereke [2] (Employment) and Seldte (Labour) were dismissed; Hugenberg (Economy; Food and Agriculture) was forced to resign in June, his duties being split between two new Nazi Ministers, Dr Schmitt (Economy) and Walther Darré (Food and Agriculture). Other Nazis who joined the Cabinet were Kerrl and Goebbels and, in December, Hess and Ernst Roehm, both 'without portfolio'.

The principal sanctions against his opponents which Hitler employed were the immediate, open forces of intimidation, the SA, whose daily presence in the streets constituted an unveiled threat to all, and the menace of arrest and imprisonment in the Nazis' own 'correction' centres, which Göring called concentration camps (Konzentrationslager).[3] Their origin is typical of the *ad hoc* methods the Nazis employed and their total disregard for civil liberties. Camps were set up, with widely varying degrees of official cognisance or control, as places in which the SA, the SS, or the secret political police could confine their victims. Göring established his camps in Prussia; Himmler founded what he held to be a 'model' camp at Dachau on 22nd March 1933, and as Acting Police President of the City of Munich published a notice to this effect in the local press. Speaking at Nuremberg, Göring affirmed that he ordered the closure of any unauthorized camps which came to his notice. Göring put his own camps under the control of Rudolf Diels; when questioned whether brutalities took place, he could only answer: 'Of course I gave instructions that such things should not happen. That they did happen and happened everywhere to a smaller or greater extent I have just stated. I always stressed that these things should not happen, because it was important to me to win over some of these people to our side and to re-educate them.' Then he added, 'Wherever you use a plane, you can't help making splinters.'[4] By the close of 1933 there were possibly as many as fifty camps of very varying size and character spread through Germany, the leading 'official' ones being at Oranienburg (later Sachsenhausen) near Berlin, founded by Göring, and Dachau in the south, founded by Himmler. Both these camps were destined to last as long as the régime itself. There were some 27,000 internees in the camps by Christmas 1933; a few were released as the result of a much publicized amnesty, which it had originally been proposed should apply to all.

Having dealt in this way with his enemies, Hitler turned next to the problem of *Gleichschaltung* as it affected his friends. The balance of power in Germany still rested on relationships which, to say the least, were uneasy. There were a number of armed forces in the State; foremost were the relatively undisciplined ranks of the Storm Troopers commanded by Ernst Roehm, whose number stood at some three million; alongside them (and still technically under Roehm's command, but holding themselves increasingly aloof) were the 'élite' forces of the SS, under the control of Himmler, and through him, after April 1934, linked with the political police, the Gestapo. The numbers of the SS (with its severe racialist marriage code of 1932) had been indiscriminately enlarged during the period of 1933–4, growing from some 32,000 in 1932 to some 300,000 by 1934; there were also the normal police forces for maintaining civil law and order; and, finally, there was the Army itself, the Reichswehr still limited by the Versailles Treaty to a ceiling of 100,000 men. Other partly alien forces, notably the Stahlhelm, he had managed with some difficulty to absorb into the SA by converting Seldte, his former Minister of Labour and leader of the Stahlhelm, into a National Socialist, and arresting those Stahlhelm officers who raised objections to the amalgamation

By 1934 Hitler's problems in maintaining his authority in the face of these divergent forces reached a level of tension which was far more serious than anything Strasser had ever represented in the ranks of the Party in 1932. The Army owed its allegiance to Hindenburg, as President and supreme Commander; the Minister in direct charge of the Reichswehr was, however, General von Blomberg, the fifty-five-year-old Minister of Defence, and, at this stage, very much Hitler's man.[5] Since his appointment as Chancellor, Hitler had done his best to carry the Army with him, promising the generals and admirals, only three days after becoming Chancellor, that he would restore Germany's armed strength. He had also guaranteed (to their relief) that as far as he was concerned they would not become involved in any civil war. Hitler's problem, therefore, did not lie so much with the Army itself, since he kept them as uninvolved in his 'revolution' as possible, as in the attitude of his most formidable aide, Ernst Roehm, commandant of the SA and, technically, of Himmler's SS as well. Hitler was well aware that the SA, though inordinately proud of their Führer, were very restive about what they held to be his tardy delivery of the spoils of conquest. Control of the offices of state meant nothing to them; they were at heart little but gangsters on parade—they wanted to loot, despoil, practise violence on helpless opponents and be given lucrative rewards for having brought Hitler to power. Among the 'opponents' were the Reichswehr, the uniformed and class-conscious 'caste' soldiers whose social position and privileges they, the SA officers, envied and regarded as rightfully due to them. At best they wanted to replace the Reichswehr; at worst to be integrated with them, outnumbering them well over twenty to one. Roehm, himself a professional soldier, wanted to become Minister of Defence, combining his forces with those of the Reichswehr, and assuming total command of all the forces of State. He had the backing of his own SA commanders, many of whom were ex-Army officers whose service after the War had been continued, *ex officio*, in the paramilitary Freikorps movement a decade and more previously. Rauschning reports a significant conversation with Roehm as early as the spring of 1933, shortly after the seizure of power:

> His scars were scarlet with excitement. He had drunk a few glasses of wine in quick succession.
>
> 'Adolf is a swine,' he swore. 'He will give us all away. He only associates with reactionaries now. His old friends aren't good enough for him' ...
>
> He was jealous and hurt.
>
> 'Adolf is turning into a gentleman. He's got himself a tail-coat now!' he mocked. .... 'Adolf knows exactly what I want. I've told him often enough. Not a second edition of the old imperial army. Are we revolutionaries or aren't we? ... If we're not, then we'll go to the dogs. We've got to produce something new, don't you see? A new discipline. A new principle of organization. The generals are a lot of old fogeys. They never have a new idea. Adolf has learnt from me. Everything he knows about military matters, I've taught him. War is something more than armed clashes. You won't make a revolutionary army out of the old Prussian NCOs. But Adolf is and remains a civilian, an "artist", an idler. "Don't bother me," that's all he thinks. What he wants is to sit on the hilltop and pretend he is God. And the rest of us, who are itching to do something, have got to sit around doing nothing. .... Hitler puts me off with fair words. He wants to let things run their course. He expects a miracle. Just like Adolf! He wants to inherit an army all ready and complete. He's going to let the "experts" file away at it. When I hear that word, I'm ready to explode. Afterwards he'll make National Socialists of them, he says ... I'm the nucleus of the new army, don't you see that?'[6]

Hitler, warily and very late in the day, gave Roehm Cabinet status alongside Blomberg, but only in December 1933. Roehm bitterly resented Hitler's tardy attitude; he failed to understand that, once he had achieved absolute political power, Hitler had his own ambition—to become himself absolute Commander of the Army on Hindenburg's death, which he, like everyone else, knew by the spring of 1934 could only be a matter of months. Roehm's overweening ambitions were a deep embarrassment in Hitler's delicate relationship with the Reichswehr's High Command; the vast, unemployed 'army' of the Storm Troopers had now outlived their usefulness. Their violence and atrocities, their lack of discipline and radical views were a blot on the régime which had now to achieve 'status' in the eyes of the German people and in the world outside.

Hitler was not slow to realize that the only force he required now to exercise civil control was represented by Himmler's 'élite' guards, the SS, with their pretensions to social quality and racial purity. Himmler, too, was loyal, indeed almost absurdly dedicated to the Nazi doctrine of Germanism and 'Aryan' racial supremacy. He had in three years built up the SS, with their handsome black uniform trimmed with silver braid, from a handful of guards policing political meetings, into a salvation army for Nazism; princes, generals, even one or two archbishops, accepted honorary rank, and wore the desirable uniform on ceremonial occasions. Himmler despised the SA rabble, with its lack of culture and Germanic idealism, its indifference to personal racial purity, its squalid morals and reputation for homosexual practices among the hierarchy of the leadership. There was nothing Himmler wanted more than total dissociation from the SA and all its works. Nor, in spite of his admiration for the Army, in which he had been too young to see active service during the War, did he desire the SS to become amalgamated with the Reichswehr. His ambition lay in more secret channels—control of the secret police, the Gestapo, and its ultimate amalgamation with the SS for the political supervision and purification of the State. However, at this stage he sought no open quarrel with Roehm.

All this Hitler took into account. During the initial months of 1934 he pondered long and deep about the consequences of this total situation. Hitler had so far tried to stiffen the self-discipline of the SA on numerous occasions with such statements as, 'The army of the political soldiers of the German Revolution has no wish to take the place of our Army or to enter into competition with it.'[7] In response, Heiden reports an inflammatory speech made by Roehm to a large gathering of SA. According to Heiden:

On 5 November 1933 before 15,000 National Socialist officials gathered in the Sportpalast in Berlin, Roehm attacked the renewed insolence of the reactionaries: 'One often hears voices from the bourgeois camp to the effect that the SA have lost their reason for being.' But this is what he wanted to say to these gentlemen: the bureaucratic spirit, which had barely changed after 30 January 1933, 'must still be changed in a gentle, or if need be, in an ungentle manner'. By no means could the National Socialist revolution be regarded as completed. At this there was thunderous applause.[8]

Open hostility broke out on the anniversary of the former Kaiser's birthday, celebrated by monarchist groups at an annual dinner held on 27th January. A gang of SA men burst in and broke up the 1934 celebrations; the presiding officer, the elderly General von Horn, suffering from shock, died of a stroke two days after. Hitler himself was forced to deny in public the many rumours that the monarchy was to be restored. In April, leaders in the Stahlhelm with anarchist leanings were arrested and put in concentration camps. Meanwhile in the previous month, a dispute between Blomberg and Roehm was brought to Hitler's attention. This concerned the special recruitment and training of some six thousand or more SA men, armed with rifles and machine guns. In April Hitler reached a new accord with the generals and admirals when he made a unique sea trip on board the cruiser *Deutschland*; it was during these naval manœuvres that it is believed he first broached the question of the Army's reaction if he himself assumed the powers of the Presidency on Hindenburg's death, which could now happen at any time. In return, he is thought to have agreed to delimit Roehm's powers.

Nor was alarm at the unruly nature of the SA limited to Germany. In February 1934 Anthony Eden, Britain's Lord Privy Seal, had visited Germany on behalf not only of the British government, but of the French as well. Hitler, as we have seen, had withdrawn Germany from the League of Nations the previous October, and turned his back on the discussions concerning disarmament at which previous German Chancellors had been present. Eden had been astonished at the readiness with which the Chancellor agreed that paramilitary organizations were undesirable. Not only was Hitler eager to use international pressures as an excuse to limit the powers of the SA, he was also anxious to seem more reasonable than his reputation with this youthful but none the less important visitor from the Power on which he was soon to practise his duplicity. Eden found that his age (he was thirty-seven) and his war service appeared to appeal to Hitler, who thought of diplomats as dodderers. Eden describes their first meetings:

> We were received in a vast room of *palais de danse* proportions, which we approached through many passages lined with guards

and the trappings of dictatorship. Hitler had just completed his first year as Chancellor. Smaller and slighter than I had expected from his photographs, his appearance was smart, almost dapper, despite his incongruous uniform. He was restrained and friendly. Though talking at some length when once he got going, he was always quite ready to accept questions and interruptions. I was told that he was quieter than usual. Certainly he listened to what I had to say at each meeting, waiting patiently for the translation. There were neither fidgets nor exclamations. As I spoke he fixed me quietly with his pale, glaucous eyes, which protruded slightly, a feature often associated with an over-active thyroid. Hitler impressed me during these discussions as much more than a demagogue. He knew what he was speaking about and, as the long interviews proceeded, showed himself completely master of his subject. He never once had need to refer either to von Neurath or to any official of the Wilhelmstrasse.[9]

Later, Eden raised the matter of Germany possessing, over and above the recognized Army, large paramilitary forces:

We discussed the topic of paramilitary organizations at some length. Here it appeared that our arguments had an effect. Hitler seemed willing to make concessions. He told me that if a convention were concluded, he would give a guarantee for the future, to the effect that the SS and SA would have no arms, receive no instruction in the use of arms, take no part in manœuvres and undergo no training by officers of the army. The fulfilment of these assurances would be subject to verification by a system of control.

This offer was beyond Eden's most liberal expectations, but was only to be fulfilled in so far as it suited Hitler's purposes. Eden also met Roehm, of whom he gives a revealing description:

Roehm, then very much a leading personality, was a ... flamboyant figure, scarred and scented, with a jewelled dagger at his waist. ... But he was not just a perverted swashbuckler, he had intelligence of a kind and, a rarity in the modern world, he was a man who boasted of his bravery, yet was brave. But he was hardly of the modern world; a condottiere of the Middle Ages might have looked and behaved like that.

Hitler in the end agreed privately to a reduction of the SA by two-thirds. The offer was even repeated to the British government in April, after his excursion in the *Deutschland*. Thus his need to placate the Army coincided neatly with his need to placate the Allied Powers, and both needs matched his own desire to curtail the SA itself and Roehm's unseemly ambitions.

In spite of the embarrassment Roehm was causing him, and indeed had caused him once before, in the 1920s, Hitler was in his own way attached to the SA commandant. He permitted the use of the intimate 'du' between them, a familiarity denied to other Nazi leaders of long standing. He addressed a tactful letter of greeting to Roehm, his newly appointed Minister, early in the New Year:

> My dear Chief of Staff,
> The fight of the National Socialist Movement and the National Socialist Revolution were rendered possible for me by the consistent suppression of the Red Terror by the SA. If the army has to guarantee the protection of the nation against the world beyond our frontiers, the task of the SA is to secure the victory of the National Socialist Revolution and the existence of the National Socialist State and the community of our people in the domestic sphere. When I summoned you to your present position, my dear Chief of Staff, the SA was passing through a serious crisis. It is primarily due to your services if after a few years this political instrument could develop that force which enabled me to face the final struggle for power and to succeed in laying low the Marxist opponent.
> At the close of the year of the National Socialist Revolution, therefore, I feel compelled to thank you, my dear Ernst Roehm, for the imperishable services which you have rendered to the National Socialist Movement and the German people, and to assure you how very grateful I am to Fate that I am able to call such men as you my friends and fellow-combatants.
> In true [*herzlicher*] friendship and grateful regard,
> Your Adolf Hitler.[10]

This letter was supposed to put the SA firmly in their due place in the State.

Roehm only came to learn the import of Hitler's private discussions with the Reichswehr and with Eden about the delimitation he planned for the SA when rumours to this effect appeared in the foreign press. The annual period of a month's leave for the SA came in July, and Hitler's plan was to stand down large numbers of the rank and file in August when their leaves expired. Roehm protested about what he had heard, but found himself opposed in the Cabinet by von Blomberg and Göring, who was still beside himself with satisfaction at having been made a General the previous August. Roehm had no one to whom he could turn, and a whiff of the old gunsmoke of intrigue tinged the air when it was rumoured that Schleicher, now living in retirement, was sounding out Roehm concerning these dissensions in the Party hierarchy.[11] These contacts were built up by Göring and his (temporary) ally Himmler, recently appointed the proud controller of Germany's secret police by deed of gift from Göring. It was at this period that Brüning—whose name was being used, without his consent, by those who wanted to make capital out of the troubles—decided it would be safer for him to leave the country. Meanwhile, Göring and Himmler proceeded to build up their dossiers against Roehm and Schleicher, as well as the whole leadership of the SA, in order to convince Hitler that an SA *coup d'état* was being planned. They pressed for an immediate purge.

But Hitler's instinctual wariness, as well as his notorious predilection for Roehm as an 'old comrade', made him hesitate before deciding on any firm, irrevocable line of action. The records pass now behind a cloud of obscurity, for the events of June 1934 were to be expunged from Nazi archives. Only the broader outlines are clear, coupled with the accounts, more or less reliable, of surviving witnesses and participants, such as Göring, Papen, Goebbels and, of course, Hitler himself in his lengthy speech to the Reichstag on 13th July. All had vested interests in bending the record for their own purposes. There are also the highly coloured reminiscences of Hans Bernd Gisevius, a minor official in the civil service (even, briefly, in the Gestapo), whose dramatic intervention in the Nuremberg trial satisfied his ego at the expense of Göring's, as well as certain affidavits made by witnesses for this and other trials.

June was to be a restless month for Hitler, with the tensions of indecision mounting to a violent climax by Saturday the thirtieth. On the evening of 4th June Hitler spent five hours in confrontation with Roehm. The only direct account of this meeting is Hitler's own, as he gave it to the Reichstag some five weeks later:

> At the beginning of June I made a last attempt and had yet another talk with Roehm which lasted nearly five hours and was prolonged until midnight. I informed him that from numberless rumours and from numerous assurances and statements of old, loyal comrades and SA leaders I had gained the impression that by certain unscrupulous elements a National-Bolshevist rising was being prepared which could only bring untold misery upon Germany. I explained to him further that reports had also come to my ears of the intention to draw the army within the scope of these plans. I assured the Chief of Staff, Roehm, that the assertion that the SA was to be dissolved was an infamous lie and that I refused to make any

comment upon the lie that I myself intended to attack the SA, but that I should at any moment be ready personally to oppose any attempt to raise chaos in Germany and that anyone who attacks the State should know from the outset that he will have me for his enemy. I implored him for the last time to oppose this madness of his own accord—let him at the same time use his authority so as to stop a development which in any event could end only in catastrophe. I raised afresh vigorous protests on the score of the impossible excesses which followed one after another, and demanded the immediate and complete elimination of these elements from the SA in order not to dishonour, through a few unworthy individuals, the SA itself together with millions of decent comrades and hundreds of thousands of old fighters. The Chief of Staff left this interview after assuring me that the reports were partly untrue and partly exaggerated, and that moreover he would for the future do everything in his power to set things right.[12]

Roehm, Hitler went on to explain to a still-stunned Reichstag assembly, had considered an SA *coup d'état* to be necessary because of 'my own inability to come to any decision', 'disability' which 'would be removed only when faced with an accomplished fact'. Again, according to Hitler, Schleicher was involved, negotiating with Roehm through his 'intermediary', General von Bredow. 'Strasser was brought in,' added Hitler, curtly and significantly.

This, however, was Hitler's chosen interpretation of events. What is on record, historically speaking, is that on 7th June, three days after the meeting between Hitler and Roehm, the SA was ordered by Hitler to go on annual leave for the whole month of July. At the same time Roehm issued a statement that he intended to go away immediately on sick-leave, and added a personal directive to the SA which was published in the press on 10th June:

> I expect then on 1 August that the SA, fully rested and strengthened, will stand ready to serve the honourable tasks which People and Fatherland may expect from them. If the foes of the SA are nursing the hope that the SA will not return from their leave or that a part only will return we are ready to let them enjoy this hope for a short time. At the hour and in the form which appears to be necessary they shall receive the fitting answer.[13]

Hitler had meanwhile agreed that he would meet the SA leadership in conference at Roehm's health resort of Bad Wiessee on 30th June. It seems unlikely that even as late as mid June Hitler had as yet the violent purge in mind which was to take place on that day. But it might have seemed at least advantageous to have Roehm and his intimates gathered in one place for any action, violent or otherwise, which the immediate future demanded. As for Strasser, his brother Otto claims that Hitler met him on 13th June and offered him the Ministry of National Economy; Strasser is said to have refused unless Göring and Goebbels were dismissed. The whole incident, as reported, seems most unlikely.[14]

Meanwhile, according to Hitler, Roehm's contact with Schleicher had hardened into a positive agreement.[15] Hitler outlined these terms to the Reichstag, no doubt presenting them in the form which best suited his case against Roehm:

–The present régime in Germany cannot be supported.
–Above all, the army and all national associations must be united in a single band.
–The only man who could be considered for such a position was the Chief of Staff, Roehm.
–Herr von Papen must be removed and he himself would be ready to take the position of Vice-Chancellor, and that in addition further important changes must be made in the Cabinet of the Reich.[16]

Rumours of an impending purge had been circulating since the previous month; on the strength of these Brüning finally left Germany. Schleicher, however, had merely gone on holiday to the Starnberger See. If, as some think, a form of purge was timed for 16th June, it had to be postponed. Hitler was invited at short notice to meet Mussolini in Venice; he flew there on 14th June, wearing civilian clothes, only to find Mussolini in a dashing uniform which would have done credit to Göring. Hitler, deeply depressed, played a secondary role at this first meeting between the two dictators. Mussolini lectured him on the need to keep the left wing of his Party in order, and severely criticized National Socialist policy in Austria. It was the first time, apart from war service in France, that Hitler had been in a foreign country outside Austria and Germany. He returned in time to meet his Party leaders on Sunday 17th June at the small town of Gera in Thuringia, and reported on this inauspicious initial meeting with Mussolini. He was in a bad mood, which was further soured when reports reached him of Papen's activities that same Sunday at the university of Marburg.

Papen was the last person from whom at this stage any strong opposition might have been expected. However, with panache and total disregard for his own safety, unparalleled at any other stage in his career, he took the opportunity of a speech he was due to give at the university of Marburg to make what proved to be a finely worded and highly critical assessment of the dangers to the State which the more destructive elements in Nazism represented.

Taking to heart the President's final words to him when he left for Neudeck—'Things are going badly, Papen. See what you can do to put them right'—Papen determined to make his gesture at Marburg. He was not, in fact, to see the President again; in little over two months Hindenburg would be dead. He and his friend Edgar Jung of the Catholic Action Group worked on the speech during June; in fact, the wording was largely by Jung, who had Jewish blood in his veins. This work was to cost him his life a fortnight after Papen had delivered the speech. Among others who advised were Herbert von Bose, Papen's secretary, and Erich Klausener, another leader in the Catholic Action Group. All these were to die at the end of the month.

Papen spoke to a packed audience in the Auditorium Maximum at the ancient university.[17] The speech was recorded on disk, and was due to be broadcast later that evening. The aim of the speech was to draw Hitler away from the influence of the radical wing in his party, notably Goebbels and Roehm. Coming at this time, however, it could only seem like an attack on Hitler and Nazism. Papen voiced the grave unease of large numbers in the nation, both of the Right and Centre, at the tyrannous policy and corrupt administration which had supervened in Germany, and he complained bitterly about the lack of freedom to criticize which had followed the Enabling Act of March the previous year. The speech contained a direct attack on Goebbels's control of the press. Papen declared that the revolution as he had conceived it to be when he had given his support to Hitler had been betrayed, and that the current rumours of a second revolution seemed to him to project a further deterioration in German affairs. Outstanding passages from the speech included the following:

> An unknown soldier of the World War who with infectious energy and unshakable faith has conquered the hearts of his fellow countrymen has set the German soul free. Together with his Field-Marshal he placed himself at the head of the nation in order to turn a new page in the German book of destiny and restore mental unity. We have experienced this reunion of minds in the intoxication of thousands, in the manifestations of the flags and festivals of a nation rediscovering itself.
>
> But now, when the enthusiasm is lessened and our labour is demanding its rights, it is clear that a catharsis of such historical dimensions necessarily produces the slag from which it must purify itself. Defects of this sort occur in all the domains of life, material as well as intellectual.

The outside world, regarding us with disfavour, points its finger at these defects and interprets them as a serious process of disintegration. Let it not rejoice too soon, however. If we can develop energy enough for freeing ourselves from these defects, that will furnish the best proof of how strong we are internally and how determined to prevent any adulteration of the German revolution.

We know that rumours and whisperings must be dragged out from the dark into which they have withdrawn. Open manly discussions would be of more service to the German people than, for instance, the present state of the German Press, of which the Reich Minister of Enlightenment and Propaganda [Dr Goebbels] has asserted 'it has no longer any physiognomy'.

This defect is beyond doubt. The press would indeed be doing a true service in informing the Government where faults have crept in, where corruption is breeding, where grave mistakes have been made, where unfit men are holding office, where sins are being committed against the spirit of the German revolution.

An anonymous secret news service, no matter how efficiently organized, can never act as a substitute for this task of the press. Editors are under a legal and conscientious responsibility, whereas anonymous purveyors of news are beyond control and are exposed to the danger of Byzantinism. When, however, the proper organs of public opinion do not clear up sufficiently the mysterious obscurity which at present seems to envelop German popular opinion, the statesman himself must intervene to call a spade a spade.

Such action should prove that the Government is strong enough to stand decent criticism—that it is mindful of the old maxim, 'Only weaklings suffer no criticism'.

If the outside world claims that liberty is dead in Germany, let it learn from the frankness of my exposition that the German Government can afford to make the burning problems of the nation the subject of debate. Such a right, however, can only be claimed by him who without reserve has placed himself at the service of National Socialism and has proved his loyalty to it.

These introductory words are necessary to show in what spirit I approach my task of giving an unreserved account of the German situation and German aims. Let me now shortly outline the situation I found when fate made me co-responsible for the conduct of German destiny.

Governmental authority was then in decay, incapable of stopping the disintegration of the nation's natural and divinely established self-respect. Leadership and energy were lacking to such an extent that there was aroused in the German people an even stronger desire for a strong hand. Opposition from combatants in the Great War and from youth was becoming irresistible. Corresponding to the splitting up into parties, there spread a fatal discouragement. Unemployment grew, and with it Social Radicalism.

That these evils could not be remedied by ordinary means but only by a mental and political turnover was realized not only by the Right-wing groups of the German people, especially by the National Socialist Party, but by all the best members of our nation not tied to any particular party. . . .

At Breslau on 17 March 1933 I pointed out that in the post-war years a sort of Conservative revolutionary movement developed in Germany which was distinguished from National Socialism in essence only by its tactics. After the German revolution and its fateful consequences the new conservatism consistently repudiated any further democratization and believed that the pluralistic forces might be eliminated from above.

National Socialism, on the other hand, first of all followed the methods of democracy to the end, to face at last the difficult question of how its ideas of unconditional leadership, absolute authority, the principle of aristocratic selection and the organic orderings of the nation could be effected. History has endorsed the soundness of the National Socialist tactics; it was this recognition that induced the Conservative statesmen in the decisive hours of early 1933 to form an alliance with the National Socialist movement. . . .

There is no need to emphasise that this yearning for a new social order is particularly alive in Fascism and National Socialism. On the other hand, we recognize how immensely difficult it is to re-transmute into a nation the masses which have lost interconnection with blood and the soil, particularly when a sound class attachment and establishment of rank have been lost in the Liberal period.

National Socialism, therefore, attaches decisive value to winning back these masses. This is chiefly to be effected by discipline and propaganda. The National Socialist system thus performs a function for which parliamentarianism had become too weak—namely, the re-establishment of direct contact with the masses. Thus there arises a sort of direct democracy which succeeds in regaining the interest of the masses in the State.

But behind this temporary and limited end there is a much greater evolutionary goal—namely, the creation of a social order which will rest on universally valid principles and not merely on adroit domination of the masses. While the French Revolution created fundamental bonds in Parliament and universal suffrage, the goal of Conservative revolution must be to push forward to universally valid principles.

We in Germany have one single party in place of the multi-party system (which lately and justly has disappeared from Germany).

This I regard as only a transition stage and justified only so long as it is necessary for safeguarding the revolution and until a new selection of personalities begins functioning, for the logic of anti-Liberal development requires the application of the principle and organized formation of political sentiment, which must be based on the spontaneity of all the members of the nation. Only organic attachments can overcome the party system and create that free popular community which must be the goal of this revolution. . . .

If one desires close contact and unity with the people, one must not underestimate their sagacity. One must return their confidence and not everlastingly keep them in leading strings. The German people realises the gravity of its situation, its economic distress, and discerns clearly the defects of many laws born of emergency. It has a keen eye for coercion and injustice and mocks at clumsy attempts to deceive it with whitewash.

No organisation, no propaganda, however excellent, would be able alone to maintain confidence in the long run. I have therefore all along held a different opinion of the propaganda movement against so-called critics. Not by incitement, especially of youth, not by threats against the helpless part of the nation—only by a confidential talking things over with people can confidence and devotion be maintained. The people are aware that heavy sacrifices are demanded of them. They follow the Leader in unshakable loyalty if they are permitted to co-operate in council and deed, if every critical word is not interpreted as malevolence and if despairing patriots are not branded as enemies of the State.

Goebbels, who was in Gera where Hitler was due to speak, had his ear close to the ground. Before the Vice-Chancellor's recorded words could be broadcast, Papen found they had been banned alike on the air or in the press. The speech, however, had already been printed in pamphlet form, and reproduced in part in the *Frankfurter Zeitung* before the edition containing it was withdrawn from circulation. However, copies managed to reach many hands, both inside and outside Germany, including diplomatic circles; the contents of the speech were freely quoted abroad, and Papen became the hero of the day outside Nazi circles. He received a telegram of congratulation from the President; when on 24th June he represented him at the German equivalent of the Derby race meeting at Hamburg, he was greeted by the crowds when he appeared in the President's box with shouts of 'Heil Marburg!' Goebbels was also present, and took great offence.

Papen had been incensed by Goebbels's prompt action in forbidding publication of the speech. Broadcast, it could have been like a tocsin for the nation. Hitler was equally angry, and referred in his speech at Gera to the 'pygmy who imagines he can stop . . . the gigantic renewal of a people's life'. The moment Hitler had returned to Berlin, Papen sought an interview with him. Papen gives his own account of this meeting, which took place on 20th June:

> I told him that I had considered it my duty to take a firm stand in a situation which had become critical. I hoped he realized what great value I still attached to our partnership and begged him to give serious consideration to the points I had raised. It was, I told him, a time for decision. The Vice-Chancellor of the Reich Government could not tolerate a ban by a junior minister on the publication of an official speech. I had spoken as a trustee for the President and had given an account of the developments of the previous eighteen months. I told him that Goebbels's action left me no alternative but to submit my resignation from the Government. I would advise Hindenburg of this immediately, unless the Goebbels ban was lifted and Hitler declared himself prepared to adopt the policy I had outlined.
>
> Hitler tried to calm me. He admitted that Goebbels had blundered, and assumed that he had been trying to avoid an increase in the prevailing tension. Hitler then launched into a tirade against the general insubordination of the S.A. They were making life increasingly intolerable for him and they would have to be dealt with. He said that he would instruct Goebbels to lift his ban, and asked me to withhold my resignation until he himself had gone with me to Neudeck to see the President. He suggested a joint interview.[18]

If this account is to be trusted, Hitler was evidently still temporizing, anxious about the possible sanctions which could still be imposed by Hindenburg, who was not, after all, dead yet. He had received a warning through Blomberg that Hindenburg was ready to impose martial law. This would mean independent action by the Army, displacing Hitler's rule.

The following day, 21st June, Hitler flew to Neudeck to see the President. He did not take Papen with him. At Neudeck he was received by Blomberg, who accompanied him into the President's room. Hindenburg saw the Chancellor for a few minutes only, and repeated the warning that, unless Hitler acted at once to ease the tension in Germany, he would indeed take the matter out of his hands and declare martial law.

The pressures brought to bear on Hitler within his own immediate circle were at last beginning to take decisive effect. Matters had to be brought to some head. According to Frick's testimony at Nuremberg, it was Himmler who finally convinced Hitler that a *Putsch* was indeed being planned. 'The Führer ordered Himmler to suppress the *Putsch*,' he said.[19] The final plan was for Hitler to take action in Bavaria, where the SA leaders were due to meet, while Göring took charge of the purge in Berlin.

Gisevius, the civil servant who in 1944 was in Frick's Ministry of the Interior, and who gave dramatic evidence at Nuremberg, was equally forthright:

> First I have to say that there never was a Roehm putsch. On 30 June there was only a Göring-Himmler putsch. I am in a position to give some information about that dark chapter, because I dealt with and followed up this case in the police department of the Ministry of the Interior, and because the radiograms sent during these days by Göring and Himmler to the police authorities of the Reich came into my hands. The last of these radiograms reads: 'By order of Göring all documents relating to 30 June will be burned immediately.'[20]

Himmler and his deputy, Reinhard Heydrich, combed their secret files for evidence to precipitate the fall of Roehm, evidence (long ignored) of his moral depravity and that of his closest associates. Himmler was spurred to further efforts to displace Roehm (still technically his commanding officer) when he was shot at (or so he alleged) on his way by car on 19th June to witness the interment of the body of Göring's first wife, Carin, in the mausoleum he had constructed by the lakeside near his country mansion, Carinhall, situated in the forests north of Berlin.[21] By this time the lists of future victims of the great purge were growing longer, awaiting action on the 'day', whenever this should be.

Hitler wanted to get away from these unpleasant prospects, and left for Bavaria after his distressing interview with the President. Nevertheless, Hitler's self-assurance was at its height at this time. In an interview he gave to the distinguished English correspondent, Vernon Bartlett, published in the London *News Chronicle* on 25th June, he is reported as saying, 'I will tell you that this Movement will go on for a thousand years. The people are more behind me today than they were a year ago. They follow me wherever I go and they will continue to do so. We are not the sort of men to capitulate before any difficulties. We are all self-made men who have grown strong in the struggle.'[22] Hitler had no self-doubts. The problem always was how to handle particular current difficulties in such a way as to turn them to the best advantage in order to enhance his all-powerful position.

Friedrich Karl Freiherr von Eberstein—an SS Gruppenführer (Lieutenant-General) and one of the many members of the German nobility who had joined the SS, and who had a command in Saxony and Thuringia of some 15,000 SS men—claimed, while giving evidence at Nuremberg, that at about this time he was ordered to Berlin by Himmler. Here, to quote his words, Himmler 'officially informed me that Roehm was planning a *coup d'état*, and gave me orders to hold my SS men in a state of quiet readiness for an emergency'.[23] On Sunday 24th June Himmler held a conference of the SS High Command in Berlin, while the following day the Army was put on an alert; all leave was cancelled, and the men were confined to barracks. On 28th June Roehm was expelled from the German Officers' League, thus losing one of his old links with the Army, while the following day, Blomberg published an article in the Nazi *Völkischer Beobachter* pledging the Army's loyalty to the President and to the National Socialist State. Ernst, the SA commander in Berlin, had that day placed his men on an alert, though he himself was about to go away on his honeymoon.

Hitler, restless and disturbed by the thought of the holocaust which he must at some stage launch, had continued with his tours in order to cover the preparations his lieutenants were making. Only just back from Bavaria, he had set off with Göring for Essen on 28th June, the day on which formal orders were issued to all police and SS contingents to stand by. At Essen, Hitler visited the Krupp plant, and then went on to attend the wedding of the Gauleiter, Josef Terboven. The wedding, indeed, became the cover for lengthy conferences between Hitler, Göring and Himmler, with hasty visits from Berlin. Göring and Himmler returned immediately to the capital, to take charge of the action to be staged there. Hitler passed the daylight hours of 29th June inspecting labour camps, moving on to the hotel Dreesen at Bad Godesberg in the evening. The following day, Saturday, he was due to address the conference of SA leaders in Bad Wiessee; indeed, he telephoned Roehm confirming that he would be there, and would meet senior officers of the SA at Wiessee at ten o'clock on Saturday morning. The officers had already been summoned to be present.

But at Godesberg Hitler completed the preparations for a visitation of a very different order from that which Roehm was expecting. Roehm appears to have been totally unprepared for anything but some kind of social event; he was alone with his homosexual friends and quite unguarded. Goebbels arrived at Godesberg with the news of the SA alert in Berlin, called the very day before the men were due to go on leave. However, with Ernst actually going on leave himself, all the indications are that the SA was utterly unprepared to undertake any kind of *coup d'état* at this time, whatever might have been in mind for later in the year.

Hitler had already telephoned Sepp Dietrich, leader of the SS Wachbatallion in Berlin, and ordered him to fly immediately to Godesberg.[24] Dietrich had left Berlin by air around five o'clock in the evening, arriving at the Hotel Dreesen at about seven o'clcok. Hitler invited Dietrich to dine with the company which had by this time assembled—Hitler, Göring, Goebbels, Paul Koerner, Göring's Secretary of State, and Hitler's adjutants, Wilhelm Brueckner and Julius Schaub, both trusted old-time supporters. After dinner, Hitler instructed Sepp Dietrich to fly immediately to Munich, and telephone him on his arrival. Dietrich did so. Hitler was still in Godesberg, and received Dietrich's phone call from Munich at midnight. He told Dietrich to be at Kaufering railway station at five o'clock that morning.

In Godesberg Hitler now also had with him, in addition to Goebbels and the rest, Otto Dietrich (his Party press chief), and Viktor Lutze, an SA officer who was entirely loyal. Göring had left for Berlin. Dietrich wrote subsequently:

> The real reason for his much-publicized presence at this wedding in the Catholic Cathedral at Essen, however, was his desire to cover up his plans. No one could suspect that the attack on Roehm was already on his schedule. That same evening he drove to Godesberg, and then to the airfield of Hangelaar near Bonn. His destination was Munich. We who were in his party had no idea what was up until his adjutant told us, while we were sitting in the plane, that we had better release the safety catches on our guns.[25]

On the way to the airport, Schaub remembers Hitler's state of excitement, and his remark to others in the car that he was going to arrest Roehm, and that it might be 'tough'. Roehm might have many armed men with him. They left the airfield at 2 a.m., arriving at Munich airport two hours later. It was a summer dawn on Saturday 30th June, and a day of reckoning in German history.

It was intended that the main action in Bavaria should be conducted by a detachment of some 700 SS gunmen, a special unit commanded by Sepp Dietrich due to be transported by rail overnight from Berlin. The unit had originally been based in Bavaria; they had only recently been transferred to Berlin to act as Hitler's personal guards. Meanwhile, before their arrival, certain SA leaders had already been rounded up and were being held to await the Führer's pleasure.

When Sepp Dietrich arrived at Kaufering station in the early light of 30th June, he was met by an Army unit under a Captain Fuchs, and only then told that two companies of his own SS Wachbatallion were on their way by train. They arrived shortly after, armed with infantry rifles, and in the charge of SS Captain Reich. Reich told Dietrich they had been entrained by order of the Army in Berlin. Dietrich still did not know what he was required to do, and only received the next phase of orders when Dr Karl Werner Best, of SS Intelligence, arrived to give him instructions to take his men by Army transport to Bad Wiessee, via Bad Tölz. Meanwhile, they were to go to Landsberg artillery barracks, where breakfast was to be provided, and vehicles prepared. It was mid-morning before they were ready to leave on the forty-mile journey.

Hitler, sleepless and tense, summoned his energies to exact vengeance. In the words of Otto Dietrich, who watched him: 'On 30 June, 1934, the monstrous side of Hitler's nature for the first time broke loose and showed itself for what it was.' The moment he had got down from the aircraft, he tore the Nazi insignia from the uniform of Roehm's deputy in Bavaria, SA General Schneidhuber, one of the senior SA officers who had been taken to the airport by his captors, local men under SS command, for this symbolic purpose. Surrounded by his old and trusted SS comrades, who showed their loyalty with every symptom of emotion, Hitler set off in a fleet of cars to raid the sanatorium where Roehm and his friends were still in bed.

The cars sped swiftly along the autobahn in the early morning light. On either side of the near-deserted road dark trees stood like silent sentinels brushed by the wind of the passing cars. Soon the waters of Tegernsee appeared, and the column of vehicles turned onto the lakeside road on their way to Bad Wiessee. Hitler was nervous and unpredictable, twice stopping the cavalcade to deal personally with men in isolated cars who had sought to overtake him.

No exact record survives of what then took place. The cars pulled up outside the sanatorium, the Hanselbauer Hotel. The main purpose of the visit was to arrest Roehm, Edmund Heines and any other of Roehm's intimate circle to be found there. Heines, apparently, was discovered in bed with a youth. Hitler, enraged, had them both taken out and shot, the execution undertaken by Emil Maurice, Hitler's driver, and Christian Weber, a former jockey who had been one of the original members of the SS.[26] Hitler is also said to have struck with a whip Count Spreti, another of the SA homosexuals, because he had appeared to be drawing a pistol. When he faced Roehm, who was alone in his bedroom, he is said to have challenged him to commit suicide. Otto Dietrich gives an eyewitness account: 'I can still see him as he entered the house in Wiessee where he arrested Roehm. . . . He paced up and down . . . with huge strides, fiery as some higher being, the very personification of Justice.' He is also quoted by Heiden as saying that Heines's room, adjoining Roehm's, 'presented a disgraceful picture', when Heines was discovered in bed with his 'homosexual boy'.[27] According to Schaub, Hitler entered Roehm's bedroom, accompanied by Schreck, the other chauffeur, and Police Commissioner Schmid-hauer. Schaub, who claims he was standing near the door, saw Roehm get out of bed and dress; he watched him being escorted downstairs by two police officers. Schaub also claims that Hitler dealt personally with a unit of twenty armed SA men belonging to Roehm's Stabs-Wache (Special Guard) who arrived suddenly in a lorry. He went over and addressed them, sending them back to Munich. Eventually the members of Roehm's staff already at Wiessee were rounded up, arrested, and sent by car to Munich were they were taken to the Stadel-heim prison. On the journey back, all SA officers whom they met travelling by car to Wiessee for the conference called for ten o'clock, were stopped, and told to report instead to the Braunhaus in Munich.

Hitler, suffering from nervous exhaustion, returned himself to the Braunhaus. Here, in the so-called Senate Hall, he made around noon a speech which was his first official statement about the Roehm purge. His audience was primarily members of the SS and SA. He explained that Roehm had been planning a *coup* against himself and the Army, and that all those involved would be shot.

The great purge had begun throughout Germany—strangely enough more hesitantly in Munich, where Hitler appeared to lose interest in directly supervising the action, than was the case in Berlin, where Göring and Himmler worked day and night to complete the roster of assassinations. In Munich there was distinct confusion; some 200 SA leaders were in the end placed under arrest, but no further action was taken against them until later in the day.

Meanwhile, Sepp Dietrich's men, on their journey to Wiessee, had received counter orders. Between Tölz and Wiessee, their column of lorries had been stopped by police, with new instructions that they were to return to Munich. Dietrich, by now completely in the dark as to what he should believe, considered trying to contact the Braunhaus by telephone, but this presented some difficulties where he was, out on the open road. Fortunately, two officers of SS Intelligence in search of him arrived almost immediately to confirm the advice to return to Munich. It was already approaching noon.

When Dietrich and his men finally arrived at the Braunhaus he found

Hitler angry at the time all this movement had taken. Dietrich blamed this on the condition of the Army vehicles. Hitler then ordered him to take his men to the Pioneer barracks, and then come back for further orders. By the time he got back to the Braunhaus it was afternoon, and he was kept waiting by Hitler until near five o'clock. All he could hear were raised voices inside. Hitler asked him whether the men were in 'good shape', and then gave him a long list of names (said to be 110) ordering him to select a squad of six to shoot those on the list who, he claimed, were guilty of high treason. They were to be shot at Stadelheim prison forthwith. Dietrich was to see to this.

Accompanied by Josias Prince zu Waldeck und Pyrmont, one of the aristocratic officers of the SS with the rank of Lieutenant General, Dietrich picked six sharp-shooters and hurried with them to Stadelheim. However, the prison governor, Dr Koch, was unwilling to allow such independent action to take place without the knowledge and consent of Hans Frank, the youthful Bavarian Minister of Justice (he was thirty-four), who arrived shortly after.[28] Frank was appalled by the situation confronting him. Dietrich claimed the order was a 'Führerbefehl', the term for a Hitler-command, which in this case supplanted the normal forms of justice. Frank, however, refused to authorize the executions without a legal warrant.

According to Frank, Dietrich managed to contact Hitler by telephone at the Braunhaus. Hitler spoke to Frank, shouting at him, 'I am Reich Chancellor and this is a Reich matter which in no way comes under your authority . . . I and the Reich decide about them, not Bavaria.' Frank, still desperate what he should do, telephoned Berlin and asked to speak to Hess, who he felt would be more reasonable. Hess, says Frank, was at least calm, and as a result of his intervention only nineteen men who were held to be wholly incriminated were executed on 30th June, while the rest were held for legal investigation.

According to the evidence given twenty-three years later at Sepp Dietrich's trial in Munich, Prince Waldeck chose the spot in the courtyard where the execution of the six high-ranking SA officers was to take place. They were shot at seven in the evening, protesting their innocence of any act or intention of treason up to the last, and demanding a trial. Ignoring their protestations, Dietrich had read out the sentence, and then witnessed the execution along with the Prince. Dötter, a medical orderly who was the only man at Stadelheim with any medical knowledge, inspected the dead; the bodies were bleeding profusely, and one officer, Heydebreck, appeared to be still alive. He was given a final, mortal shot. The Prince then took the night train to Berlin, while Dietrich returned to the barracks where the rest of his men were waiting. He was to fly back to Berlin the following day, while his troops were to return by train.

Roehm, along with many other SA officers, remained under arrest. According to the evidence given at Munich, Michael Lippert, then second-in-command under Theodor Eicke of the SS Wach-Kommando based on Dachau concentration camp, went to Munich by car with Eicke and a detachment of their men during the afternoon of Sunday 1st July. They saw Dr Koch at Stadelheim and demanded custody of Roehm, telling him the SA Commandant was to be given a pistol and told to kill himself. Koch reported the position immediately to Frank, as Bavarian Minister of Justice, who wisely told him to make a formal report in writing of anything that took place.

Eicke and Lippert were then taken to the door of cell 474, where Roehm was being held. Eicke produced a pistol and loaded it with a single shot, and the two officers entered the cell. Eicke put a copy of that day's *Völkischer Beobachter* on the table in front of Roehm, pointing to the front page report of the sentence Hitler had pronounced upon him. Then, placing the pistol on the newspaper, he said: 'Roehm, you have forfeited your life. The Führer offers you the chance of carrying out the sentence yourself.' They then turned, and left the cell.[29]

They gave Roehm ten minutes, and then went back. Roehm stood there, still alive. Eicke and Lippert ordered him to bare his chest. They both took aim very deliberately and shot him simultaneously. Roehm fell, and then one of them, muttering there should be a *coup de grâce*, fired a third shot at the prone man. There were a number of police witnesses of this execution. Koch finally inspected Roehm's body.

The previous evening, 30th June, after his brief stay at the Braunhaus, Hitler felt the urge to fly back to Berlin. He had not slept now for some forty hours. Still accompanied by Goebbels and Otto Dietrich, he reached Tempelhof as the sun was setting. Gisevius has given a graphic picture of this scene, since, for some unexplained reason, he was among those, led by Göring and Himmler, who were gathered on the runway to receive the Führer:

> The plane from Munich was announced. In a moment we saw it, looming swiftly larger against the background of a blood-red sky, a piece of theatricality that no one had staged. The plane roared down to a landing and rolled towards us. Commands rang out. A guard of honour presented arms. Göring, Himmler, Koerner, Frick, Daluege, and some twenty police officers went up to the plane. Then the door opened and Adolf Hitler was the first to step out.
> His appearance was 'unique', to use the favourite word of Nazi

commentators. A brown shirt, black bow tie, dark brown leather jacket, high black army boots—all dark tones. He wore no hat; his face was pale, unshaven, sleepless, at once gaunt and puffed. Under the forelock pasted against his forehead his eyes stared dully. Nevertheless, he did not impress me as wretched, nor did he awaken sympathy, as his appearance might well have done. I felt quite indifferent to him. It was clear that the murders of his friends had cost him no effort at all. He had felt nothing; he had merely acted out his rage.

First Hitler silently shook hands with everyone within reach. Nebe and I, who had taken the precaution of standing some distance away, heard amid the silence the repeated monotonous sound of clicking heels. Meanwhile, the other members of his entourage got out of the plane: Brueckner, Schaub, Dietrich, and the rest. All of them showed grave faces. At last a diabolic, grinning caricature of a face appeared: Goebbels.

Hitler walked slowly and laboriously past the guard of honour as if he were wading through sloshing mud. He seemed to be moving with such an effort that we felt he might bog down at any moment.

On the way to the fleet of cars, which stood several hundred yards away, Hitler stopped to converse with Göring and Himmler. Apparently he could not wait a few minutes until he reached the Chancellery. He listened attentively as the two made their report, though he must have been in constant telephone communication with them all day.

From one of his pockets Himmler took a long, tattered list. Hitler read it through, while Göring and Himmler whispered incessantly into his ear. We could see Hitler's finger moving slowly down the sheet of paper. Now and then it paused for a moment at one of the names. At such times the two conspirators whispered even more excitedly. Suddenly Hitler tossed his head. There was so much violent emotion, so much anger in the gesture, that everyone noticed it. Nebe and I cast significant glances at one another. Undoubtedly, we thought, they were now informing him of Strasser's 'suicide'.[30]

Retribution had been far better administered in Berlin. Göring, assisted by Himmler and Heydrich, had conducted the whole operation from his official residence on the Leipziger Platz, which had been cordoned off by an SS unit. The purge had started during the night while Hitler was flying to Munich. It was essential that Frick, locally responsible for law and order at the Prussian Ministry of the Interior, be kept outside this special operation; Göring knew that the formalities of justice could only lead to frustration and delay, as had happened in the south.[31] He therefore created his own private state of martial law while the officials were in their beds, ordering arrests according to the lists drawn up by Himmler, identifying the victims as they were thrust before him, and demanding their immediate extermination by a detachment of his police, whose firing-squads stood ready at the chosen place of execution, the former cadet school in Lichterfelde. Göring and Himmler worked without ceasing, while liveried footmen handed round food and drink to keep them and their aides refreshed. The men whose lives were forfeit were seized in their homes and rushed by car to Göring's residence, where they were left standing under guard in an ante-room, fearful and apprehensive, uncertain what was to happen. Those outside the room where Göring's inquisition was at work could hear him from time to time shouting orders, 'Shoot him! Shoot him!'

Little by little, piece by piece, fragments of eye-witness evidence have been assembled over the years uncovering something of the secret violence of 30th June. No one responsible knew, or cared to investigate, how many were killed—officially the figure was to stand at seventy-seven, including suicides and 'accidents'; unofficially the estimates rose to more than a thousand as rumour was added to rumour throughout Germany when the news of the purge leaked out.[32] Göring broke away from his assize to meet an anxious gathering of journalists. He met them at the Chancellery during the late afternoon and spoke briefly and curtly about the *coup d'état* which he had been able, he said, to catch in time. Someone asked about Schleicher who, it was rumoured, had been killed a few hours before. Göring replied with an ironic smile, 'Yes. I know you journalists like a headline. Well, here it is. General von Schleicher had plotted against the regime. I ordered his arrest. He was foolish enough to resist. He is dead.' Then he left them and returned to his duties. Later that evening he went to the airport to meet Hitler and report progress in the killings.

Schleicher indeed was dead; so too was Strasser. The exact circumstances of Schleicher's death, and that of his wife, were the subject of an affidavit made soon after by Marie Güntel, who had been Schleicher's housekeeper since 1918. She was fifty-three, and suffered from shock to such an extent that she eventually took her own life a year later in July 1935. On 2nd July, two days after the assassination, she gave the details of what happened at the urgent request of Schleicher's friends[33]:

On Saturday 30 June at 12.30 I was in the study of the Herr General to hand over the household accounts and a balance of

M. 100. Present were Herr General sitting behind his desk and Frau von Schleicher sitting with some knitting in an armchair next to the desk. At this moment the garden door bell rang for an unusually long time and very vehemently. I went to the front door, asked through the window who it was, and got the answer in a male voice: 'Wir müssen zu Herrn General.' I opened the door and five men pressed forward, one of whom asked where the Herr General was. This man may have been 30 and he wore a dark suit. The other men seemed rather younger and all of them wore light civilian clothes. I said first that the Herr General was not at home, and had gone for a walk. Whereupon the man in the dark suit pushed past me and shouted I should speak the truth. All five men had their hands behind their backs, but I could see almost at once that they were carrying revolvers. Realising that I could not stop them, I said: 'I'll have a look whether he is in', and went through the ante-room towards the study. The man in the dark suit ordered the others: 'Follow her!' As I entered the study one or two of the men, or maybe, three or four followed. Before I could say anything I heard a voice behind me: 'Are you General von Schleicher?' The Herr General, still sitting behind the desk, turned half right and said, 'Jawohl'. Within that split second there were three shots, almost simultaneously. I know for certain that apart from the half-right turn of head and shoulders the Herr General made no movement whatever before the shooting; I am quite sure he did not reach for his pocket or his desk. There could be no question of any sort of defensive action on the part of the Herr General. There would have been no time anyway, since there was hardly more than a second between the question, 'Are you General von Schleicher?' and the shooting. I distinctly remember that the general's 'Jawohl' and the shots were almost simultaneous. I stood in the midst of the room and Frau von Schleicher was seated as quietly as her husband. Whilst I screamed in fear and ran out of the room I heard Frau von Schleicher scream too and, almost immediately, some further shots. I seem to remember that the man who did most of the shooting had a grey, pin-striped suit and was at most twenty-five, but there were shots from at least two of the others. After rushing in panic around the lobby and the dining room, I ran into the garden through the winter-garden. I had another glimpse of the man in the grey suit carrying his revolver.

I went to find Frau von Schleicher (the general's cousin), and when we approached the study from the garden, all the men had left. It must have been less than two minutes between the first ringing of the doorbell and the final disappearance of the men. The actual assassination happened within a few seconds.

According to Gisevius and other sources, Gregor Strasser died an equally terrible death.[34] He was taken to the Gestapo's prison on Prince Albrechtstrasse, and, like Roehm, shot down in his cell, one bullet piercing an artery which gushed blood over the walls. He was left to bleed to death.

It would appear that Göring regretted Schleicher's death. He was to tell Meissner later, when they both shared captivity for a while after the war, that he wanted Schleicher alive rather than dead, and had decided to take him into 'protective custody', as he was able to do in the case of Papen. But, Göring claimed, when his men reached Schleicher's house to bring him in, he had already been killed by 'ein wildes SS Roll-Kommando', an irregular SS unit. On the other hand, Göring's unit can only be said to have arrived very late, several hours after securing the safety of Papen.[35]

Only Papen, as Hitler's Vice-Chancellor, was spared, though his close associates who had worked on the speech at Marburg were arrested and shot—Edgar Jung and Erich Klausener of the Catholic Action Group, and Papen's secretary, Herbert von Bose. Papen has left a detailed account of what happened to him personally; the sparing of his life was deliberate, since Hitler continued to recognize the debt he owed him. Göring was in consequence careful to isolate him from his associates early on 30th June, and so secure his personal safety during the height of the danger. Papen only pieced together the significance of what was happening as he lived from hour to hour through the period 30th June to 2nd July:

> I got to the office at nine o'clock, to find that Goering's adjutant, Bodenschatz, had already rung several times asking me to call on Goering immediately. Still without any hint as to what was going on, I hurried over to his home in the garden of the Air Transport Ministry, and I remember being amazed to find that the whole area was full of S.S. guards armed with machine-guns.
>
> Goering was in his study with Himmler. He told me that Hitler had had to fly to Munich to put down a revolt headed by Roehm, and that he himself had been given powers to deal with the insurgents in the capital. I protested immediately at this, and pointed out that as I was the Chancellor's deputy, in his absence such powers could only be granted to me. Goering would not hear of this, and declined flatly to delegate his authority. With the police and the air force troops under his command, he was certainly in the stronger position. I then said that it was essential to tell the Presi-

dent what was happening, declare a state of emergency, and bring in the Reichswehr to restore law and order. Again Goering refused. There was no need to disturb Hindenburg, he said, since, with the help of the S.S., he was in complete control of the situation.

Tschirschky, who was outside in the waiting-room, told me afterwards that while I was with Goering, Himmler had gone to the telephone and had spoken to someone very quietly. Tschirschky could only distinguish the words, 'You can go ahead now.' This was apparently the signal for a raid on the Vice-Chancellery.

Our discussion became distinctly heated, and Goering cut it short by stating that my own safety demanded I should return to my home immediately and not leave it again without his knowledge. I told him that I would accept full responsibility for my own safety and was not prepared to submit to what amounted to arrest. While this was going on, Himmler kept passing messages to Goering. I did not understand them at the time, but later realized that they were reports of the occupation of my Vice-Chancellery by the S.S. and the Gestapo. Presumably Himmler had made Goering call me to his office, assuming—rightly, I may add—that I would have refused to permit this occupation, and that his thugs would have had to deal with me on the spot. My presence would, no doubt, have been an additional embarrassment.

In the Vice-Chancellery—and all this had to be pieced together later—Bose had been shot out of hand, for 'offering resistance'. My secretary, Baroness Stotzingen, Savigny and Hummelsheim had been arrested and carted off to gaol or concentration camps. This was a back-handed way of making my own position impossible although I could not understand the arrest of Hummelsheim, who had never been a member of our inner circle. The offices were searched for secret documents and then sealed. A row of safes in the basement—the building had been a bank—were blown open and found to be empty.

In the end, Goering, who had a flood of incoming messages to deal with, more or less threw me out. . . .

My home was surrounded by an S.S. detachment armed to the teeth. The telephone was cut off, and in my reception room I found a police captain, who had had orders that I was to have no contact with the outside world and that no one was to be allowed to see me. Later he told me that he was responsible with his own life for preventing any Brownshirts or Gestapo from attempting to abduct me, unless he received direct orders from Goering. I must say it would have been nice to have known this a little earlier. My unfortunate wife and two of our daughters had accepted an invitation to visit friends in Bremen, and I could well imagine what her state of mind must have been when she heard reports of what was happening.

I spent the next three days completely alone. I had no idea what was going on in Berlin or in the country as a whole, and expected to be arrested and probably shot at any moment. I had no doubt that Goebbels, Himmler and Heydrich had made up their minds that it was time for the Marburg reactionary to be liquidated. As I learnt later, the only man who stood between me and this fate was Goering. He probably felt that my liquidation would only complicate matters more.[36]

Hitler, meanwhile, had returned to the Chancellery from Tempelhof airport on the night of 30th June. His spirits seem to have lightened. He was due to give a garden party at the Chancellery on Sunday afternoon, 1st July, and saw no reason to cancel this. The sporadic killings were still continuing in Germany as Hitler moved among his guests. According to Ambassador Dodd of the United States, the streets of Berlin were quiet; he drove slowly past the house of his friend, Papen, but could see nothing amiss. Sepp Dietrich reported to the Chancellery that evening around 7.30, and found Hitler in lively conversation with, among others, Fritsch, Blomberg and Guertner. Dietrich formally reported the execution he had supervised in Munich, and Hitler promoted him an SS General on the spot.

The impudent gloss put upon the purge, first by Hess (8th July)[37] and then by Hitler (13th July) and made later by Göring at the Nuremberg Trial, is deeply characteristic of Nazism, portraying the gravest of crimes as heroic deeds undertaken for the security of the state. Meanwhile, on 3rd July a law had been published which stated in a single sentence: 'The measures employed on 30 June, 1 and 2 July 1934 for the suppression of treasonable attacks are declared to be legal as taken in defence of the State.' While Goebbels muzzled the German Press, Hitler prepared his own public acknowledgment of the purge as the climax of his speech in the Reichstag on 13th July, two weeks later. It was ironic that the speech was the first to be given in the old Reichstag building, restored after the fire some eighteen months previously. Meanwhile, Viktor Lutze had been appointed Chief of Staff of the SA in Roehm's place, and as early as 1st July Blomberg had issued a statement to the Army, which had been kept inactive during the purge. The generals were no doubt glad to see the destruction of the menace which Roehm had represented. Blomberg wrote:

The Führer with soldierly decision and exemplary courage has himself attacked the traitors and murderers. The army, as the bearer of arms of the entire people, far removed from the conflicts of domestic politics, will show its gratitude through devotion and loyalty. The good relationship towards the new SA demanded by the Führer will be gladly fostered by the army in the consciousness that the ideals of both are held in common. The state of emergency [*Alarmzustand*] is terminated everywhere.[38]

Hitler saw to it that Hindenburg gave his presidential approval to the illicit action. Two telegrams were despatched from Hindenburg, now only within a month of his death; the first was addressed to Hitler:

From the reports presented to me I realize that through your determined action and through the courageous intervention of your own person you have nipped in the bud [*im Keime erstickt*] all treasonable plots. You have saved the German people from grave danger. For this I express to you my profound thanks and my sincere recognition. With best greetings—von Hindenburg.

The other was sent to Göring:

For your energetic and successful action in crushing the treasonable attempt I express to you my thanks and my recognition. With comradely greetings—von Hindenburg.[39]

Hitler's veiled and untruthful version of the events of 30th June was as follows:

At 1 o'clock in the night I received the last dispatches telling me of the alarm-summonses; at 2 o'clock in the morning I flew to Munich. Meanwhile Minister-President Göring had previously received from me the commission that if I proceeded to apply a purge he was to take similar measures at once in Berlin and in Prussia. With an iron fist he beat down the attack on the National Socialist State before it could develop. The necessity for acting with lightning speed meant that in this decisive hour I had very few men with me. In the presence of the Minister Goebbels and of the new Chief of Staff the action of which you are already informed was executed and brought to a close in Munich. Although only a few days before I had been prepared to exercise clemency, at this hour there was no place for any such consideration. Mutinies are suppressed in accordance with laws of iron which are eternally the same. If anyone reproaches me and asks why I did not resort to the regular courts of justice for conviction of the offenders, then all that I can say to him is this: in this hour I was responsible for the fate of the German people, and thereby I became the supreme Justiciar [*oberster Gerichtsherr*] of the German people!

Mutinous divisions have in all periods been recalled to order by decimation. Only one State has failed to make any use of its Articles of War and this State paid for that failure by collapse— Germany. I did not wish to deliver up the young Reich to the fate of the old Reich. I gave the order to shoot those who were the ring-leaders in this treason, and I further gave the order to burn out down to the raw flesh the ulcers of the poisoning of the wells in our domestic life and of the poisoning of the outside world. And I further ordered that if any of the mutineers should attempt to resist arrest, they were immediately to be struck down with armed force. The nation must know that its existence—and that is guaran-teed through its internal order and security—can be threatened by no one with impunity! And everyone must know for all future time that if he raises his hand to strike the State, then certain death is his lot. And every National Socialist must know that no rank and no position can protect him from his personal responsibility and therefore from his punishment. I have prosecuted thousands of our former opponents on account of their corruption. I should in my own mind reproach myself if I were now to tolerate similar offences in our own ranks. . . . Every people is itself guilty if it does not find the strength to destroy such noxious creatures. If people bring against me the objection that only a judicial procedure could precisely weigh the measure of the guilt and of its expiation, then against this view I lodge my most solemn protest. He who rises against Germany is a traitor to his country, and the traitor to his country is not to be punished according to the range and the extent of his act, but according to the purpose which that act has revealed. He who in his heart purposes to raise a mutiny and thereby breaks loyalty, breaks faith, breaks sacred pledges, can expect nothing else than that he himself will be the first sacrifice. . . .

A foreign diplomat explains that the meeting of Schleicher and Roehm was of course of an entirely harmless character. That matter I need not discuss with anyone. In the political sphere conceptions of what is harmless and what is not will never coincide. But when three traitors in Germany arrange and effect a meeting with a foreign statesman which they themselves characterize as 'serviceable', when they effect this meeting after excluding every member of their staff, when they give strict orders that no word of this meeting shall reach me, then I shall have such men shot dead even when it should prove true that at a consultation which was thus kept secret from me they talked of nothing save the weather, old coins, and like topics.

The penalty for these crimes was hard and severe. Nineteen

higher SA leaders, thirty-one leaders and members of the SA, were shot, and further, for complicity in the plot, three leaders of the SS, while thirteen SA leaders and civilians who attempted to resist arrest lost their lives. Three more committed suicide. Five who did not belong to the SA, but were members of the Party, were shot for taking part in the plot. Finally there were also shot three members of the SS who had been guilty of scandalous ill-treatments of those who had been taken into protective custody.

In order to prevent political passion and exasperation venting itself in lynch justice on further offenders when the danger was removed and the revolt could be regarded as suppressed, as early as Sunday 1 July strictest orders were given that all further retribution should cease.

Thereby from the night of Sunday 1 July the normal state of affairs was re-established. A number of acts of violence which do not stand in any connection with the plot will be brought before the ordinary courts for judgment.[40]

Göring's account at the Nuremberg trial was as brutal as it was pre-varicating; for example, he spoke of Roehm as if he were some junior officer:

I knew Roehm very well. I had him brought to me. I put to him openly the things which I had heard. I reminded him of our mutual struggle and asked him unconditionally to keep faith with the Führer. . . . He assured me that, of course, he was not thinking of undertaking anything against the Führer. Shortly afterwards I received further news to the effect that he had close connections with those circles that were strongly opposed to us. There was, for instance, the group around the former Reich Chancellor Schlei-cher. There was the group around Gregor Strasser, the former member of the Reichstag and organizational leader of the Party who had been excluded from the Party. These were groups which had belonged to the former trade unions and were rather Leftist-minded. I felt it my duty to consult the Führer on this subject. I was astonished when he told me that he, too, already knew about these things and considered them a great threat. He said that he wished, however, to await further developments and watch them carefully.

Of the assassinations he said:

In the course of the arrest of the former Reich Chancellor Schlei-cher, it happened that both he and his wife were killed. An investi-gation of this event took place and it was found that when Schleicher was arrested, according to the statements of two witnesses, he reached for a pistol, possibly in order to kill himself, whereupon the two men raised their pistols, and Frau Schleicher threw herself upon one of them to hold him, causing his revolver to go off.

We deeply regretted that event.

In the course of that evening I heard that other people had been shot as well, even some people who had nothing at all to do with this Roehm revolt. The Führer came to Berlin that same evening. I learned this later that evening or night, and went to him at noon the next day, and asked him to issue an order immediately that any further execution was, under any circumstances, forbidden by him, although two other people who were very much involved and who had been ordered to be executed were still alive. These people were, in fact, left alive. I asked him to do that because I was worried that the matter would get out of hand as, in fact, it had already done to some extent, and I told the Führer that under no circumstances should there be any further bloodshed. . . . As my final remark on the Roehm *Putsch* I should like to emphasize that I assume full responsibility for the actions taken against those people—Ernst, Heidebrecht and several others—by order of the Führer which I executed or passed on, and that, even today, I am of the opinion that I acted absolutely correctly and from a sense of duty. That was confirmed by the Reich President, but no such confirmation was necessary to convince me that I had averted what was a great danger to the State.[41]

Göring assumed at the trial as far as ever possible, the mask of the frank humanitarian—the man who had always exercised moderation in times of violence, but who was always prepared to stand by the orders he had given when these still seemed to his easy conscience to represent some honourable execution of duty.

Nevertheless, it was Göring who, according to Gisevius, took most care to see that all official records of the purge were destroyed once a halt to the killings had been ordered.[42] Giving evidence at Nuremberg, Gisevius said, when cross-examined by Mr Justice Jackson:

GISEVIUS: I estimate that 150 to 200 persons lost their lives, which, at that time, was an incredible figure. I myself, together with Minister of Justice Guertner, compared the lists of the number of the dead which had been given him by Hitler and Göring, and we ascertained that the list which contained the names of 77 dead, who had supposedly been killed justly, was exceeded by nearly one hundred per cent. This we ascertained through those names which we had received from the prosecuting authority or through calls for help coming from relatives through the Ministry of the Interior.

JACKSON: Now, did you ascertain who selected the men who were killed in that purge?

GISEVIUS: To begin with, we ascertained that Himmler, Heydrich and Göring had compiled exact lists of those to be murdered, because I myself heard in Göring's palace, and this was confirmed by Daluege who was present, that not one of those who were killed was mentioned by name; all that was said was, 'Number so and so is now gone', or, 'Number so and so is still missing', or, 'It will soon be number so and so's turn'. There is, however, no doubt that Heydrich and Himmler also had a special list. On that official list there were several Catholics—Klausener and others— and so I cannot, for example, say under oath in this courtroom whether Schleicher was murdered by order of Göring, or whether he was a man who was on Heydrich's and Himmler's special list.[43]

The American ambassador, William E. Dodd, formerly professor of history at the University of Chicago, gives a running comment on the events of the period as he experienced them from the diplomatic angle. On 30th June he had received a formal note from Roehm's office in Berlin saying he would be unable to come to dinner at the Embassy on 6th July. On 1st July he notes certain details of Hitler's raid in Wiessee which are correct in broad outline as generally known. On 5th July he called off a lecture he was due to give at the University of Berlin; the diary is full of references to tension in the capital, no one knowing exactly what had happened or might happen in the immediate future. On 6th July, in conversation with Neurath, he was solemnly told that Hitler, Göring and Goebbels were to have been killed the previous Saturday, and the rest of the Cabinet put in jail. Schleicher and Roehm, said Neurath, were to stage a *coup d'état*, which would have led to civil war. Dodd was shocked to hear such stuff from Neurath, whom he had regarded as one of the 'wiser men of the régime'. On the same day a note he sent to Papen was confiscated by the secret police. On 9th July he was further shocked by the arrest and confinement in a concentration camp of Professor Morsbach on the grounds (it appeared) that he was a friend of Roehm; Morsbach was well known to Dodd through being in charge of foreign student exchange fellowships. On 13th July he refrained from attending Hitler's speech that evening to the Reichstag; during the afternoon he had walked in the Tiergarten with the French ambassador, François-Poncet, who was very angry that he was being charged in certain Nazi quarters with having 'conspired' with Schleicher and Roehm, both of whom he had known fairly well.[44]

On 15th July he received a visit from his friend, Papen, who explained in confidence that Hitler was putting pressure on him 'to remain in the Cabinet and to co-operate'. Papen said he had told Hitler 'he could not promise anything at the moment'; he was too distressed at the death of Bose, without any proof of his guilt being produced, and at the imprisonment of others of his staff, 'their heads shaved, with no knowledge of what would happen to them from day to day'. 'This,' he said, 'was Hitler's treatment of all who are suspected of disloyalty.'

Twelve days after Hitler's speech to the Reichstag, violence was carried beyond the German frontier. The Austrian Chancellor, Engelbert Dollfuss, was shot down by Austrian Nazis with the same brutality as Schleicher; he was left to bleed to death on a sofa in his Chancellery. Whatever Hitler may have felt about this assassination, he did not want at this stage to be considered as in any way implicated. This Nazi *Putsch* had failed in Austria, and Hitler was always unwilling to be associated with failure.

His mind, in any case, was fixed on higher things. The news now from Neudeck was that Hindenburg was at last approaching his end, and on 2nd August he died, murmuring a passage from the Bible he could no longer see to read, but knew by heart. Within three hours of the President's death, Hitler announced that the offices of President and Chancellor would be merged, thus making him not only supreme head of state but also Commander-in-Chief of the Army. That same day, before they had time to ponder the implications of these changes, the Army, both officers and men, were called upon to assemble, wherever they might be, and swear allegiance to Hitler in person: 'I swear by God this holy oath: I will render unconditional obedience to the Führer of the German Reich and People, Adolf Hitler, the Supreme Commander of the Armed Forces, and will be ready, as a brave soldier, to stake my life at any time for this oath.'

Hitler, though, was still careful to give this final stage in his seizure of supreme power the full gloss of legality. Hindenburg's funeral on 7th August, an occasion for pageantry in the imperial style, was preceded the day before by Hitler's respectful oration in the Reichstag; Hitler left it in no doubt that Hindenburg had in his wisdom bequeathed Germany to the Chancellor. Further, a plebiscite was announced for 19th August, at which the German people would be able to endorse their late President's wish that Adolf Hitler take the control of Germany's destiny in his hands.

But yet another feat of timing was to be achieved. The existence of Hindenburg's testament was known to Hitler; it had, in fact, been drafted initially by Papen himself earlier in the year in a form which included a recommendation that the monarchy be restored after the

President's death. However, the final testament, as redrawn by Hindenburg in May, was addressed to the German people, but made no mention of the restoration of the monarchy; this was contained in a private letter to Hitler in which Hindenburg recommended him to consider restoring the imperial family.

As soon as the President's funeral was over, Hitler demanded to see any testament which Hindenburg had left. Both documents were finally produced for him by Papen and Oskar von Hindenburg. Hitler suppressed the letter, but published the testament, since it contained favourable if brief references to himself.[45] The letter was never mentioned again. On the eve of the plebiscite, Oskar von Hindenburg broadcast to the nation saying: 'My father had himself seen in Adolf Hitler his own direct successor as Head of the German State, and I am acting according to my father's intention when I call on all German men and women to vote for the handing over of my father's office to the Führer and Reich Chancellor.' The Hindenburgs had sold out to Hitler.

The plebiscite produced the expected overwhelming majority in Hitler's favour—over 38 million voted for him, only 4.25 million against, while 0.75 million spoiled their papers. Only some 2 million of the 45.5 million eligible did not go to the polls.

Following this great vote of confidence by the German people, Hitler could proudly proclaim during the Party rally at Nuremberg the following month that 'the form of German life was finally determined for the next millennium'. It was, in fact, established for only the next eleven years. But the cost in Europe of its overthrow was to be some 35 million lives lost,[46] 15 million persons displaced, and a total re-structure of the balance of power in Europe.

The question of whether Hitler could have been displaced at any time between 1932 and 1934 remains open. What becomes evident is that no single politician, soldier, or social leader in Germany was a match for him, and that only by means of a firm and lasting combination of opposing forces could he have been successfully resisted during these formative years of his power. The division in Germany's narrow-minded political life made such a combination of forces impossible.

As a character, like Napoleon before him, Hitler remains unique in history. In spite of his nondescript background, he was possessed of a magnetic force of personality and an intuitive judgment of people and political situations which amounted to genius. Yet genius is normally associated with rare creative powers of the highest order, which result in some great furtherance of the scope of art, science, culture or statesmanship. But that there is also such a thing as negative genius, a unique capacity to destroy and to lead others to destruction, is exemplified in the character and personality of Hitler. Without his intuitive sense of weakness in his opponents, without his continual insistence on waiting for absolute power to come his way, in the face of every temptation to compromise and accept a second best, he would never have achieved dictatorship in so great a country as Germany, with its vast authoritarian establishment which was for the most part set against him. Lacking conventional conscience himself, he chose able men to help him whose only ethic was to give him their individual service. With no initial resources save his tongue, he was to gather the might of arms around him and make millionaire industrialists his servants. And all this he achieved, effectively, in little more than four years, between 1930 and 1934.

Hitler lived to see his empire stretch from the Atlantic seaboard to the gates of Moscow and the hinterland of the Ukraine, and from the Arctic Circle south to the countries of the Mediterranean and the deserts of North Africa. But it was then that his genius began to crumble and his intuitive judgment wane. Sick in mind and body, his megalomaniac powers moved into the spheres of fantasy; men became statistics, and armies symbols marked on maps. Though it took the combined armies of the British, Americans, Russians and their many allies to defeat him, Hitler carried in himself the seeds of his own destruction, for the price of negative genius is that it can do nothing but destroy. It is genius without productive future.

Hitler died by his own hand on 30th April 1945. His territory then had shrunk to the narrow confines of a bunker set beneath the garden of his grandiose Chancellery. But his legacy remains in the changing face of Europe with its ideological divisions. It also remains in the enigma of his character. No man in human history has combined so swift a rise to absolute power with so savage an instinct for the destruction of mankind.

Notes

The primary published sources on which we have drawn include such standard works as Alan Bullock's *Hitler* (revised edition 1964), Franz von Papen's *Memoirs* (used with reservations), Goebbels's carefully edited diary of the period, *My Part in Germany's Fight* (used with even further reservations), J. W. Wheeler-Bennett's study, *Hindenburg, The Wooden Titan*, W. M. Knight-Patterson's *Germany from Defeat to Conquest*, Erich Eyck's *A History of the Weimar Republic*, and Norman H. Baynes's admirably edited *The Speeches of Adolf Hitler*. We have also drawn continually on the transcript of the Trial of the major War Criminals in Nuremberg; the edition of the latter referred to below as IMT is that published by HMSO in London in 22 volumes. We have also drawn extensively on the American volumes of documents used during the trial entitled *Nazi Conspiracy and Aggression*, and on *Documents on British Foreign Policy*, second series, 1929–38. In the Notes below the present authors are indicated individually as R. M. and H. F.

As far as possible we have gone back to original documents rather than quote them from secondary sources. Wherever it has been possible to conduct interviews with surviving participants in the events of this period, we have endeavoured to do this.

Throughout this book we have also drawn on material held in the German Federal Archives in Koblenz (referred to below as Koblenz) and the Institut für Zeitgeschichte in Munich (referred to as Munich), in the Military Archives at Freiburg (ref. Freiburg), in the Research Centre for National Socialist History at Hamburg (ref. Hamburg), as well as in the Wiener Library in London.

Part 1   CONFRONTATION 1932

1 Article 48 of the Constitution regulated emergencies, and gave the President substantial powers. If public security, law and order were, in the President's view, threatened, he could take measures to

restore order, if necessary with the help of the armed forces. He could assume emergency powers which enabled him to disregard temporarily articles 114, 115, 117, 118, 124, and 153 of the Constitution, which severally guaranteed the freedom of the individual, freedom of expression of opinion, the right of assembly, the right to form unions and associations, and rights relating to ownership of property. The Reichstag, on the other hand, could demand that the measures be cancelled.

2 An extension of Hindenburg's Presidency required parliamentary backing in the form of an amendment to the Constitution passed by not less than a two-thirds vote in the House. There was a precedent in October 1922 in the case of President Ebert. See Eyck, 1964, II, p. 352.

3 H. F. has had many conversations with Ernst Hanfstaengl, who was an intimate friend of Hitler at this time, concerning Hitler's relationship with his wayward niece. Hitler was inordinately jealous of her, and Hanfstaengl has claimed he saw what he called pornographic drawings of her by Hitler. The whole affair of her suicide had to be hushed up by Franz Guertner, the Bavarian Minister of Justice, who was one of Hitler's supporters. See Hanfstaengl, 1970, pp. 304–8.

4 The Stahlhelm was an ex-servicemen's military association. The difficult relationship between Hitler and the Stahlhelm leaders is reflected in the letters exchanged between them, and published in Düsterberg's *Der Stahlhelm und Hitler* (Wolfenbüttel, 1949), pp. 15–33.

5 See Schacht, 1955, p. 290.

6 See Bullock, 1964, p. 191.

7 Heiden, 1944, p. 342.

8 Unpublished diary preserved at Munich. Schaeffer was to be Schwerin-Krosigk's Undersecretary of State. He was later to become a director of the celebrated publishing house of Ullstein. Hermann Pünder was a senior civil servant in the ministries of Justice and Finance.

9 For the curious relationship between Roehm and Schleicher, see Heiden, 1944, pp. 355–6. Schleicher even toyed with the idea of trying to detach Roehm and the SA from Hitler. See Bullock, 1964, p. 205. Letters proposing meetings between Roehm and Schleicher are held at Freiburg.

10 These and subsequent quotations from Goebbels's diary can be found in *My Part in Germany's Fight*, under the appropriate dates. It is necessary once again to warn the reader to take everything Goebbels says with due regard to the fact that he edited his journal after the events he describes in order to achieve the greatest propaganda effect.

11 The Weimar Constitution required the President to be a German national. See Eyck, 1964, II, p. 354: 'Frick had already attempted, as a minister of Thuringia, to effect Hitler's naturalization through the back door by appointing him director of land police in Hildburghausen. But this had been too blatant a deceit even for Hitler, and so the Nazi leader had declined. The Brunswick minister (and later SS Gruppenführer) Dietrich Klagges approached the problem in a more sophisticated way; he appointed Hitler adviser (Regierungsrat) to the Brunswick Legation in Berlin.' Hitler paid one visit only to the Legation to swear himself in, and thus acquire German citizenship. A memo signed by Groener addressed to the Chancellery and dated 4th Feb. 1932 challenges the legality of this naturalization process, with reference to the Hildburghausen appointment. It was later decided that the Brunswick appointment was sufficiently satisfactory legally to pass muster, since Frick controlled the Brunswick administration. These documents are preserved at Koblenz.

12 Günther Gereke (1972), reveals how Hindenburg's campaign was financed (p. 183). I. G. Farben contributed a million marks. Krupp and others contributed substantially. Another million came from secret Reichswehr funds controlled by Schleicher. (Later Schleicher was to offer to pay the oustanding printing bills of the Nazi Party, said to be some 7 million marks, if Strasser would collaborate fully with him, using similar secret funds.)

13 After the first indecisive presidential election the idea was mooted of both Hindenburg and Hitler retiring in favour of the Crown Prince, son of Kaiser Wilhelm II. A messenger went to the ex-Kaiser at Doorn, to Hindenburg, and to Hitler. This was Joachim von Ostau, who told H. F. he found Hitler not entirely averse to the suggestion, at least at first, since he did not welcome facing a second defeat by Hindenburg. However, Goebbels persuaded him not to withdraw, and Ostau was sent back to the Crown Prince, who lived at Oels, near Danzig, to tell him of Hitler's refusal. Brüning, however, regarded the Crown Prince as 'quite intelligent', but 'unreliable'. See conversation recorded in Hans Schaeffer's unpublished diary preserved at Munich; entry for 7th June 1932.

14 The principal evidence was the discovery of the so-called Boxheim papers—documents drawn up by the Nazi legal adviser, Dr Werner Best, following discussions by local Nazi leaders in the state of Hesse and relating to the establishment of a local Nazi government with authoritarian powers in the event of a Communist rising. Hitler probably knew nothing of this. See Bullock, 1964, p. 202; Eyck, 1964, II p. 364 et seq. *See also* Part III, Note 34 below.

15 Rauschning, 1939, p. 28.

16 Goebbels, 1938, p. 64.

17 For further background on the negotiations behind the scenes leading up to the SA being banned, see Eyck, 1964, pp. 266–9.

18 The position of the other 'armies' caused some difficulty. For example, Hindenburg was the honorary president of the Stahlhelm, the 'army' of the Right. The Reichsbanner, the 'army' of the Left, like the Stahlhelm, were not disbanded officially at the same time as the SA, which numbered over 400,000 men. See Wheeler-Bennett, 1936, p. 376 et seq.

19 Goebbels, 1938, p. 70.

20 Goebbels, 1938, pp. 86–7. On 5th June, in other provincial elections, the Nazis polled 49 per cent in Mecklenburg, and 44 per cent the following month in Hesse.

21 According to Hans Schaeffer's unpublished diary (Munich), it 'may be a good thing that Hindenburg was not elected first go. His majority will become much larger and it'll damage the Nazis psychologically. Schwerin-Krosigk begs to differ. He says the "Alter Herr" was very disappointed to have been left in the lurch by "his people".' (14th March 1932.)

22 This was the celebrated Osthilfe, in its original form a sensible scheme, both socially and economically, proposing to settle landless peasants on vast Junker estates which had declined through mismanagement, with substantial funds set aside to compensate the landowners. The Left soon attacked the scheme as a means of bringing subsidy to the landowner rather than helping the industrious peasant. The Right, on the other hand, were only too ready to believe the opposite, that the whole scheme was a form of dispossession fostered by the Left. The Osthilfe scheme became a source of 'scandal' exploited by the Left and the Right alike.

23 Groener was vulnerable at this time; he had recently married,

and his wife had produced a child five months after the ceremony, which caused scandal in the Army. (See Heiden, 1944, p. 362.) He was also in ill-health, and unable to withstand heckling in the House. Most bitter of all was the sudden betrayal by Schleicher, whom he looked upon as a son, and employed in his Ministry. The ultimate cause of the conflict with Schleicher was their differing attitude to Hitler, to whom Groener was always bitterly opposed. See the statements made by Groener himself and, after his death, by his daughter, Dorothea Groener-Geyer, preserved at Freiburg.

24 Heiden, 1944, p. 361.

25 Goebbels, 1938, p. 77.

26 See *Deutsche Rundschau* (edited by R. Pechel, July 1947) for a 22-page letter by Brüning analysing the political situation during 1932. Schaeffer in his unpublished diary considers Meissner as responsible for Brüning's downfall as Schleicher; Schaeffer was involved in the discussions. Behind these domestic disputes were the imminent discussions at Lausanne on reparations; Britain was taking a soft line in contrast with the hard line of France. On disarmament, Brüning's policy had been that general disarmament must follow automatically upon German disarmament. On reparations, he favoured at the worst postponement of payment with instalments stretched over as long a period as possible.

27 Goebbels, 1938, p. 86.

28 On 26th June Hitler held a gathering of SA leaders near Berchtesgaden and lectured them about the 'legal' policy he was determined to follow, counselling them to practise patience. See Heiden, 1944, p. 368.

29 It is significant that Eyck in his authoritative *History of the Weimar Republic* has a very low opinion of Papen, and regards his memoirs as completely untrustworthy. He quotes the French ambassador, André François-Poncet, as approving the general opinion in diplomatic circles in Berlin that Papen was 'superficial, confused, and untrustworthy ... vain, ambitious and scheming'. Wheeler-Bennett also classes him as 'fifth-rate', while the British ambassador described him after his fall as a man of 'second-rate ability'. For a very negative interpretation of Papen's part in German politics, see Eyck, 1964, II, Chapters XIII et seq.

30 Principals in Brüning's and Papen's cabinets were, Brüning: Groener (Defence; Interior), Dietrich (Finance), Stegerwald

(Labour), Joel (Justice), Schiele (Agriculture), Schlange (Osthilfe); Papen: Neurath (Foreign Office), Gayl (Interior), Schwerin-Krosigk (Finance), Warmbold (Economy), Guertner (Justice), Schleicher (Defence), von Braun (Agriculture).

31 Papen, 1952, p. 162.

32 There were 461 political riots in Prussia between 1st June and 20th July 1932, with 82 people killed, and 400 seriously injured. In the Prussian Diet the Nazis and the Nationalists held some 200 seats, the Social Democrats and Centre Party about 160, and the Communists 57. The new Diet passed a law confiscating the property of all Jews who had come to Prussia from eastern Europe after 1914, together with other anti-Jewish legislation.

33 The free German trade unions had some 5 million membership. But the inaction by the workers in the face of Papen's action was due to the widespread unemployment; a national strike was impossible to call at this time. Men feared losing such jobs as they had. See Eyck, 1964, II, p. 414, Heiden 1944, p. 372, Knight-Patterson, 1945, p. 536.

34 Goebbels, 1938, p. 100. Graf Wolf Heinrich von Helldorf was SA leader in Berlin; Edmund Heines was an officer in the SA, a homosexual, highly corrupt, and a close friend of Roehm.

35 Goebbels, 1938, p. 101.

36 Goebbels, 1938, p. 114.

37 The murder of Pietzruch, a Communist miner, in Potempa, happened at this time. It was the work of five uniformed Storm Troopers, who kicked their victim to death before his mother's eyes. They were given death sentences on 22nd August by a special court in Beuthen, which was packed with Nazi supporters led by Edmund Heines who created an uproar when the sentences were announced. Hitler took the risk of defending the assassins in public. He attacked Papen in the *Völkischer Beobachter* for betraying 'the blood of national heroes'. He sent the murderers a telegram: 'My comrades, in the face of this most monstrous sentence of death I regard myself bound to you in limitless fidelity. From this day on your release is a matter of our common honour, and the fight against the government under which the sentence was possible, our common duty.'

38 Papen, 1952, pp. 195–7. Hitler was accompanied on this occasion by Roehm and Frick, not Göring, as Meissner states in the affidavit following, which he made some thirteen years later at Nuremberg.

39 Meissner's affidavit at Nuremberg, ND 3309–PS.

40 Schacht, 1955, p. 281.

41 IMT, IX, p. 68.

42 Goebbels, 1938, p. 134.

43 Brüning in his *Memoiren 1918–34* (Stuttgart, 1970), p. 628, claims that the Centrist vote *for* the Communists' motion was due to confusion. The Centrist deputy Oberfohren refrained from voting against the motion, as he was supposed to do; Brüning gives no reason for this.

Part 2 THE HUNDRED DAYS—I

1 For some account of Hitler's sources of finance at this time, see Appendix I.

2 The drop in the vote recorded in favour of the Nazis led to disastrous wishful thinking abroad. Eyck, 1964, II, p. 441, quotes Harold Laski's words in the London *Daily Herald* of 19th November 1932: 'The day when they [the Nazis] were a vital threat is gone. . . . Accident apart, it is not unlikely that Hitler will end his career as an old man in some Bavarian village who, in the Biergarten in the evening, tells his intimates how he nearly overturned the German Reich.'

3 Papen, 1952, p. 210. The official figures for unemployment were 2,019,000 in the autumn of 1929, 3,484,000 by mid November 1930, 3,762,000 by 1st December 1930, 3,977,000 by mid December 1930, 4,367,000 by New Year 1931, and 4,765,000 by mid January 1931. A further million was added to this figure during 1932.

4 Nuremberg Documents, D 633.

5 Koblenz (File R43 I/1309) preserves documentation showing that Dr Schaeffer (Bavarian Volkspartei) saw Papen on 16th November 1932 to urge him that Hitler should be brought into the government if needs be as Chancellor, but that there ought to be 'safety measures by distributing posts in such a way that Hitler's freedom of movement was reasonably restricted'. On 18th November Seldte and Düsterberg of the Stahlhelm wrote to Hindenburg 'imploring him to maintain an authoritarian regime' since proper forms of parliamentary government were impossible after the election results of 6th November.

6 Nuremberg Documents, D 634.

7 This record, and the following correspondence between Meissner (writing on behalf of Hindenburg) and Hitler, can be found in *Jahrbuch des öffentlichen Rechts*, vol. 21 (1933–4).

8 The reference to Reich-Prussia signifies that Prussia's being by far the largest state, with its administration working side by side with that of the federal authorities, led to much wasteful overlapping.

9 Strangely enough, though innumerable decrees were put through by virtue of Article 48, the Reichstag hardly ever availed itself of its right to declare such legislation invalid unless supported by a majority vote on some subsequent occasion.

10 Text preserved in the Koblenz archive, K644165–7.

11 Nuremberg Documents, 3901–PS.

12 IMT, XVI, pp. 271–2. The staff officer whom Schleicher summoned to the cabinet meeting was Major Eugen Ott, who was later to become Hitler's ambassador to Tokyo. In conversation with H. F., Schacht claimed that Schleicher approached him late in November (a few days before Papen's resignation) with the suggestion that he might consider being proposed for Chancellor. This revealed that Schleicher preferred to be the power behind the throne rather than its occupant. When H. F. suggested that the proposal, which Schacht refused to take seriously, was a counsel of despair, Schacht's response was that it was a counsel of embarrassment. Gereke, however, told H. F. that he considered Schacht was lying; he was close to Schleicher at the time, and no such suggestion had reached his ears. Schacht also confirmed to H. F. that it was his considered opinion after the Nazi success in the July election that the Party must be brought into the government. As for himself, 'I was never a politician, you know,' he said. 'But I was of course interested in developments.'

13 Hitler's anti-socialist views had been apparent enough in his debate on Socialism with Otto Strasser, Gregor's brother, on 22nd May 1930. He had declared that 'the term Socialism in itself is unfortunate [*schlecht*], but it is essential to realize that it does not mean . . . businesses must be socialized, it means only that they *can* be socialized if they offend against the interests of the nation. As long as they do not do that, it would be simply a crime to destroy business life [*Wirtschaft*]. . . . The only thing which the present system lacks is the ultimate responsibility to the nation. There can never be a

system which is based on any other principle. . . . This sharing of the workers in possession and control is simply Marxism.' (See Baynes, 1942, I, pp. 111–12.)

14 Gregor Strasser also said on 10th May in the Reichstag: '. . . the rise of the Nazi movement signifies the nation's protest against a state refusing the right to work . . . , protest against economic order thinking only in terms of profit and dividends.'

15 Notes taken by Hinrich Lohse, and preserved in Hamburg.

16 Schwerin-Krosigk's published diary, 13th November 1932.

17 Leipart, however, was under instruction not to enter into any form of collaboration with the Nazis. See also Gereke, 1972, pp. 204 et seq.

18 Leipart's position is summed up in a message to the trade union officials sent late in 1932: 'We are agreed that the ultimate aim of the working-class is the realization of socialism. But you know that the trade unions were established in order to improve the situation of the working-class in the framework of the present economic order.' (See Heiden, 1944, p. 395.) Schleicher was considered a reactionary by the trade union movement, however, and it is inconceivable that co-operation between him and Leipart could ever have matured.

19 Otto Braun, the Premier of Prussia, claims (1940, pp. 430 et seq.) that Schleicher told him during a meeting shortly after Schleicher's appointment as Chancellor, that 'Gregor Strasser will soon be appointed Vice-Chancellor'. However, it is perhaps significant that Eyck (1964, II, p. 451) does not consider Schleicher ever went so far as to offer Strasser the Vice-Chancellorship. But on the other hand, most authorities accept without any doubt that Strasser was very seriously considered as a potential Vice-Chancellor. For example, Gereke, 1972, p. 212, records Schleicher's acute disappointment when Strasser virtually retired from politics.

20 This was Kaufmann's memory of the meeting, as he recalled it to H. F., over thirty years later. According to Heiden, writing in the United States during the war as an historian, Strasser defended himself at least to the extent of claiming he was trying to save the Party, and that it was Hitler who was destroying it. (See Heiden, 1944, p. 396.) Kaufmann, who as a Reichstag deputy was present at this humiliation of Strasser, and was indeed one of Strasser's friends, confirmed to H. F. in 1967 that Hitler chose the technique

he knew would hurt Strasser most. Strasser was a relatively sensitive man, and would loathe being shouted at in public.

21 This account follows Hinrich Lohse's record at the Hamburg Institute.

22 Goebbels, 1938, pp. 180–2. The text of Strasser's letter does not survive. According to Kaufmann, it was brief. In addition to Goebbels's description of it, Heiden (1944, p. 397), without indicating his source, claims it contained personal attacks on Goebbels and Roehm, as well as taking up 'differences which went back to 1925'. The author of the commentary in the 'opposition press' was undoubtedly Hans Zehrer, who had originally proposed to Schleicher his 'axis' with Strasser and Leipart. The journal involved was the *Rundschau*, which from time to time acted as Schleicher's mouthpiece.

23 Another account of the search for Strasser claims that Frick persuaded Hitler to allow him to go out and look for the missing man. Frick, however, the story goes, failed to find Strasser.

24 A series of official statements followed. Hitler's *Völkischer Beobachter* for 10th December published Hitler's 'decree': '(1) As from today and until further notice I personally assume the direction of political organization; (2) As my chief adjutant for political organization I appoint Party Comrade Dr Ley, formerly Reichsinspekteur; (3) On Wednesday 14th December I will issue new instructions for strengthening the movement following the appeal of 6th January 1932—Adolf Hitler.' On 11th December Roehm issued the following: 'To the SA and SS. While Gregor Strasser is on sick-leave, the Führer is putting in force some organizational changes in the movement. SA and SS are not concerned in such measures. Being the soldierly kernel [*Kerntruppe*] of the movement and fully conscious of their duties and responsibilities they loyally stand in front of the Führer. (signed) Ernst Roehm.' On 19th December Strasser himself issued a statement through a news agency, the Telegraph Union: 'Member of the Reichstag Gregor Strasser asked us to state that he is remote from all press speculations about the alleged motives for his resignation from Party offices.'

25 In conversation with H. F., Schwerin-Krosigk said that Strasser was the first Nazi he ever met to engage in discussion. He found him a most reasonable man, the only Nazi in a senior position who might have steered the mass movement he represented into some kind of democratic channel. He was, however, an administrator rather than a leader. The second Nazi Schwerin-Krosigk met was Hitler him-

self, and that only an hour or so before being sworn in as a member of Hitler's first Cabinet.

26 According to Bredow (Freiburg, file N 97/2), he was informed that Strasser was still in Munich on 13th December, and on that day fetched his files and personal property from the Braunhaus.

27 Preserved at Freiburg.

28 Both letters preserved at Freiburg.

29 Among Strasser's more prominent supporters until Hitler's firm intervention were Wilhelm Frick (who did nothing, however, behind Hitler's back, merely supporting Strasser's compromise policy), Gottfried Feder, who had headed an economic planning department in the Party, Karl Kaufmann, Nazi Gauleiter of Hamburg and Reichstag deputy, Wilhelm Kube, Hinrich Lohse, H. Hinkel. Kaufmann claimed to H. F. that after Strasser's resignation he organized a petition, with thirty-two signatures, urging Hitler to reinstate Strasser. Among the signatories were Count Reventlow, Joseph Wagner, the Gauleiter Bürckel, and Murr of Stuttgart.

30 Heiden, 1944, p. 399. Wheeler-Bennett (1936, p. 425) claims that Roehm had to quell a possible attempt on Hitler's life originating from a section of the SA. See also Heiden, 1944, p. 410.

31 Goebbels, 1938, p. 189.

32 According to Heiden, 1944, p. 393, Adolf Müller, printer of Hitler's journal, the *Völkischer Beobachter*, threatened repeatedly during November 1932 to cease printing the paper.

33 See Heinrich Brüning, *Memoiren 1918–34* (Stuttgart, 1970), p. 639.

34 See Braun, 1940; Braun had a discussion on 6th January 1933 with Schleicher during which the latter said that he was arranging for Gregor Strasser to meet the President.

35 Brüning, op. cit.

36 The statement in Heiden, 1944, p. 406, to the effect that Strasser on his return from Italy sought a reconciliation with Hitler through Mutschmann, Gauleiter of Saxony, would seem to be without foundation, and was probably influenced by the statements in Goebbels's diaries. However, there is also a reference in Helmut Klotz's Newsletter for 23rd January that Göring was arranging a meeting between Hitler and Strasser at least to ensure that Strasser retains

his membership in the Party. (Koblenz.) Lohse, however (notes on Strasser, Hamburg), claims that Strasser cold-shouldered Mutschmann's attempts at mediation.

37 Braun, 1940.

38 IMT, XVI, p. 273.

39 *Nazi Conspiracy and Aggression*, II, pp. 922–4.

40 See also Papen's account of the lunch in his *Memoirs*, pp. 227 et seq.; Papen claims his discussions were aimed at bringing Hitler into Schleicher's cabinet. Papen told H. F. that his meeting with Hitler was undertaken at the request of 'my friend', Schleicher. However, in the *Memoirs* (p. 225), Papen makes no mention of Schleicher's being involved at this stage, or indeed having any advance knowledge of the meeting. He claims that Schroeder was one of the guests at a dinner given by the Herrenklub in Berlin, and puts the initiative for setting up the meeting entirely in Schroeder's camp; Schroeder, he claims, telephoned him to make the final arrangements and he agreed a date when he was travelling back to Berlin from his home in the Saar.

Schwerin-Krosigk, however, a member of both Papen's and Schleicher's cabinets, declared to H. F. that there could be little chance of secrecy, and both he and Schleicher knew a meeting was going to take place, at which once again Hitler was to be offered the Vice-Chancellorship. There was, indeed, a great deal of advance gossip about it. Papen himself said to H. F. that the meeting was not especially secret, though in the *Memoirs* he says he was surprised to find a photographer outside Schroeder's house. At the time he was researching our book on Goebbels, H. F. met Dr Helmuth Elbrechter, a physician who had been on the fringe of the Nazi movement in the mid 1920s and an associate of Karl Kaufmann, much disliked by Goebbels. The photographer was no pressman, but Dr Elbrechter himself, and he was there (he claimed) at the request of no less a person than Schleicher. He had by then left the Nazi movement and become a close acquaintance of Schleicher. Schwerin-Krosigk thinks Papen lied when he claimed he sent a letter reporting the meeting to Schleicher immediately after it was over, writing this from the Excelsior Hotel in Cologne. H. F., in Germany at the time, remembers the sensation the press report of the meeting (and photograph) caused when it was revealed in the press the following day. Schleicher had sent a messenger by air to collect the photograph so that it could be given to the press immediately. This shows that the meeting was not only known to Schleicher, but regarded by him in a hostile light. When H. F. asked Papen about this, he gave his word that Schleicher had double-crossed him, and had the event publicized in order to blacken him in the eyes of Hindenburg.

As for the money, Papen declared on his word of honour to H. F. that he had never obtained money for Hitler. He claimed the money which relieved the situation after the Cologne meeting had come from the Warburg bank.

In order to counter the bad publicity, Papen issued his own comment to the press on 5th January 1933: 'On the occasion of a visit to Düsseldorf to see my mother I had a political conversation with Herr Hitler in Cologne. I understand that a section of the Berlin press has indulged in comments which are freely invented, such as the suggestion that my conversation with Herr Hitler was motivated by opposition to the Herr Reich Chancellor or the present government. The opposite is the case.'

Eyck, 1964, II, p. 464, as would be expected, firmly rejects Papen's apologia, quoting the historian Theodor Eschenburg who was present at the dinner at the Herrenklub on 16th December 1932, at which he claims Papen in an address to the assembly demanded that the National Socialists be given a place in a coalition government, evoking 'great distress' in many of his listeners, who thought this 'a stab in Schleicher's back'. Hitler in the *Table Talk* (21st May 1942) claims that Papen undertook the contact with him at the instigation of Hindenburg, and that he had gained the impression at Cologne that 'his prospects were excellent'!

41 Quoted by Oswald Dutch, 1940, p. 168.

42 See Schacht, 1955, p. 297. Schacht offers no account of his backing for Hitler during 1932. See also IMT, XII, pp. 375, 398.

43 IMT, XIII, p. 27.

44 Nuremberg Documents, EC–457.

45 Nuremberg Documents, EC–456.

46 Dietrich, 1955, p. 172.

47 This decision was reached by a Steering Committee, on which the Nazis were represented. The Nazis did not want the Reichstag re-convened.

48 Papen, 1952, p. 235.

49 IMT, XVI, pp. 334–5.

50 See Gereke, 1972, pp. 226 et seq., for Schleicher's 'plot' to establish a military dictatorship, deposing the President, and using the regiments at Potsdam to assert authority.

51 Papen, 1952, p. 236.

52 A meeting took place on 27th January between Hindenburg and two representatives of the Ministry of Defence, General von Hammerstein and General von der Bussche-Ippenburg. It was a routine meeting which took place monthly. In divergent reports from these generals, Hammerstein claimed he had warned the President against a Papen-Hugenberg regime, which would be likely to embroil the Army with both the SA and the forces of the Left. Bussche, on the other hand, claims Hammerstein had warned the President against the SA and its attempts to infiltrate the Army. However, both generals claim that Hindenburg concluded with the statement—'Gentlemen, surely you do not think that I would appoint this Austrian corporal Chancellor of Germany.' See Eyck, 1964, II, p. 477, and K. D. Bracher, *Auflösung der Weimarer Republik* (Stuttgart, 1955), pp. 717, 733.

53 Papen, 1952, p. 239.

54 There is evidence that Hitler had been in touch with Blomberg, and that from Hitler's point of view Blomberg could be regarded as an important link between himself and the Army.

55 Papen claims that Hitler was present, but Goebbels's diary makes it clear that he could not have been. See Goebbels, 1938, p. 206.

56 Papen, 1952, p. 241.

57 Goebbels, 1938, p. 206.

58 Papen, 1952, p. 242. And see Note 50 above. Goebbels refers to the Schleicher 'plot' in his diary (p. 206) as the 'last dangerous move planned by our adversaries'. *See also* Wheeler-Bennett, 1953, pp. 281–6.

59 Quoted by Eyck, 1964, II, pp. 484–6, from Düsterberg's *Der Stahlhelm und Hitler*, (Wolfenbüttel, 1949), pp. 61 et seq.

60 Göring, *Germany Reborn* (London: Elkin Mathews, 1934), p. iii.

61 Goebbels, 1938, p. 207.

THE HUNDRED DAYS—II

1 Papen, 1952, p. 264.

2 Hitler's 'considerate' behaviour in Cabinet meetings during the first months was noted favourably by his Cabinet colleagues. In conversation with H. F. in 1967 Schacht, Papen and Schwerin-Krosigk all confirmed this. 'He was extremely well behaved,' said Schacht. 'Always ready to accept advice, and even ask for it,' said Schwerin-Krosigk. But it was, added Krosigk, a sham. Hitler had admitted to him initially that he knew very little about financial matters, and would rely on him for constant guidance. But Cabinet meetings became more and more infrequent from 1936 as Hitler increased his hold on German life.

3 Nuremberg Documents, PS–351.

4 Quoted by Knight-Patterson, 1945, pp. 566–7.

5 IMT, XVI, p. 279.

6 Papen, 1952, p. 265.

7 IMT, XVI, p. 279.

8 See Baynes, 1942, I, p. 252.

9 Nuremberg Documents, EC–439.

10 Nuremberg Documents, D–203.

11 Papen, 1952, p. 256.

12 The other, non-Nazi, members of Hitler's cabinet were: Neurath (Foreign Affairs), Blomberg (Defence), Schwerin-Krosigk (Finance) Guertner (Justice), Hugenberg (Economic Affairs and Agriculture), Seldte (Labour), Ruebenach (Communications and Post), Gereke (Employment).

13 Papen, 1952, p. 260.

14 The Communist Party leadership spoke of 'Trojan Horse tactics', an illusion in that many of their rank and file merely went over to the Brownshirts.

15 Quotation from Manvell and Fraenkel, 1962, p. 76.

16 See Manvell and Fraenkel 1962, pp. 77–8, for this and the following quotation.

17 See *Documents on British Foreign Policy*, Second Series, vol. IV, No. 246.

18 See Manvell and Fraenkel, 1962, p. 78.

19 Göring, *Germany Reborn* (London: Elkin Mathews, 1934), pp. 126–7.

20 See Papen, 1952, p. 269.

21 Hanfstaengl, 1957, pp. 201–2.

22 Goebbels, 1938, pp. 222–3.

23 IMT, IX, pp. 194–5.

24 Nuremberg Documents, PS–1856.

25 For an account of these divergencies concerning the origin of the Reichstag fire, see Appendix II.

26 According to Papen (1952, p. 270), quoting Rudolf Diels, some 4,000 Communist officials were arrested. Others fled to Moscow. H. F., the co-author of this book, himself escaped from Berlin at this dangerous period.

27 These Bulgarian Communists were arrested on the grounds of association of events, the arson in Sofia Cathedral in 1925. Dimitroff was the leader of the Central European section of the Communist International.

28 *Documents on German Foreign Policy 1918–1945*, Series C, Vol. I, pp. 93–4. For Papen's statement, see Papen, 1952, p. 269.

29 Torgler was retained in custody, but Dimitroff was later released and left Germany. (For the full story behind his release, see Manvell and Fraenkel, 1962, p. 350, note 13.)

30 Heiden, 1944, p. 440. According to Wheeler-Bennett (1936, p. 440), Papen even considered during this difficult period placing the President under protection. There is no mention of this in Papen's *Memoirs*.

31 Goebbels, 1938, p. 225.

32 The Ritter von Epp had been Roehm's original commanding officer. Epp had also been the original financial sponsor of the first newspaper associated with the Nazi party, the *Völkischer Beobachter*.

33 The origin of Heinrich Himmler's power stems from this 'take-over' of the State police. Later in the year, starting in October, Himmler gradually began to acquire authority over the Political Police (parallel to Göring's Gestapo force in Prussia) in the various

states. By March 1934 his authority was complete, except in Prussia. Already head of the SS, Himmler was formally granted control of the Gestapo in Prussia on 10th April 1934, Göring stepping back since he had other, more popular and grander duties to undertake. Himmler's impregnable status as head of the SS and of the national Gestapo, the political police, was now confirmed. See Manvell and Fraenkel, 1965, Chap. II.

34 In the Reichskanzlei files (R431/2683), Koblenz, there is a note by Groener concerning the voluminous evidence up to February 1932 alone on instances of Nazi terrorism reported by the public. At that stage it amounted to eight 'fat volumes'.

35 Rauschning, 1939, pp. 57–60.

36 See Knight-Patterson, 1945, pp. 583–5; and R. d' Harcourt, *The German Catholics* (London: Burns Oates, 1939). The Catholic Centre Party dissolved itself the following July.

37 Quoted by Knight-Patterson, 1945, p. 579.

38 The swastika (*Hakenkreuz*) was first used as a symbol by the newly established German National Socialist Workers' Party in May 1918. The Nazi flag took the form of a black swastika on a white circle on a red background, a design specially created by Hitler. The swastika itself is an ancient Indian symbol for vitality and fertility.

39 Actually, a term derived from motoring, 'everything *geared* the same way'.

40 See Baynes, 1942, I, p. 499.

41 Nuremberg Documents, PS–2962–63.

42 Rauschning, 1939, p. 87.

43 This ceremony had considerable historical significance, or was so intended by Hitler. The opening of parliament, the Reichstag, had always taken the form of a religious ceremony in the period of the Prussian Kings and German Emperors. Potsdam was associated with the Hohenzollerns, and the Garrison Church contained the grave of Frederick the Great. The choice of venue, therefore, was in pointed contrast to that chosen for the National Assembly in November 1919—Weimar, with its literary associations with Goethe and Schiller. The date, 21st March, was the same as that on which Bismarck had opened in 1871 the first Reichstag of the German Empire. (See Bullock, 1964, p. 267.) Hindenburg had stood

in the same church as far back as 1866, a subaltern returned from the Austro-Prussian war.

Hitler's enumeration, 'Third Reich', omitted any reference to the Weimar Republic, historically the proper Third Reich. The first was the Empire of Charlemagne, the second that established under Bismarck. Hitler claimed his régime to be the Third Reich in the history of Germany.

44 Both speeches are quoted in full in Knight-Patterson, 1945, pp. 568–70.

45 Text of bill given in Knight-Patterson, 1945, pp. 572–3.

46 See Knight-Patterson, 1945, p. 574.

47 The Centre Party was tricked by Hitler into modifying any opposition it might have entertained to the Enabling Bill. Hitler promised to send them a letter (which he never wrote) assuring them that all parties who supported him would be permitted to share in government in the form of a working party. They did, however, receive a letter from Hindenburg assuring them that Hitler had promised him as President not to use his powers without prior consultation. See Wheeler-Bennett, 1936, p. 448 for the text of this letter. See also Bullock, 1964, p. 226, and Heiden, 1944, p. 451.

48 See Knight-Patterson, 1945, p. 573.

Part 3 AFTERMATH—THE NIGHT OF THE LONG KNIVES

1 See Hilberg, 1961, pp. 90, 258; Manvell and Fraenkel, 1967, p. 224.

2 Günther Gereke was a Reichstag deputy, officer, jurist, landowner. He had been organizer of the Hindenburg Committee during the Presidential elections. After becoming Reich Commissioner for Re-Employment in Schleicher's government, he was retained in Hitler's Cabinet, but excluded in April 1933. In 1934 he was framed on an embezzlement charge by the Nazis and imprisoned for a while. He was later implicated in the July Plot of 1944. His memoirs, *Ich war königlich Preussischer Landrat*, were published in East Berlin in 1972.

3 Göring took great delight in claiming that the British originated the concentration camp system during the Boer War. See Manvell and Fraenkel, 1962, p. 89.

4 IMT, IX, p. 78.

5 Blomberg was created Field-Marshal in 1936. He was Minister of Defence up to 1938, when his dismissal was brought about by exposing his 'scandalous' marriage to a former prostitute. By this time he was out of favour with Hitler. He died in 1946 while acting as a witness at the Nuremberg Trial.

6 Rauschning, 1939, pp. 154–5.

7 Baynes, 1942, I, p. 554.

8 Heiden, 1944, p. 573.

9 Eden, 1962, p. 61; the quotations below from pages 62 and 71.

10 Baynes, 1942, I, p. 289.

11 Bullock supports the idea that Goebbels, the 'radical' in the Nazi hierarchy, had considerable sympathy for Roehm's standpoint. See Bullock, 1964, pp. 291, 297; Heiden, 1944, p. 578; Manvell and Fraenkel, 1960, p. 134. Goebbels's movements during June have been the subject of some suspicion. This is largely due to Otto Strasser, who claimed in his book *Hitler and I* that Goebbels had a secret meeting in mid June with Roehm in Munich at the Bratwurst-Glöckle inn, the results of which he reported to Hitler on his return. Hitler possibly used Goebbels as a go-between. In any event, the landlord and head waiter at the inn are said to have been among those purged on 30th June, on the grounds they had witnessed this, and possibly other meetings.

12 Baynes, 1942, I, pp. 315–16.

13 Baynes, 1942, I, pp. 287–8.

14 Strasser, 1940.

15 For a while the French Ambassador was under suspicion of aiding the supposed *coup d'état*, being involved with both Schleicher and Roehm. Later this was officially denied by the German Foreign Office. See Bullock, 1964, p. 295, and François-Poncet (the Ambassador concerned), 1946, pp. 138–41.

16 Baynes, 1942, I, p. 311.

17 A full version of the speech appears in Oswald Dutch's biography of Papen (1940), pp. 191–209. The original pamphlet version of the text of the speech was entitled *Rede des Vizekanzlers von Papen vor dem Universitätsbund, Marburg, am 17 Juni 1934* (Berlin: Germania-Verlag).

18 Papen, 1952, pp. 310–11.

19 Frick affidavit, Nuremberg Documents, PS–1852. Reproduced in *Nazi Crime and Aggression*, vol. II, p. 258.

20 IMT, XII, pp. 211–12.

21 For an account of this strange incident, see Manvell and Fraenkel, 1965, p. 43.

22 Baynes, 1942, I, p. 224.

23 IMT, XX, p. 249.

24 A case for aiding and abetting manslaughter during the Roehm purge was heard before judge and jury in Munich in May 1957, the defendants being Sepp Dietrich and Michael Lippert, both former officers in the SS. The verdict went against them, and they each received an 18 months' sentence. Among the witnesses were Dr Koch, governor of Stadelheim prison at the time, Prince Waldeck, who assisted Dietrich in carrying out the initial executions at Stadelheim, Dötter, a medical orderly who inspected the bodies, and Schaub, Hitler's chauffeur. All witnesses in a position to judge voiced their conviction that there was no danger whatsoever of an SA *Putsch* at the time Hitler initiated this action, whatever might have been the position at some later date. The counsels for the defence had attempted to call Hess as a witness, but the Allied authorities had refused to allow him to be approached.

25 Dietrich, 1955, p. 174.

26 For a fairly full account of the events of the day, see Gerald Reitlinger, *The SS* (London, Heinemann, 1956), pp. 64–5. Hanfstaengl (1957, pp. 350 et seq.) states that Roehm was under sedation. Hanfstaengl and Roehm had the same doctor, and the latter told him that he was himself at the Wiessee sanatorium overnight on 29th June, and as part of his treatment for Roehm's condition had put him under sedation.

27 Dietrich, 1955, pp. 28–9.

28 This account follows Frank's possibly biased statements in *Im Angesicht des Galgens* (Graefelfing: 1953), pp. 142–3. See also Manvell and Fraenkel, 1961, pp. 56–9.

29 Some historians, for example Gerald Reitlinger in *The SS* (London: Heinemann, 1956), p. 65, give the date of Roehm's death as 2nd July 1934. Testimony at the Munich trial gives the date as 1st July.

30 Gisevius, 1960, pp. 160–1.

31 According to Gisevius, giving evidence at the Nuremberg trial, Frick (Minister of the Interior) 'rushed out of the room [at the ministry]—it may have been about ten o'clock—in order to drive to Göring to find out what had happened in the meantime, only to be told by the latter that he, as Police Minister of the Reich, should go home now and not worry about what was still going to happen. In fact, Frick did go home, and during those two dramatic days he did not enter the Ministry.' (IMT, XII, p. 212.)

32 A typical regional reflection of events at the centre of the purge was given at the Nuremberg trial when Friedrich Karl Freiherr von Eberstein was giving evidence in relation to the SS. He was based as an SS commandant in Weimar, Thuringia. Eberstein reported, 'In the course of that day, 30 June, a certain SS Obersturmbannführer [Lieutenant-Colonel] Beutel came to me from the SS with a special order which he had received from Heydrich. He was a young man, this Beutel, and he did not know what he should do, and he came to me to obtain advice, as an older man. He had an order in which there were approximately 28 names and a postscript from which it appeared that some of these men were to be arrested and others were to be executed. This document had no signature on it and therefore I advised this officer to get positive clarification as to what should take place, and warned him emphatically against any rash action. Then, as far as I know a courier was sent to Berlin and then this courier brought back eight orders of execution which came from Heydrich. This order read approximately as follows: "By order of the Führer and Reich Chancellor" and then followed the name of the person concerned "so and so is condemned to death by shooting for high treason". These documents were signed by Heydrich. The signature was undoubtedly genuine and the documents were stamped with the official stamp of the office which Heydrich directed in Berlin; and on the basis of these documents eight members of the SA and the Party too, eight persons in all, were shot by the political police of Saxony in Dresden.' (IMT, XX, p. 250.)

33 The text of the document is preserved at Freiburg, N 42/93. Joachim von Ostau corroborated these facts in conversation with H. F. The American Ambassador, William E. Dodd, has an interesting entry in his published diary for April 13, 1935: 'From SS circles, I hear that General von Schleicher's next of kin, incited by the head of the army, General von Fritsch, are suing the German state for damages in connection with the shooting of their distinguished

kinsman last June. It will be recalled that the Reichswehr Ministry refused to give back to the SS the files and records of the shooting, after having obtained them for examination. The day before yesterday, four SS men called on the major in the Reichswehr Ministry in whose keeping these files are held. At the point of a pistol they demanded the records. Feigning to acquiesce, he bent down as if to take the documents out of his desk drawer but instead pressed an alarm button concealed there and gave them other papers to gain time. Shortly thereafter, the guards responded to the bell and came and arrested the four SS men, took them to the cellar of the building and there shot them. The ashes of the bodies were sent in a box to Himmler.' (Dodd, 1941, pp. 241-2.)

34 Gisevius, 1960, p. 158.

35 See Meissner, 1950, pp. 369-70.

36 Papen, 1952, pp. 315-17. Bodenschatz, Göring's aide, was Karl von Bodenschatz (later General) in the Luftwaffe. Baron Fritz-Günther von Tschirschky was Papen's personal adjutant who, according to Papen, 'in 1935, with the Gestapo after his life, emigrated from Vienna to England'. Bose was Papen's press councillor, Savigny his legal adviser.

37 Hess delivered a speech at Königsberg on 8th July 1934 in defence of the purge; it was linked with an appeal for peace addressed to the so-called Front-line Fighters of other countries. The text appeared in the *Frankfurter Zeitung*, 9th July 1934. The latter part of the speech appeared in a special English translation, *Germany and Peace: a Soldier's Message*, published for private circulation, with an Introduction giving an official account of the purge. See Murphy, 1941, pp. 9-14, and Baynes, 1942, II, p. 1714.

38 Baynes, 1942, I, p. 332.

39 For Hindenburg's telegrams, see Baynes, 1942, I, p. 332.

40 Baynes, 1942, I, pp. 321-4. For the term 'night of the long knives' see p. 315. Speaking of the 'second revolution' which Hitler alleged was being planned by an inner circle in the SA, the Führer claimed their term for it was the 'night of the long knives'. Heiden, 1944, p. 586, quotes a Nazi verse: 'Sharpen the long knives on the sidewalks, so that they can cut the priests' bodies better. . . . When the hour of retribution strikes, we will be ready for mass-murder.'

41 IMT, IX, pp. 84-5. The lie that it was Frau Schleicher's intervention which caused her accidental death was the specious invention

of the Nazis. Joachim von Ostau, a friend of the Schleichers, confirms the account given by Marie Güntel in her affidavit. He has done so personally to H. F.

42 For the hideous story of the accidental killing of Dr Willi Schmid, a distinguished music critic, in mistake for Willi Schmidt, an SA leader, see Manvell and Fraenkel, 1971, pp. 58–9.

43 IMT, XII, p. 265.

44 See the reference to this above in Hitler's speech to the Reichstag, p. 181.

45 The text of Hindenburg's testament can be found in Wheeler-Bennett, 1936, pp. 470–5.

46 The official figures of war deaths including the genocide campaign in Europe are:

German armed forces	2,850,000 killed
	200,000 lost PoWs
German civilian deaths	3,000,000 (some 500,000 through air raids)
West European losses	610,000 armed forces
	690,000 civilians
U.S. losses (total armed forces all fronts)	590,000
Deaths in Austria and Italy	750,000
Deaths in Poland	6,000,000
Deaths in the U.S.S.R.	13,600,000 armed forces (including 3.7 million while in captivity)
	7,000,000 civilians

This totals 35,290,000

Appendices

I Hitler's Policy of 'Legality' and the degree of support he received from the major industrialists and the middle classes

(i) The Policy of 'Legality'

General Groener, as Minister of Defence, issued an order in January 1930 forbidding Nazi propaganda to be spread within the Army; this, he maintained, was an act of treason. The Army must keep aloof from party politics. Nevertheless, young men with Nazi backgrounds had been infiltrating into the Army, and in the spring of 1930 three young officers of the garrison at Ulm were arrested and charged with spreading Nazi propaganda. The matter eventually had to come before the Supreme Court at Leipzig owing to a leak to Hitler's newspaper, the *Völkischer Beobachter*; Groener had hoped to be able to keep the hearing quiet by dealing with it internally at a court martial.

The trial opened shortly after the Nazi landslide in the Reichstag elections of September 1930, and Hitler was called on to act as star witness by Hans Frank, counsel for the defence. Hitler regarded the situation as a challenge. He declared, under oath, that the Nazis had no intention of replacing the Army; rather to create a great future for it. He asserted that he was only interested in attaining power by constitutional means: 'When we do possess constitutional rights, then we will form the State in the manner which we consider to be the right one.' When the President asked him if this also would be achieved by constitutional means, Hitler answered, 'Yes'. Questioned again by the President about his statement in 1923, before the Munich *Putsch* which had failed, that when he was victorious 'heads will roll in the sands', Hitler replied, 'I can assure you that when the National Socialist movement is victorious in this struggle ... the November 1918 revolution will be avenged and heads will roll.' Hitler's statements were fully reported in the *Völkischer Beobachter*.

According to K. D. Bracher in 'Die Technik der nationalsozial-
istischen Machtergreifung' (*Die Weg in die Diktatur*, pp. 151–74;
Munich: Piper Verlag, 1963), the weakness of the Weimar constitution
was 'that the very substance of the constitution could be eroded by
constitutional means'. This is what Hitler set out to do in the Reichstag.
As Hitler put it himself, 'The constitution merely indicates the place
of our struggle but not its aim. By entering all the legal units [*gesetzliche
Körperschaften*] we will make our party the decisive factor. But once we
control the constitutional powers we will put the state into the shape
we consider the right one.'

Baynes, in *The Speeches of Adolf Hitler*, gives many instances of
Hitler's stress on his policy of 'legality'. After the failure of the *Putsch*
in 1923, he said to Kurt Lüdecke:

> When I resume active work it will be necessary to pursue a new
> policy. Instead of working to achieve power by an armed *coup*,
> we shall have to hold our noses and enter the Reichstag against
> the Catholic and Marxist deputies. If out-voting them takes longer
> than out-shooting them, at least the results will be guaranteed by
> their own Constitution. (I, p. 168.)

To Brüning in 1931 he said:

> Herr Chancellor, if the German nation once empowers the National
> Socialist Movement to introduce a Constitution other than that
> which we have today, then you cannot stop it. Statesmen are
> primarily responsible for that which springs from their spirit
> and from their action, not for that which another brings about
> at a later time. . . .
>
> The German nation does not live for a Constitution, but it
> gives itself that Constitution which serves its life, and when a
> Constitution proves itself to be useless for that life, the nation
> does not die—the Constitution is altered. . . .
>
> We National Socialists respect the Constitution in our fight for
> political power, and we hope that we may be able to give the
> German people a new and a better Constitution. And here and now
> I promise you that we will respect whatever Constitution may be
> in force—and respect its spirit—more truly than the present
> system respects the Weimar Constitution. (I, p. 164.)

At the time of the Presidential elections he said: 'I had no personal
ambition to become President of Germany. . . . I opposed President
von Hindenburg on the sole ground that this system which we have
sworn to overthrow was taking refuge behind his reputation and
authority.' (I, p. 165.)

When asked about his refusal to enter the Papen government, he said:

> I will never sell my Movement for a mess of pottage. There can be no compromise. You cannot expect heroism from a people if the leaders make so-called bearable compromises. My lieutenants forgive me if I make a mistake. They would never do so if I renounced my principles. (I, p. 165.)

In October 1932 Hitler said in a speech in Munich:

> One cannot replace a parliamentary system by the mere creation of a new cabinet composed of men who belong to that system. If one wishes to supersede the parliamentary organization that cannot be done through a clique which seeks to impose its will on the people. That can only be done by means of an unparliamentary organization which has grown up already from below and has proceeded from the people. (I, p. 166.)

In April 1933 he spoke of the time he had to refuse to give way when others would have him join the cabinets of Papen or Schleicher:

> I know how hard it was for many always to keep their faith that after all the hour would come at last. We almost doubted in justice and in Providence. ... And then came the time when we had to say No, when for the first time it seemed that the way to power was opening before us, tempting us: and yet despite this we had to remain hard and say, 'No, it is not possible that way.' And for a second time the doors seemed to open and for the second time we had to say 'No, impossible'. And then at the third time the hour came and that was given to us which we could not but desire, which we had a right to desire, and at last the National Socialist movement entered into the great period of its historic action.

Papen's essential mistake, indeed the universal mistake of those who advocated so strongly during 1932 that Hitler must be brought into the government, lay in his belief that once Hitler was involved in some form of coalition cabinet, he, and through him his movement, could be tamed.

(ii) *Hitler and the Industrialists in 1932*

It would seem that the degree of financial support Hitler and the Nazi party actually received from the major industrialists before 1933 has been greatly exaggerated. Various authors, including Shirer, have supported this traditional view that big business was substantially responsible for bringing Hitler to power—for example, H. F. Hallgarten in *Hitler, Reichswehr und Industrie* (Frankfurt, 1955), Arthur

Schweitzer, *Big Business in the Third Reich* (London: Eyre & Spottiswoode, 1964), and Franz Neumann, *Behemoth: the Structure and Practice of National Socialism* (London: Gollancz, 1942). The Marxists in particular have enjoyed making capital out of exposing the capitalists. Louis P. Lochner has also studied the problem in *Tycoons and Tyrants* (Chicago: Regnery, 1954).

Schroeder, following the lunch with Papen and Hitler on 4th January 1933, is said to have managed to obtain financial support for Hitler, possibly amounting to a million marks. But there appears to be no hard evidence that there was any considerable sum subscribed on this occasion; indeed Hitler had to appeal for further help the following month. Papen categorically denied to H. F. obtaining money for Hitler on 4th January. Göring, Himmler and Strasser received unspecified sums of money to support their specialized interests, notably from Keppler's group of business 'friends', who at a later period were to give substantial sums to the SS. But any money given initially remained comparatively modest. Strasser, as a 'moderate', received some money from the coal industry (Bergbau-Verein).

It is more realistic to assume that the Nazis, apart from occasional windfalls, survived more by bluff than by payment. They were normally heavily in debt—for example, to their printers and to the Kaiserhof hotel. Hitler owed some 400,000 marks in back taxes (see Eyck, 1964, II, p. 466). Income, however, came in from various sources—royalties from *Mein Kampf* (some 15,600 marks in 1929), fees charged for giving exclusive interviews to American journalists, but most of all from gate money at political rallies. Dietrich (1955, p. 171) is categorical about this being the prime source of Party funds: 'Hitler's large-scale propaganda tours in the decisive year of 1932 were financed solely by the entrance fees at the gigantic mass demonstrations at which fantastic prices were often paid for seats in the first rows.' He holds that the funds contributed by industry during 1932 'were insignificant in amount'. However, Schacht, when interrogated prior to the Nuremberg Trial, claimed that the industrialists who assembled at Göring's house to hear Hitler speak on 20th February 1933 (see IMT, XIII, p. 29; and Bullock, 1964, p. 259) just prior to the March elections, collectively subscribed three million marks to be divided among the coalition parties of the Right. But this was after Hitler had become Chancellor.

It is the opinion of Heinrich August Winkler, Professor at the Free University of Berlin, writing in the *Vierteljahrshefte für Zeitgeschichte* (April 1972), pp. 175–91, that:

> ... the financial support from heavy industry could not bear

comparison with the mass-support from the middle strata; yet in the decisive three months before 30 January 1933 it helped substantially to reverse the political significance of Hitler's election set-back in November 1932, and to invalidate the last possible alternative to Hitler through Schleicher's attempts to branch out. Even more important and immediate at that particular phase, and one of the more direct causes of the Nazis' ascent to power, was the gratitude of the East-Elbe country squires. It was largely their fear of having the Osthilfe 'scandal' exposed which led to intense activity by the *Reichslandbund* in December 1932 and January 1933 to secure a government 'of national concentration'.

In a recent re-examination of the problem, Henry A. Turner Jnr ('Big Business and the Rise of Hitler'; *The American Historical Review*, 1969 pp. 56–70), has shown how little hard evidence there is concerning the extent of financial support Hitler received from the major industrialists in 1932, and how little real research into the matter has so far been undertaken. He shows that big business, dedicated to its own self-interest rather than to politics as such, was disillusioned with the Weimar government and the predominant Social Democratic Party, because of what they held to be the government's socialistic leanings. They tended, therefore, to align themselves with the Right-wing groups.

Thyssen and the octogenarian Emil Kirdorf were untypical of big business in turning, as they did, for a period to Hitler. Most of the more prominent industrialists feared radical elements in the Nazi Party. This was why Hitler increasingly went out of his way to stress the opposite at his various meetings with industrialists. On the whole, the industrialists (such as Friedrich Flick and the I. G. Farben enterprise) preferred to distribute such political contributions as they made among the various Right-wing parties, the Nazis receiving their share of this. These contributions were designed as a kind of insurance policy.

Only twenty industrialists, few of them really prominent, signed the 1932 petition to Hindenburg to give Hitler government office. Increased support for Hitler followed on Schleicher's appointment as Chancellor. Schleicher was thoroughly disliked by the businessmen for what they regarded as his radical views; the man they really preferred was Papen.

Hitler's more private view of the industrialists was expressed to Rauschning (1939, p. 30): 'I shall not be deceived by these captains of industry either! Captains indeed! I should like to know what ships they navigate! They are stupid fools who cannot see beyond the wares they peddle! The better one gets to know them, the less one respects them.' 'The question of finance,' adds Rauschning, 'has never troubled him much.'

(iii) *Who voted for Hitler?*

There has been considerable division of opinion on this issue between sociologists; for example, Reinhard Bendix in *Class, Status and Power* (edited by S. M. Lipset and R. Bendix; Glencoe, Illinois, 1953) began by asserting the commonly held view that the sudden rise in Nazi support at the Reichstag elections between 1928 (2·6 per cent of the vote) and 1930 (18·3 per cent) was due to the disaffected of all classes in the community. Subsequently, however, Lipset convinced Bendix that the shift of non-voters to the Nazis came only in 1933, whereas in 1930 their principal support came from middle-class extremists. However, in 'Who Voted for Hitler?' (*The American Journal of Sociology*, vol. 74, No. 1, July 1968; University of Chicago Press), Karl O'Lessker, subjecting the available statistics to more sophisticated analysis, including the use of a computer, reviewed the voting returns and reached the conclusion that a combination of former non-voters (the apathetic, roused by social distress and other factors) and traditional men of the Right gave Nazism its first great success, and the bulk of the middle-class vote went to Hitler only after the Nazis had established themselves as the largest non-Marxist party in Germany. What have to be explained are the following incontrovertible facts:

May 1928	Nazi share of vote 2·6 per cent (0·81 million out of 30·75 million votes cast); 10·47 million voters abstained.
September 1930	Nazi share of the vote 18·3 per cent (6·38 million out of 35 million votes cast, representing over 4 million extra votes); 8·02 million voters abstained.
July 1932	Nazi share of the vote 37·3 per cent (13·7 million out of 36·9 million votes cast, representing almost 2 million extra votes); 7·34 million voters abstained.
November 1932	Nazi share of the vote 33·1 per cent (11·73 million out of 35·5 million votes cast, representing a loss of 1·4 million votes); 8·92 million voters abstained.
March 1933*	Nazi share of the vote 43·9 per cent (17·27 million out of 39·34 million votes cast, representing 3·9 million extra votes); 5·34 million voters abstained.

*After Hitler's accession to the Chancellorship.

Quoting O'Lessker on the 1930 election:

> The most important single source of the new Nazi strength in 1930
> came from voters who had formerly supported the conservative,
> ultranationalist DNVP: in statistical terms, fully 38 per cent of the
> variance in the Nazi vote can be attributed to this source. But a
> close second in importance, accounting for some 32 per cent of the
> variance, were the previous non-voters: that group which in
> Lipset's analysis, appeared to be wholly unrelated to the group of
> new Nazi voters. And third in importance—much weaker than the
> preceding two but by no means negligible—were those who had
> formerly voted for non-Catholic middle-class parties; these
> accounted for perhaps 23 per cent of the total variance. . . .
>
> It was a combination of new voters and defecting Nationalists
> that transformed the Nazi party into a true mass movement in
> September 1930.

O'Lessker supports Lipset's comment on the July 1932 election:
'the Nazis gained disproportionately from the ranks of the center and
liberal parties rather than from the conservatives.' The explanation for
the drop in the November 1932 election favoured by O'Lessker is:
'those who stayed away from the polls in November were predomin-
antly those customary non-voters who had been lured to the polls for
the first time in 1930 by the incendiary appeals of Nazism.'

July 1932 saw the virtual collapse of the non-Catholic middle-class
parties, Nazism appearing to their former voters as the best insurance
against a Communist take-over. In November, however, it appears to
O'Lessker that while the middle-class voters stayed with Hitler, over
800,000 of the Nationalists went back to their original parties, and some
1·2 million of the apathetic, who had voted Nazi before, stayed away
from the polls. The Communists achieved their maximum votes in
1932—5·28 million (14·3 per cent of the vote) in July and 5·98 million
(16·85 per cent) in November.

The significant point is that the 'legitimate peak' of the July elections was really an embarrassment for the Party, which could hardly
make further headway at the polls. It was not that electoral triumph
that took Hitler to power but the setback in November, with the loss of
2 million voters and 34 seats. The 'Bolshie Bogy' played its part in
creating the feeling that the country could not afford to let the NSDAP
break asunder.

II Who Fired the Reichstag?
by Heinrich Fraenkel

The Reichstag was ablaze on the night of 27th February 1933, exactly four weeks after the lavish torch parade of 30th January to celebrate Hitler's appointment as Chancellor. The historic consequences of the event were as speedy as they were momentous. Within twenty-four hours, on 28th February, the aged President had been induced to sign the emergency decree suspending all civil liberties in the cause of 'the protection of the people and the State'; just over three weeks later, on 23rd March, those 'emergency' powers were perpetuated by passing the Enabling Act which 'constitutionally' changed the Coalition Government of 30th January (Hitler's cabinet had nine non-Nazis to three Nazis in it) into a police state with dictatorial powers for the Führer.

The new, young régime, and certainly no other Party, had everything to gain from the Reichstag fire, so it was immediately assumed that they had caused the arson themselves, all the more so when their strenuous efforts to saddle the Communists with the crime came to nothing. Not a shred of real evidence could be produced. For almost thirty years no one seriously doubted that the Nazis had been behind the arson, using the half-demented young Dutchman as their cover. But during the past ten years there has been much controversy concerning a book published by Fritz Tobias in 1962, in which he claimed that van der Lubbe caused the fire single-handed. We have never accepted this claim, which would seem now to be refuted conclusively by recent, very thorough research which is still in process of being compiled and published.

This controversy about who caused the fire needs some elucidation, however brief. It is necessary to go back over the key events starting three days prior to the fire. On 24th February Göring initiated what was to become the annihilation of the German Communist Party. Its headquarters, the Karl Liebknecht House, were raided, and in its cellars, which Göring called the 'catacombs', was found what he claimed to be documentary evidence of planned insurrection, the assassination of the principal members of the cabinet, and a map alleged to be marked for key-points of a *Putsch*—though he only made this claim on 2nd March, *after* the fire. Göring claimed he would publish the documents; however, he did not do so. What had actually been confiscated in the 'catacombs' was normal party literature.

Arriving at the scene of the fire within half an hour of the first sighting of van der Lubbe with his torch, Göring lost no time in making his accusations that the Communists were the culprits, and that the fire was part of a Communist conspiracy against the new government. Goebbels claimed that Communism had made its last attempt to cause disorder by means of fire and terrorism, while Hitler, standing in the stench of the ruined building, cried: 'This is a beacon [*Fanal*] from Heaven!'

The great fire trial months later at the Leipzig Supreme Court was intended to be a display of Nazi rectitude and Communist culpability, but it turned out to be the only serious setback sustained by the régime during its first triumphant years. After seven months of careful preparation the trial started on 21st September and lasted till 23rd December. In the dock, apart from the young Dutchman, was Torgler, leader of the Communists in the Reichstag, who had left the House less than an hour before the discovery of the fire, as well as three Bulgarian Communists, including the fiery Dimitroff who, on 4th November, was to succeed in making Göring lose his temper when he was acting as a witness, and indeed make a fool of himself in front of the world's journalists assembled for the trial. The prosecution had hoped to make the Bulgarians suspect by linking the Reichstag fire with the arson of the Sofia cathedral in 1925, some seven years earlier. But they had in the end to be acquitted whilst van der Lubbe, a willing victim, was sentenced to death and executed.

During the summer, in advance of the Leipzig trial a 'Legal Enquiry into the causes of the Reichstag fire' took place in London on the premises of the Law Society under Lord Marley's chairmanship and with Sir Stafford Cripps among a group of prominent lawyers from various countries, such as Dennis Pritt, the London K.C., Moro Giafferi and Gaston Bergery from France, Georg Branting from Sweden and Arthur Garfield Hays from the United States.

While, obviously, this 'legal enquiry' gained much support from international Communism, it would be wrong to say (and, indeed, disproved by the names of the distinguished lawyers mentioned above) that it was Communist-inspired. However, the much-publicized *Brown Book of the Hitler Terror* was published in Paris under Communist auspices in 1933 with the primary object of incriminating

Göring; this was followed up by a second Brown Book a year later. One could certainly claim that the factual research involved in the Brown Books was indifferent; it could hardly be otherwise in circumstances of closed frontiers, strict censorship, and incarcerated witnesses. However, the crimes and bestialities actually committed during the first months of concentration camps, arbitrary arrests and unchecked torturing and plundering, were so numerous that some part of the documentation was authentic. But much was exaggerated, distorted, and some was sheer invention, such as the celebrated Oberfohren document, the alleged confession by a right-wing politician who (it was claimed) had been murdered because he knew too much.

The inaccuracies and inventions of the Brown Book provided a field-day for Fritz Tobias who was able to produce carefully documented refutations even of such items as the Oberfohren document, which was known to be a Communist forgery long before Tobias set to work. But he was primarily concerned to advance his astonishing (and we think impossible) thesis that Marinus van der Lubbe was the sole fire-raiser, unaided by the Nazis and quite unknown to them. Dr Tobias was a civil servant in Hanover, and a long-time member of the Social Democratic party; he was most certainly not some kind of neo-Nazi intent on exculpating the Hitler régime. Weight was lent to his argument when, before its appearance in the form of a bulky book, it was serialized in the distinguished and progressive journal, *Der Spiegel*. As a result, it gained rather more credence than it deserved, and was accepted uncritically by eminent historians in this country and elsewhere, especially in Germany.

More recently, though, there has been a steady swing against Tobias's argument. Professor Bracher in Cologne is among a number of distinguished historians who deny the possibility of Lubbe as the sole fire-raiser. Foremost among those who take a special interest in the subject is Professor Walther Hofer of Berne University, aided by equally well-known historians such as Professor Eugen Kogon and Professor Golo Mann.

For some years a group of experts headed by Professor Hofer have been conducting a thorough investigation of the Reichstag fire, and have recently published the first of three volumes to deal with the matter conclusively. In this first volume, *Der Reichstagsbrand* (Arani Verlag, Berlin, 1972) a painstakingly precise investigation of the technical aspects of the fire is set out by experts in the field of chemistry, fire-fighting, and other specialities involved in the starting of a fire of such magnitude. It is established beyond any doubt that, given the brief time involved and the primitive means available to Lubbe, it would have been utterly impossible for any one man to set the building alight on this scale, let alone a man without knowledge of the premises and gravely handicapped, both mentally and physically, as Lubbe undoubtedly was. (Precisely the same conclusion was reached by the experts heard in the Leipzig court.)

Tobias had ignored Lubbe's incapabilities, along with certain other evidence which failed to fit his thesis. Following a cruel practical joke played on him in his youth by his workmates—they pulled a mason's bag over his head and some of the chalk entered his eyes—Lubbe became almost totally blind. Simon Harteveld of Leiden, who trained Lubbe as a mason's apprentice, among others who had known him, confirmed to me that in order to read or write he had to bring a paper to within an inch or two of his eyes. Tobias ignores the implications of this, merely mentioning that he was *sehbehindert*, which implies that his sight was slightly impaired.*

More important than this physical handicap were his mental idiosyncrasies. He was a compulsive exhibitionist and it is wrong for Tobias to claim as an achievement that Lubbe, as an athlete, seriously attempted to swim the English Channel. He did, in fact, make more than one 'attempt', though there is no evidence he was in any way an exceptional swimmer. He never had the money to afford to have a boat to accompany him, which all genuine channel-swimmers must have. But he did not need one. All that happened was that he made an exhibition of his body being greased before an audience and a press photographer. Then he would wade in, swim for a hundred yards or so, and return, claiming the currents were unsuitable and that he would try again later.

My research into Lubbe's earlier history produced various accounts of significant actions of his, such as his behaviour during a major strike at the Tielemann factory. When the management asked for the 'ringleaders' to reveal themselves, Lubbe (who was far too young at the time to have had anything to do with the strike organization) stepped forward, claiming to be the only 'ringleader' and to be prepared to accept any punishment, provided none of his comrades was victimized. A similar incident on a minor level took place at another factory, where he claimed to have smashed several windows single-handed, when the damage had in fact been done by some of his workmates.

Four important witnesses for eliciting the truth about Lubbe's connection with the Reichstag fire are not mentioned at all in Tobias's book. One of these is Dr Stomps of Haarlem, a lawyer sent by the Dutch authorities to attend the Leipzig trial. He was given the opportunity to see Lubbe in his cell in the presence of an official interpreter who quietly sat in a corner making his notes and not interfering. The inter-

*For more detail on this and the points below, see Manvell and Fraenkel, 1962, pp. 380–2.

view lasted an hour, during which Lubbe adopted his usual 'hangdog' attitude, his head bowed, his face expressionless. Dr Stomps had brought letters, photographs, and messages from Lubbe's family and friends; Lubbe thrust them into his pocket without a glance, and hardly seemed to listen when the lawyer explained what could and should be done for his defence. After much wasted argument, Dr Stomps lost patience and demanded: 'So you don't want us to help you? You don't want us to try to save you from the hangman?' Now for the first time Lubbe looked up with a grin, and uttered the only word he spoke during the interview, 'Nej! No!'. He shook his head vigorously and was taken away, still grinning.

Another vitally important witness to Lubbe's character is Simon Harteveld, to whom I spoke before his death in Leiden. Harteveld not only trained Lubbe when he was a mason's apprentice, but more importantly became his political mentor. Nothing could be more significant than Harteveld's indignation, almost thirty years after the event, when he told me how Otto Katz (later to be called André Simon, and hanged in the Prague Slansky trial) had tried to persuade him to come to London to take part in the 'legal enquiry' mentioned above. The old man shook his head angrily, saying 'Fancy such people asking *me* to appear as a witness!' He said 'such people' whenever he referred to anyone representing the official Communist party line. Otto Katz was a party man, sent by Willy Münzenberg. Harteveld's own politics, in which he indoctrinated Lubbe in his youth, envisaged the 'direct action' used by the Soldiers' and Workers' Councils of 1918–19.

Among witnesses pointing positively in the direction of Nazi involvement is Bertus Smit, who as head of the then Dutch equivalent of the SA was a close friend of the German Brownshirt leader, Karl Ernst, later shot during the Roehm purge. He told me about a convivial meeting he had with Ernst a few weeks after the fire; when asked whether he and other Storm Troopers had been involved in the fire, he answered, 'If I said Yes, I'd be a bloody fool; if I said No, I'd be a bloody liar!' The Dutchman looked up his diary for the exact words, and the very term (*blöder Hund* for bloody fool) seemed to me to ring true, in fact too true to have been made up by a foreigner not all that conversant with German vernacular.

Further revealing evidence was provided by Mimi Storbeck who, when I went to see her early in 1962, was a naturalized Dutch subject in charge of a children's home in Haarlem. Twenty-nine years earlier, when she was barely twenty (and, incidentally, the daughter of a Social Democrat Reichstag deputy), she was a district nurse in Berlin and in that official capacity, a few days before the fire, she had had to deal with Lubbe, a vagrant who wanted 20 marks while he was waiting, he said, for a job he hoped to get. He was accompanied by two 'friends' who were known to her as local Storm Troopers, and who did most of the talking. She testified to the near-blindness of the Dutchman, whose request for maintenance money was rejected; he was offered, instead, a rail ticket to the Dutch frontier. The SA men created such a storm over the rejection of Lubbe's demands for money that the police had to be called upon to get rid of them. This testimony supports other evidence that the Dutchman had made some initial contacts on the lowest SA level which would make it appear likely that this odd foreign vagrant with his strange predilections should be brought to the notice of people higher up in the Brownshirt movement. Karl Ernst was head of the SA in Berlin.

It is important to our argument that Lubbe represented an almost textbook case of what psychiatrists term the 'Herostratus complex'. Herostratus burned the temple of Ephesos merely to achieve fame, and can be regarded as successful since his name is used to this day in connection with fire-raising. But in Lubbe's case, as we have seen, his complex was coupled with an equally compulsive desire to 'do good', usually in the context of what he held to be some form of social justice. It was obvious from his attitude throughout that he was proud to be the man who set the Reichstag alight for who knows what 'good cause' in his muddled mind.

It might well be argued, of course, that for the student of history all that matters are the consequences of the fire—that is, the emergency decree the following day and the Enabling Act of 23rd March voted by a firm majority in an assembly reduced to a rump. It matters, perhaps, little whether the establishment of a police state in Germany was precipitated by a crime of arson devised by the Nazis themselves or by a fluke which happened to play into their hands. Even so, it is the duty of historians to try to ascertain the facts. The problem, in any case, is one of peculiar fascination.

To sum up, in our view, more especially following the evidence given at the Leipzig trial and the current investigations of Professor Hofer and his associates,

(i) a group of trained Nazis (probably SA men) entered the Reichstag building during the evening of 27th February, using some unspecified means of entrance which may or may not have been the underground passage connecting the building with the Reichstag President's palace, which was, of course, under Göring's control;

(ii) this group sprayed the assembly hall and other areas of the building with the inflammatory chemical which it was well-known the Nazis had been using to burn down the election displays of opposition parties;

(iii) this group then withdrew, and left Lubbe alone in the impregnated area of the building with torches and primitive firelighters adequate to set the wooden parts of the edifice alight. Although the arson involved not only the great assembly hall, but other areas as well, it was demonstrated during the Leipzig trial that it would just be possible for Lubbe to set all this alight in the limited time testified by the witnesses who saw the start of the fire. During the trial the very willing Lubbe was able to demonstrate the route he followed with his torch, and he was timed by stopwatch.

III Hitler's Own Account of His Seizure of Power

Looking back on the period some ten years later, Hitler gave his own biased and far from factually accurate account of the seizure of power in his 'table talk' of May 1942. (*Hitler's Table Talk*, p. 495 et seq.)

When I roundly refused to consider any compromise and accept the Vice-Chancellorship in a von Papen Cabinet, and after the vain and treacherous attempts of General Schleicher, supported by Gregor Strasser, had failed to split the solid unity of the Party, political tension reached its zenith. Not only did Schleicher fail to win over a log-rolling majority in the Reichstag, but as a result of his go-slow policy as regards national economy, the number of unemployed rose, during the first 15 days of his regime, by no less than a quarter of a million. In January 1933—one month, that is, after his assumption of office—Schleicher saw no other alternative but to dissolve the Reichstag and form a military Cabinet, upheld solely by the support of the President of the Reich.

But the idea of a military dictatorship, in spite of his great confidence in General Schleicher, filled old von Hindenburg with the liveliest apprehension. For in his heart of hearts the Old Gentleman was opposed to soldiers meddling in politics; besides that, he was not prepared to go further in the delegation of political plenipotentiary power than he felt himself able to do in accordance with his constitutional oath.

Faced with this situation of extreme political tension, von Hindenburg, through the intermediary of von Papen, approached me, and in the famous Cologne conversations explored the ground. For myself, I had the impression that all was going well for me. I made it quite clear, therefore, that I would not hear of any compromise, and threw myself, heart and soul, personally into the Lippe electoral campaign.

After the electoral victory at Lippe—a success whose importance it is not possible to over-estimate—the advisers of the Old Gentleman approached me once more. A meeting was arranged at Ribbentrop's house with Hindenburg's son and Herr von Papen. At this meeting I gave an unequivocal description of my reading of the political situation, and declared without mincing words that every week of hesitation was a week irretrievably wasted. The situation, I said, could be saved only by an amalgamation of all parties, omitting, of course, those fragmentary bourgeois parties which were of no importance and which, in any case, would not join us. Such an amalgamation, I added, could be successfully assured only with myself as Reich Chancellor.

At this juncture I deliberately neglected my work within the Party in order to take part in these negotiations, because I considered it of the highest importance that I should legitimately take over the Chancellorship with the blessing of the Old Gentleman. For it was only as constitutionally elected Chancellor, obviously, and before undertaking any measures of reconstruction, that I could overcome the opposition of all the other political parties, and avoid finding myself in constant conflict with the Wehrmacht. My decision to obtain power constitutionally was influenced primarily by my knowledge of the attitude of the Wehrmacht vis-à-vis the Chancellorship. If I had seized power illegally, the Wehrmacht would have constituted a dangerous breeding-place for a *coup d'état* in the nature of the Roehm *Putsch*; by acting constitutionally on the other hand, I was in a position to restrict the activities of the Wehrmacht to its legal and strictly limited function. . . .

On 24 January 1933—the day after the SA assault on the Karl Liebknecht-Haus in Berlin had resulted in a tremendous loss of prestige for the Communist Party and caused great indignation in Berlin—I was again invited by von Papen to a conference. Von Papen told me at once that Schleicher had formally asked the Old Gentleman for plenipotentiary powers to set up a military dictatorship, and that the latter had refused and had stated that he proposed inviting Adolf Hitler, in the role of leader of a national front, to accept the Chancellorship and to form a Government, with the proviso that von Papen should be nominated vice-Chancellor.

I replied that I took cognisance of the offer, and, without permitting any discussion of detail, stated the conditions under which I was prepared to accept. These were the immediate dissolution of the Reichstag and the organization of new elections. Under the pretext that I should be away from Berlin, I avoided a tentative suggestion that I should have a ten-minute talk with the Old Gentleman. Mindful of the experiences of the previous year, I was anxious to avoid giving rise to any undue optimism within the Party, such as was invariably the case whenever I was received by the Old Gentleman.

I took the opportunity in this conversation with Herr von Papen of pressing home my advantage and carrying a step further the negotiations started by Göring for the tentative formation of a Government. It was with the German Nationalists that the negotiations proved most difficult, for Geheimrat Hugenberg displayed a greed for portfolios out of all proportion to the strength of his party, and, because he feared that he would probably lose a great number of votes in any new elections, he would not hear of an early dissolution of the Reichstag. On 27 January, after a short absence from Berlin, I had a personal conference with Hugenberg, but we were unable to agree.

The negotiations for the formation of a Government were further complicated by General Schleicher and his clique, who did all in their power to wreck them. General von Hammerstein, Schleicher's most trusted colleague and Commander-in-Chief of the Army, was even stupid enough to have the impertinence to ring me up and tell me that 'under no circumstances would the Wehrmacht sanction my acceptance of the Chancellorship'. If Herr Schleicher and his friends really imagined that they could shake my determination with puerilities of this sort, they were grievously mistaken. My only reaction was to impress emphatically on Göring to accept as Minister of the Reichswehr only a General who enjoyed my confidence, such as General von Blomberg, who had been recommended to me by my friends in East Prussia.

On 28 January the Weimar Republic finally collapsed. Schleicher resigned, and von Papen was instructed to sound the various parties with a view to the formation of a new Government. For my part, I at once declared that any half-measures were now unacceptable to me. The 29th, naturally, was buzzing with conferences, in the course of which I succeeded in obtaining Hugenberg's agreement to the dissolution of the Reichstag in return for the promise to give him the number of seats in the new Government which he had originally demanded for his Party, convincing him that with the Reichstag in its present form it would be impossible to achieve anything.

The next afternoon Göring brought me the news that on the morrow the Old Gentleman proposed officially to invite me to accept the Chancellorship and the task of forming the Government.

Late in the afternoon, we were surprised by a completely insane action by Schleicher and his clique. According to information received from Lieut.-Colonel von Alvensleben, General von Hammerstein had put the Potsdam garrison on an alarm footing; the Old Gentleman was to be bundled off to East Prussia to prevent his interference, and the Wehrmacht was to be mobilized to stop by force the assumption of power by the NSDAP.

My immediate counter-action to this planned *Putsch* was to send for the Commander of the Berlin SA, Graf Helldorf, and through him alert the whole SA of Berlin. At the same time I instructed Major Wecke of the Police, whom I knew I could trust, to prepare for a sudden seizure of the Wilhelmstrasse by six police battalions. Through Herr von Papen I informed the Old Gentleman of the Schleicher clique's intentions. Finally, I instructed General von Blomberg (who had been selected as Reichswehr Minister elect) to proceed at once, on arrival in Berlin at 8 a.m. on 30 January, direct to the Old Gentleman to be sworn in, and thus be in a position, as Commander-in-Chief of the Reichswehr, to suppress any possible attempts at a *coup d'état*.

By eleven o'clock on the morning of 30 January, I was able to inform the Old Gentleman that the new Cabinet had been formed, and that the majority in the Reichstag required by constitution to enable it to function had been acquired. Shortly afterwards I received at the hands of the Old Gentleman my appointment as Chancellor of the German Reich. . . .

Apart from the difficulties inherent in the formation of a Government, I very quickly realized that the Old Gentleman had called upon me to accept the Chancellorship only because he could see no other constitutional way out of the political impasse. This was obvious from the number of conditions he imposed. He informed me, for instance, that all questions connected with the Reichswehr, the Foreign Office and overseas appointments remained in his hands. He further decided that von Papen must be present whenever he received me officially; and it was only after much hesitation and the intervention of Meissner that the Old Gentleman was pleased to sign the order for the dissolution of the Reichstag, which I had managed to rattle through during the session of 31 January.

Within a week or so, however, my relations with Hindenburg began to improve. One day, when he wanted to see me about something or other, I invited his attention to the custom he himself had established—namely, that I could not visit him except in the company of von Papen—and pointed out that the latter was at the moment away from Berlin. The Old Gentleman replied that he wished to see me alone, and that in future the presence of von Papen could be regarded as unnecessary. Within three weeks we had progressed so far that his attitude towards me became affectionate and paternal. Talking of the elections fixed for 5th March, he said, 'What are we going to do if you fail to get a majority? We shall have the same difficulties all over again.' When later the first results of the elections began to come in, our relations had attained such a degree of frank cordiality, that the Old Gentleman exclaimed in a voice charged with real satisfaction: 'Hitler wins!' And when the overwhelming victory of the National Socialists was confirmed, he told me straight out that he had always been averse to the parliamentary game and was delighted that the comedy of elections was now done with, once and for all. . . .

For the fact that the Old Gentleman so faithfully followed my lead and always did his utmost to understand my intentions, I am deeply grateful. Once I had won him over to my side the Old Gentleman's solicitude towards me was truly touching. Again and again he said that he had a Chancellor who was sacrificing himself for his country, and that often he could not sleep at night for thinking of 'his Chancellor flying from one part of the Reich to another in the service of the people'. What an eternal shame it was, he added, that such a man must belong to one Party.

The most glaring of the inaccuracies in this 'table talk' is Hitler's claim that in the first fifteen days of Schleicher's Chancellorship the number of unemployed rose by 250,000. The very opposite is the case, and it is indeed significant that the economic crisis had been abating ever since the late autumn. The significance lies in the fact that all through the fourteen years of struggling for power Hitler's ups and downs were in a precisely inverse ratio to the prosperity of the country. His first bid for power in November 1923 happened on the very day on which inflation ($1 = 4.2 million million Marks) reached its absolute peak. A decline of the Party came at the time of Locarno and the Stresemann-Briand era envisaging 'prosperity round the corner'. With the economic crisis of the late 1920s the Party grew commensurate to ever more millions of unemployed, the 'peak' of the July elections coinciding with the peak of the dole statistics.

Bibliography

ADOLPH, HANS, 1971. *Otto Wels und die Politik der Deutschen Sozial-demokratie 1894–1930.* Berlin.

BAYNES, NORMAN H., 1942. *The Speeches of Adolf Hitler.* 2 vols. London, Oxford University Press.

BERNARD, GEORG, 1933. *Die Deutsche Tragödie: Selbstmord einer Republik.* Prague, Orbis.

BRAUN, OTTO, 1940. *Von Weimar zu Hitler.* 2nd edition. New York, Europa Verlag.

BREDOW, KLAUS, 1934. *Hitler rast.* Saarbrücken.

BULLOCK, ALAN, 1964. *Hitler: a Study in Tyranny.* Revised edition; first published 1952. London, Odhams.

DIETRICH, OTTO, 1955. *The Hitler I Knew.* London, Methuen.

DODD, WILLIAM E., 1941. *Ambassador Dodd's Diary.* London, Gollancz.

DUTCH, OSWALD, 1940. *The Errant Diplomat: the Life of Franz von Papen.* London, Edward Arnold.

EDEN, ANTHONY (the Earl of Avon), 1962. *The Eden Memoirs: Facing the Dictators.* London, Cassell.

EYCK, ERICH, 1964. *A History of the Weimar Republic.* London, Oxford University Press.

FLEDERLEIN, MARTIN FRIEDRICH, 1966. *Der Deutsche Osten und die Regierungen Brüning, Papen, Schleicher.* Würzburg (doctoral thesis).

FRANÇOIS-PONCET, ANDRÉ, 1946. *Souvenirs d'une Ambassade à Berlin.* Paris, Flammarion.

GEREKE, GÜNTHER, 1972. *Ich war königlich Preussischer Landrat.* Berlin (East), Union Verlag.

GISEVIUS, H. B., 1960. *Bis Zum Bitteren Ende.* Revised edition. Originally translated as *To the Bitter End.* London, Cape, 1948.

GOEBBELS, JOSEPH, 1938. *My Part in Germany's Fight.* London, Paternoster Library.

HANFSTAENGL, ERNST, 1957. *Hitler—the Missing Years.* London, Eyre and Spottiswoode.

1970. *Zwischen Weissem und Braunem Hause.* Munich.

Bibliography

HEIDEN, KONRAD, 1944. *Der Führer*. London, Gollancz.

HILBERG, RAUL, 1961. *The Destruction of the European Jews*. London, W. H. Allen.

HITLER, ADOLF, 1939. *Mein Kampf*. London, Hurst and Blackett.

1953. *Hitler's Table Talk 1941–44*. London, Weidenfeld & Nicolson.

HORN, WOLFGANG, 1972. *Führerideologie und Parteiorganisation in der NSDAP*. Düsseldorf, Droste Verlag.

INTERNATIONAL MILITARY TRIBUNAL. *The Trial of the Major War Criminals. Proceedings*, vols I–XXIII. *Documents in Evidence*, vols XXIV–XLII, Nuremberg 1947–9. The *Proceedings* were also published by His Majesty's Stationery Office (HMSO) in London in 22 parts (the edition referred to in this book). Translations into English of many of the documents used in evidence were published by the U.S. Government Printing Office under the title *Nazi Conspiracy and Aggression* in eight main and two supplementary volumes.

KNIGHT-PATTERSON, W. M., 1945. *Germany from Defeat to Conquest*. London, Allen and Unwin.

KORDT, ERICH, 1947. *Wahn und Wirklichkeit*. Stuttgart, Deutsche Verlagsanstalt.

MANVELL, ROGER, and FRAENKEL, HEINRICH, 1960. *Dr Goebbels*. London, Heinemann.

1962. *Hermann Göring*. London, Heinemann.

1965. *Heinrich Himmler*. London, Heinemann.

1967. *The Incomparable Crime*. London, Heinemann.

1971. *Hess*. London, MacGibbon and Kee.

MASER, WERNER, 1971. *Adolf Hitler Legende, Mythos, Wirklichkeit*. Munich, Bechtle.

MEISSNER, OTTO, 1950. *Staatssekretär unter Ebert, Hindenburg, Hitler*. Hamburg.

MURPHY, JAMES, 1941. *Who Sent Rudolf Hess?* London, Hutchinson.

Nazi Conspiracy and Aggression. See International Military Tribunal.

NOSKE, GUSTAV, 1947. *Aufstieg und Niedergang der deutschen Sozialdemokratie*. Zürich, Aero Verlag.

PAPEN, FRANZ VON, 1952. *Memoirs*. Deutsch.

PUNDER, HERMANN, 1968. *Von Preussen nach Europa*. Stuttgart.

RAUSCHNING, HERMANN, 1939. *Hitler Speaks*. London, Thornton Butterworth.

SCHACHT, HJALMAR, 1955. *My First Seventy-Six Years*. London, Wingate.

SCHWARTZ, MAX, 1965. *Biographisches Handbuch der Reichstage*. Verlag für Literatur und Zeitgeschichtes.

SCHWERIN VON KROSIGK, Count LUTZ, 1951. *Es Geschah in Deutschland*. Tübingen.

234

SEVERING, CARL, 1950. *Mein Lebensweg.* Cologne, Greven Verlag.

SHIRER, WILLIAM A., 1960. *The Rise and Fall of the Third Reich.* New York, Simon and Schuster; London, Secker and Warburg.

STAMPFER, FRIEDRICH, 1947. *Die ersten 14 Jahre der Deutschen Republik.* Bollwerk, Verlag Offenbach.

STRASSER, OTTO, 1935. *Die Deutsche Bartholomäusnacht.* Zürich, Reso-Verlag.

1940. *Hitler and I.* London, Cape.

TREVIRANUS, G. R., 1968. *Das Ende von Weimar.* Düsseldorf, Econ.

VOGELSANG, THILO, 1965. *Kurt von Schleicher.* Göttingen.

WEIZSÄCKER, ERNST VON, 1950. *Erinnerungen.* Munich, List.

WHEELER-BENNETT, JOHN W., 1936. *Hindenburg, the Wooden Titan.* London, Macmillan.

1953. *The Nemesis of Power.* London, Macmillan.

WÖRTZ, ULRICH, 1966. *Programmatik und Führerprinzip.* Doctoral Thesis. (The Problem of the Strasser Circle within the NSDAP.)

Index

237